DISCOURSES IN READING AND LINGUISTICS

ANNALS OF THE NEW YORK ACADEMY OF SCIENCES

Volume 433

DISCOURSES IN READING AND LINGUISTICS

Edited by Sheila J. White and Virginia Teller

The New York Academy of Sciences
New York, New York
1984

Library of Congress Cataloging in Publication Data

Main entry under title:

Discourses in reading and linguistics.

(Annals of the New York Academy of Sciences, ISSN 0077-8923; v. 433)
Papers derived from a meeting of the New York Academy of Sciences, May 7-8, 1982 and from talks to the Academy's Linguistics Section between Jan. 1980 and May 1982.
Includes bibliographies and index.

1. Linguistics — Congresses. 2. Literacy — Congresses. 3. Reading — Congresses. I. White, Sheila J. II. Teller, Virginia. III. New York Academy of Sciences. IV. New York Academy of Sciences. Section of Linguistics. V. Series.
Q11.N5 vol. 433 [PS23] 500s [410] 84-27309
ISBN 0-89766-260-1
ISBN 0-89766-261-X (pbk.)

CCP
Printed in the United States of America
ISBN 0-89766-260-1 (Cloth)
ISBN 0-89766-261-x (Paper)
ISSN 0077-8923

ANNALS OF THE NEW YORK ACADEMY OF SCIENCES

Volume 433

December 28, 1984

DISCOURSES IN READING AND LINGUISTICS

Editors
SHEILA J. WHITE and VIRGINIA TELLER

CONTENTS

Part I. Reading

Part II. Linguistics

Introduction: Part I

SHEILA J. WHITE

Research Department
The Lexington School for the Deaf
Jackson Heights, New York 11370

The papers in this section are partially a reflection of a two-day meeting held at the New York Academy of Sciences on May 7 and 8, 1982 which was chaired by Drs. Elaine Fenton, Frances Podwall, Beatrice Kachuck, and myself. The meeting was entitled: "Reading and Reading Disabilities: Scanning the 80s from Left to Right," and was intended to expose practitioners to a range of problems and diversity of perspectives in literacy research. While there are still those who argue about whether "language" is innate or not, there is no argument about literacy being an *acquired* skill—and an acquired skill of a quite complex type. A child may not be reading for a wide variety of reasons. These could range from being "simply" based on a physical deficit to being caused by the inability to process linguistic elements; or they could reflect a lack of societal needs and pressures (in nonliterate societies, there is no need to read).

The variety of papers included here reflects this range of concerns. It is not a totally inclusive selection: papers on basic neurological processes and those dealing specifically with syntax or with the current area of discourse processing and text cohesion can be found elsewhere. Nonetheless, the range of topics that are covered is impressive and should serve to underline the basic message that the attainment of literacy does not represent a unitary process nor a unitary set of skills. What follows from that revelation, of course, is that approaches to remediation may have to be as varied as the processes involved.

The first paper, by Scribner, addresses the larger cultural issues and suggests that reading skills are bound up with the social milieu in which the individual learns to read, which includes the purposes for which reading is done. Using a unique situation in which three separate language systems (English, Arabic, and Vai) are available in the same culture, Scribner presents a fascinating picture of the different kinds of skill promoted by different kinds of literacy. (This is in contrast to the usual approach to the study of literacy, which seeks to examine *requisite* skills only.) A major conclusion is that one cannot ignore the socially embedded nature of reading and reading skills. Thus, treating "reading" as a unitary skill is problematic, and may account for our difficulties in teaching it, testing it, and remediating when difficulties are present.

Reading is a "mystery" because, although we can identify what component processes may be involved in its skilled accomplishment, we do not yet know how the parts are organized into a whole. We know that even though we can philosophically separate the lexical elements (words) from their organization (syntax) and meaning (semantics), all these elements interact in sig-

1

nificant (and yet not understood) ways. Aaronson and Ferres address this issue directly in their paper by presenting evidence of how lexical categories provide clues for syntactic and semantic processing. As Scribner does, they call attention to the fact that the process of reading is not unitary, but is affected by what we read and by our purposes for reading. (For example, whether we read a newspaper or a textbook and whether we read each for gist or for complete retention contributes to the strategies we use and to what we take away from the endeavor.) Aaronson and Ferres use a variety of research techniques to point up the validity of their lexical categories and they describe how they are used as cues for processing structure, meaning, or both, depending on the task at hand. One of their findings is that data from a variety of techniques support a differentiation of function between content words (emphasizing meaning) and noncontent words (emphasizing structure).

The differential responsiveness of children to content and noncontent words is the specific subject of investigation by Blank and Bruskin. The content/noncontent dichotomy is an important one, in that it contributes directly to the understanding of sentence organization: the noncontent words often do the work of putting a string of words into meaningful subunits or chunks. The paper by Blank and Bruskin presents evidence that children perceive these two categories as separate. Further, the noncontent words are mastered later and offer particular problems to dyslexic populations. Dyslexic readers make significantly more mistakes with the noncontent words whether they are presented either in isolation or in an appropriate context. If one considers that more than half of a page of text consists of noncontent words, one can understand why text might be incomprehensible to readers with problems in this domain. The authors suggest that the teaching of these two word classes should be differentiated.

Dyslexic children's problems are not only in the noncontent domain. Anderson, Podwall, and Jaffe show that dyslexic persons can be differentiated on the basis of their performance with content words also. The authors show deficits in naming by analyzing the timing of different aspects of spoken responses to graphic material, asking which aspect of the response requires the extra time. Specifically, these authors were testing an information processing model that postulates that cognitive preparation can account for some of the delays in forming the spoken response. Indeed, they found evidence that the need for extra cognitive time, rather than the need to articulate slowly, was the prime source of naming difficulties in the dyslexic children of their sample.

To further show that reading is to be understood as a complex set of physiological and psychological processes that interact together, Thatcher, McAlaster, Lester, and Cantor address ecological factors, and examine the relationship between nutritional intake and reading levels. Their line of reasoning is that what a child takes in by mouth can eventually affect the brain, thereby eventually affecting how the child handles what comes in by eye. Specifically under investigation was refined carbohydrate intake, which, in unrefined terminology, can be called "junkfood." Needless to say, a relation was found, and the paper details connections between specific minerals and reading scores in both normally performing and slower readers of differing ages.

While several of the papers consider educational implications in their concluding sections, Richardson's paper addresses this issue directly. Richardson, who postulates that a phonemic processing deficit is a primary causal factor in the reading problems of many children with developmental dyslexia, presents an instructional model which emphasizes phonics instruction. He explores the relation between phonic sounds and their association with specific graphemes which, particularly in English, can be very confusing. (For example, compare the pronunciation of "at" with "ate", and "shoe" with "hoe".) Richardson also presents preliminary results of his work on the effect of medication (Ritalin) on participation in the instructional program of hyperactive children who are poor readers.

There is great concern today about the outcomes of teaching our children to read. One constantly hears complaints about entering college students who cannot put two words together on paper. It should take no great leap of imagination to wonder what, if anything, these same students can *read*. Recognition of the scope of the problem has fostered adult literacy and remediation programs in our schools and libraries. Yet solutions are not close at hand. After a century of research, we do not yet know how to teach reading when there are problems. Many of the authors of the papers in this volume have attempted to shed light on areas that will eventually feed into educational policy decisions. These areas are cultural, linguistic, cognitive, physiological, and instructional. Although these can be separated conceptually, it is important to understand that they can and do interact with each other.

What one should come away with after reading these papers is an appreciation that an understanding of reading (and reading disabilities) requires acquaintance with a variety of disciplines. Thus it should follow that the teaching of reading by using a common set of rules for all children does not reflect the diverse nature of the research findings. We should not allow this complexity to deter us. On the contrary, we should put it to use, for it enables us to more clearly define what needs to be taught and where our research efforts should be.

The Practice of Literacy:
Where Mind and Society Meet

SYLVIA SCRIBNER

Graduate School and University Center
The City University of New York
New York, New York 10036

It is seventy-five years since Edmund Burke Huey[1] published his pioneering work on the psychology and pedagogy of reading. His research instruments were rudimentary and his knowledge base limited, but few, even now, rival his deep understanding of the phenomenon of reading and the challenge it poses to the human sciences. Huey said:

> . . . to completely analyze what we do when we read would be almost the acme of a psychologist's achievements, for it would be to describe very many of the most intricate workings of the human mind, as well as to unravel the tangled story of the most remarkable specific performance that civilization has learned in all its history. (p. 6)

Embedded in this short statement are three important concepts about reading which serve as an introduction to the topic of this paper — how cultural practices affect the reading process. I will review current research which demonstrates a link between social uses of literacy and the psychological operations required for certain reading tasks, and Huey's concepts provide a useful starting point.

First, Huey describes reading as something we *do,* "what we *do* when we read." In terms of contemporary cognitive science, Huey is claiming that reading is performance as well as competence. Whether or not one subscribes to a competence-performance distinction, it is certain that the concept of reading as performance requires us to take into account aspects of behavior that are not typically catalogued as "basic reading competencies." If reading is performance, we need to understand *why* a person undertakes to do it — the purposes and goals of reading — and we need to inquire into the conditions under which reading is carried out — the features of the social and physical settings that contextualize and constrain particular acts of reading. A performance framework of analysis requires attention not only to a *reader* and a *text* but to the *task* the reader is trying to fulfill through engagement with a text. (For current work on the influence of purpose and task on reading, see Collins *et al.,*[2] Gibson and Levin,[3] and Sticht.[4])

Huey's second concept is that reading should be viewed as the outcome of "very many workings of mind," not as some unitary process. Increasingly today, reading researchers[5-7] are turning away from attempts to work out a single-process analysis of reading, and are emphasizing that every act of reading involves processes on many levels — linguistic, perceptual, and cognitive. Huey, however, went beyond this observation to emphasize that full understanding of reading requires a knowledge of how component processes are assembled, how they are synthesized on particular occasions of performance to accomplish "reading." He likened the synthesis in reading to the synthesis that occurs in skilled motor performances such as tennis or piano playing. By making this comparison, he drew attention to the fact that an outstanding characteristic of all complex skills is their flexibility: a skilled performer adapts strategies and techniques to the task at hand.

Finally, Huey emphasizes the social dependency of reading skills. Individuals do not become expert readers as a consequence of maturation or, in Piagetian[8] terms, by passing through successive intellectual stages. Society — civilization is the term Huey used — is involved in the acquisition process. Whether or not physiologically normal individuals attain literacy skills is entirely dependent on whether written symbol systems are available in their culture and what meanings and uses are assigned to them. According to one UNESCO projection,[9] one billion people throughout the world are nonliterate today. No amount of study of reading as an individual phenomenon can account for that fact.

If Huey's concepts are brought together and paraphrased somewhat loosely, they yield a functional approach to reading which can be defined as follows: *reading* is a term that refers to a variety of performances with written language; it involves many and varied skills depending on the task and purpose of the performance; these skills and tasks are somehow bound up with the social milieu in which individuals learn to read.

The rest of this article will proceed from this functional definition of reading and will be devoted to a discussion of recent research that seeks to explicate that "somehow" — the specific ways in which the social milieu affects the reading process. Research evidence for cultural influences on reading skills will be drawn from a multidisciplinary investigation conducted among a traditional rice-farming people of West Africa, the Vai people of Liberia and Sierre Leone.[10] Because Vai society is both culturally and geographically distant, it offers us a fresh perspective from which to view literacy activities in our own society, activities whose very familiarity blurs our vision of the social factors affecting them.

BACKGROUND OF VAI RESEARCH

My colleagues and I[a] undertook the Vai research to test age-old speculations that learning how to read and write fosters the development of higher intellectual skills. Such claims have been with us ever since Plato meditated about the effect of writing on men's minds.[11] In recent years, communication

[a] This research, funded by the Ford Foundation, is fully described in S. Scribner & M. Cole, *The Psychology of Literacy* (Cambridge, MA: Harvard University Press, 1981). Other research participants and their publications are: S. Reder, "The Functional Impact of Writing on Vai Speech," Ph.D. dissertation (New York, NY: The Rockefeller University, 1977); and M. R. Smith, "An Ethnography of the Vai People," Ph.D. dissertation (Cambridge, England: Cambridge University, 1982).

specialists such as McLuhan,[12,13] Ong,[14,15] and others have popularized the notion that the processing of alphabetic writing involves a particular form of linear, logical thought. Greenfield[16] and Greenfield and Bruner[17] have argued that comprehension of written language, because it presents decontextualized information, requires a form of abstract thinking which is not necessary for the interpretation of spoken language. Another leading cognitive psychologist, David Olson,[18] has maintained that in learning how to read essayist text, individuals acquire a particular kind of logical competence—the ability to make inferences from language alone.

These claims have far-reaching implications for both theory and practice. If certain thinking skills are intimately bound up with reading and writing, it follows that there may be deep qualitative differences between the thought of literate and nonliterate individuals. If nonliterates are incapable of abstract or logical thought, it also follows that programs for economic and social advancement may be seriously handicapped by these human limitations. For these reasons, it is important to go beyond rhetoric and traditional wisdom to bring empirical evidence to the discussion. Researching the psychological impact of literacy, however, proves a difficult enterprise. One reason is that we rarely find literacy in the raw. In our own and other industrialized societies, literacy and schooling go hand in hand. As children progress through the grades learning how to read and write, they are also acquiring knowledge, becoming familiar with science, and engaging in classroom dialogue and inquiry. With these experiences all intertwined, it is difficult to determine whether literacy *in itself* is a driving force for intellectual advancement. The logical requirements for research on literacy are that we find a place where there are literate people who have never gone to school and compare their thinking with people of similar background who are neither literate nor schooled. If group differences are found on cognitive tasks, we may have identified intellectual skills uniquely associated with literacy.

While the logical requirements are simple, the logistical conditions for meeting them are not. Countries with universal schooling do not allow us to separate literacy from education. In many third-world countries, nonliterate groups are sufficiently dissimilar from literate groups in language, custom and socioeconomic status to disqualify comparisons. Vai society, however, has a configuration of literacy practices which are ideal for research purposes. The Vai are one of the few peoples in the world with an original writing system, invented 160 years ago. This system is a syllabary with approximately 200 characters representing the syllabic structure of the Vai language. The arts of reading and writing in this script are passed on from one villager to another through individual tutoring; no schooling or education in the larger sense is involved. Thus literacy in the Vai script offers an unusual opportunity to examine the cognitive implications of literacy acquired without schooling. Moreover, since literates and nonliterates alike pursue the same farming and craft occupations, group comparisons are reasonable.

Vai society is unusual, too, in hosting literacy in two international scripts in addition to the local writing system. The official language in Liberia is English and government-sponsored English schools modelled after United

States schools are scattered throughout country villages, so that English literacy is becoming increasingly widespread. In addition, the Vai are a Muslim people and have a century-old tradition of Qur'anic study. Thus three literacies, each with its own script and its own mode of transmission, flourish among a people whose primary economic activity is slash-and-burn rice farming and whose way of life remains largely traditional. These exceptional historical circumstances created in Vai society an "experiment in nature," ideally suited to testing questions about social influences on literacy and the skills uniquely associated with reading and writing activities.

SOCIAL USES OF LITERACY AMONG THE VAI

While our principal interest was in analyzing intellectual operations involved in literacy activities, it was apparent that we could not undertake such psychological analysis until we knew exactly what these activities were and how they were distributed throughout the population. The initial phase of the research, therefore, concentrated on securing a detailed description of the social functions of reading and writing. Methods were both quantitative and qualitative. We conducted a sample interview survey involving 700 adults in all parts of Vai country, and in-depth ethnographic studies of literacy practices in two typical towns.

First, some findings on the extent of literacy. Approximately one-third of Vai men are literate in one of the three scripts (few women are literate). The majority know and use the indigenous Vai script, the next largest group is literate in Arabic and the smallest in English. A substantial number of literate men are knowledgeable in both Vai script and the Arabic alphabet and a few have mastered all three scripts. Since each literacy involves a different orthography and a different course of study, multiple literacy is no mean accomplishment.

As in other multiliterate societies,[19] social functions of literacy are distributed in regularly patterned ways across the scripts. English is the official writing system of government and commerce and of institutions operating on a national scale. In the capital city of Monrovia, English writing is part of the natural landscape as it is among us — it is displayed on street signs and billboards, and English-language newspapers and books are available in stores. Upcountry, however, English has a limited role. Some chiefs retain clerks to record court matters in English and maintain official correspondence with government agencies. Some villagers who formerly attended schools use their literacy for personal affairs but even these individuals get their news by radio or word of mouth.

English is learned exclusively in government-run schools, but not all villages have schools, and commonly these continue only up to the 5th grade. Students are thus forced to leave home to pursue their education; if they contrive to complete high school, they rarely return to the farm but remain in the city seeking to win a place for themselves in the modern sector.

Arabic writing, on the other hand, is an organic part of village life. Almost every town of any size has a Qur'anic school conducted by a learned Muslim. These are usually schools without walls — groups of boys ranging in age from approximately 4 to 24 years who meet around the fire twice a day for hours of recitation and memorization of Qur'anic verses. In Islamic tradition, committing the Qur'an to memory is a holy act, and the student's progress through the text is marked at fixed intervals by religious observances and feasting. Initially, since Arabic is a foreign language to the Vai, learning is by rote repetition: students can neither decode the written passage nor understand the sounds they produce.[20] But boys who persevere learn at some point to match symbol with sound; they become able to sing out passages from the text without having heard them before and to write new verses from dictation. For those who go on to learn Arabic as a foreign language, Qur'anic reading passes through other stages until text memorization is fully supported by comprehension.[20] Memorization of the entire Qur'an requires from five to seven years of concentrated effort. Among the Vai, a few who complete the Qur'an arrange for tutorial instruction in religious, legal and other texts. Some outstanding individuals acquire libraries and lead scholarly lives in the countryside teaching, studying and participating in textual commentary and disputation. Thus Arabic literacy relates individuals to text on both the lowest level (repetition without comprehension) and highest level (analysis of textual meaning). Vai script uses, in contrast, are overwhelmingly secular, pragmatic, and personal. Script learning may begin any time in adolescence or throughout adulthood. No special occasions are set aside for it. The would-be literate arranges to get the help of a friend, relative or coworker who teaches him the characters and gives him practice in reading. Typically, this instruction begins with individual words such as names of things and progresses to text. The teacher uses whatever Vai script material he has on hand, and when he thinks the student has made sufficient progress he sends him a letter in the script with instructions to write a reply. On the average, most students are able to pass this test after two to four weeks.

While learning is individual, the practice of Vai script literacy is often a social enterprise. For reasons discussed later, the orthography is ambiguous and often hard to decipher. Accordingly, it is not uncommon to see several village men reading a letter out loud together, sometimes consulting each other about a particular character, at other times arguing about whether the author's spelling is correct or his writing style "good Vai." Reading and writing are cooperative as well as individual phenomena.

Uses of the Vai script involve both textual and nontextual materials. Nontextual uses range from very simple activities such as labelling a piece of property to systematic record-keeping. Records fulfill both social cohesion and economic functions: lists of dowry items and of funeral contributions, for example, help to regulate the reciprocal rights and obligations of the kinship system. Records also enlarge the scope and planning aspects of commercial transactions such as cash-crop farming or carpentry, tailoring, and other traditional crafts. In every village, some expert scribes keep public records for the town, maintaining lists of house tax payments, work contributions to public projects such as road or bridge-building, population counts and the like.

Letter-writing is the principal textual use of the script. Every literate interviewed reported that he corresponded with one or more people. Letters may pass from hand to hand within a town, or may be carried by taxi to distant parts of Liberia. Many Vai people who are not personally literate participate in this form of exchange through the service of scribes. For all its popularity, however, letter-writing is circumscribed in ways which simplify its cognitive demands; four out of five literates in the survey reported that they correspond only with persons already known to them and never with a stranger. Written communication among the Vai draws heavily upon shared background knowledge against which the figural news is exchanged.

As for other textual material, it is interesting to note that it is all held in private. Texts are rarely circulated to others to be read, though on occasion they might be made available for copying. This ownership arrangement has several important consequences. One is that reading typically involves familiar material (works written by oneself) rather than assimilation of new knowledge. When we showed literates an unfamiliar story written in Vai script, they often expressed surprise that we would expect them to "read" something they did not "know." Another consequence of the private holding of written materials is that existing texts reflect what individuals choose to write about and what they think writing is "for." Much of the writing is journal style; literates maintain diaries or notebooks in which they enter various items: autobiographical facts for example, snippets of town history, or family birth dates. We also discovered books of maxims for the young, clan histories, and on one occasion, a collection of traditional Vai folk tales. Texts of this kind were rare however, and certain genres entirely missing. For example, we found no poetics or expository prose or textbooks in the Vai script.

This is a brief review but it supports certain general observations. In spite of its three-script literacy, Vai society's uses of written language are considerably more restricted than those of an industrial society such as ours. Many traditional educational, cultural and economic activities are carried on without the intervention of the written word. Yet within the spheres of cultural activities in which literacy is a factor, reading and writing are used for a variety of purposes — practical, intellectual and ideological — and many routes lead to learning.

MODAL READING TASKS

Comparative studies of Vai script, Arabic and English literacy suggest that each type presents the learner and the practitioner with a particular modal reading task. Oversimplifying in order to highlight differences, we can summarize the principal goals of reading in each script as follows: In English schools, Vai students, like United States students, pass through the first grades *learning to read*, but then their major requirement is *reading to learn*. Their reading material consists overwhelmingly of expository prose material that is meant to convey new information. Once outside of school, English literates will occasionally read newspapers, government announcements, and other material communicating "news." In Vai script literacy, *reading* is importantly *related to action.* Letters typically carry news and requests of one kind or another; records are used to better carry out practical activities. Even recorded histories and stories are given instrumental significance: they are often read aloud at ceremonial occasions to instruct young people and strangers in Vai ways. As for Qur'anic literacy, much of it clearly consists of *reading to remember.* The goal of study is to ingest the holy word, literally to take it inside oneself through memorization.

Harking back to Huey's language, we can say that in these literacies people are doing different things with reading — learning, acting, remembering. They are also interacting with different writing systems — a syllabary whose characters represent syllables in the native language, and two alphabetic systems, Arabic and Roman, which represent phonemes in foreign tongues.

COGNITIVE ANALYSIS OF LITERACY SKILLS

Thus far we have been considering the social organization of literacy among the Vai and how social practices pose different kinds of reading and writing tasks to individuals. Our aim, however, was to determine what processing skills underlay these differences and whether they had any general intellectual implications. Were certain psycholinguistic and cognitive skills common to all literacies? Or were some specific to particular scripts and/or reading tasks?

To pursue these questions we turned to psychological studies. Taking advantage of the multiliteracy situation among the Vai, we set up a comparative research design to ferret out commonalities and differences among groups with different literacy experiences. One group consisted of youth and adults who either were in English school at the time or who had once attended school. Groups of Vai script literates and Arabic literates represented nonschooled literacy. In most studies we contrasted individuals who knew only one of these scripts with those who were biliterate, that is, knowledgable in both Vai and Arabic. Comparable groups of nonliterates were included and, in keeping with the social reality of literacy among the Vai, we conducted most of our studies among men only.

In the first set of studies, we administered a set of experimental cognitive tasks tapping abstraction, memory and other cognitive processes that have been speculatively linked to literacy. Results on this battery were clear-cut. In keeping with previous research, we found that schooling improved performance on many of these tasks, especially those involving verbal explanations. But there was no indication that the mere ability to use language in written form had any general impact. Vai script and Arabic literates were no different in average performance from nonliterates. Moreover, some nonliterates performed on every task as well as literates or those with schooling. If for the time being we accept these tasks as indicators of higher-order intellectual processes, the conclusion is unmistakable that literacy per se does not play a formative role. The failure of Qur'anic schooling to make a difference in general cognitive performance was interesting because of the argument, cited earlier, that alphabetic writing systems are especially likely to foster abstract forms of thinking. These conclusions are, of course, relative to the circumstances of Qur'anic and other literacies obtaining among the Vai.

The second set of studies represented a shift in research strategy from testing general hypotheses about literacy to a more functional, context-sensitive approach. Instead of relying on psychological theories to suggest literacy-related skills, we developed specific hypotheses on the basis of our ethnographic observations. We selected certain literacy activities for which we had detailed descriptions — memorizing the Qur'an, for example, and writing a letter in Vai script. We made functional analyses of the skills these activities seemed to involve, and designed experimental tasks with different content but hypothetically similar skills to determine whether practice in the original activity enhanced performance. The logic of the enterprise was to demonstrate the link between a particular literacy practice and specific cognitive skills through evidence that literates displayed those skills on a related but new task while nonliterates did not. This is a reversal of the mainstream of research on reading which asks what skills are *necessary* for literacy; through our transfer paradigm, we proposed to determine what skills are *promoted* by literacy.

Several lines of experimentation modeled processes involved in reading letters composed in Vai script. The first series focused on perceptual-linguistic processes and was prompted by our observations of how script readers went about decoding the message in personal letters that came to them by taxi or by hand. Making out the sense of a letter seemed a difficult task for many. Some difficulties appeared to be related to features of the writing system which introduce ambiguity into the written message. As previously pointed out, the Vai language is represented by its script at the level of a syllable; a single character stands for one spoken syllable. Although characters map the syllabic structure of the language in a comprehensive and systematic manner, there is not always a direct one-to-one correspondence between a single character and the unit of sound it represents. Vowel tone, a phonological feature that is semantically crucial, is not marked in the script, and, as a consequence, the same character may have more than one sound referent. Representation of vowel length, another semantically distinctive feature of the language, varies from one writer to another. Finally, writing conventions, like those of ancient Greece, do not segment lines of text into words or other semantic or syntactic units. Each syllable stands alone with space surrounding it (FIGURE 1). Since Vai words may consist of more than one syllable, readers must find a way of integrating the individual syllables on the page into meaningful chunks of language. A common solution to these problems is reading aloud — grouping and regrouping strings of syllables until they are organized into such meaningful chunks. In this recycling process, readers must keep separate syllables in mind until they can be integrated into words or phrases. We supposed that this experience might foster skills in integration of syllabic units

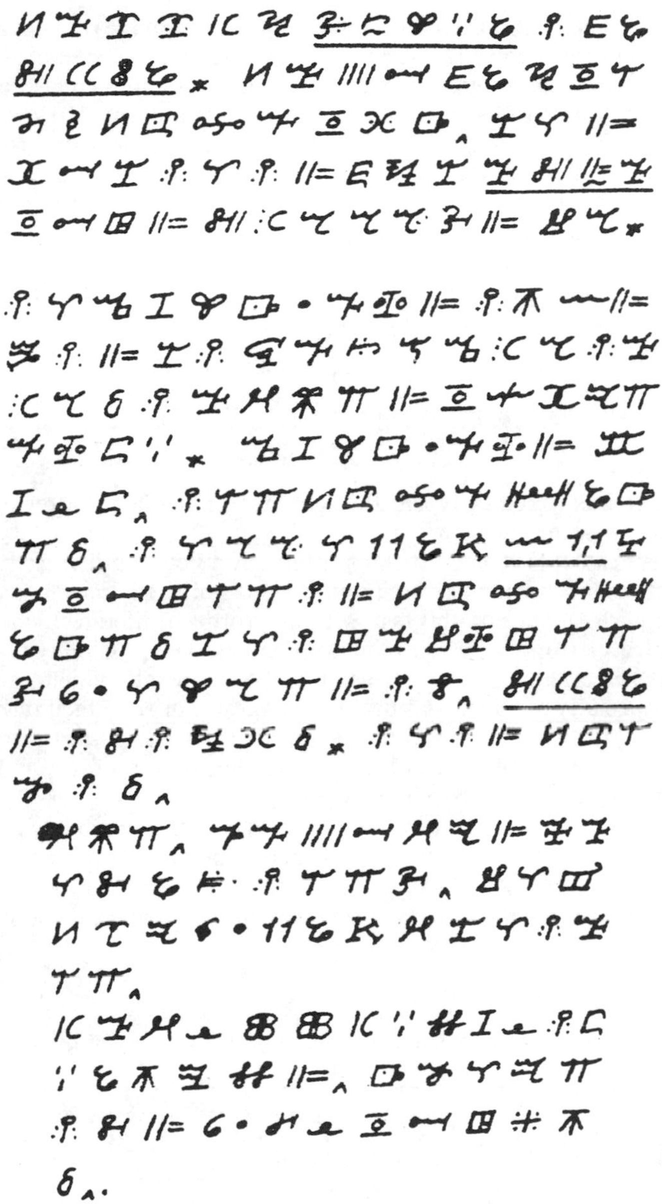

FIGURE 1. A sample of text in Vai script.

of languages and that these skills might apply to language processing in contexts that did not involve the script. To test this idea, we developed an oral language comprehension task. We asked nonliterates and members of the various literate groups to listen to tape recordings of a native Vai speaker. The speaker presented meaningful Vai sentences, one at a time, without tonal variations, pausing between linguistic units in a mimicry of early stages of reading. One set of sentences was segmented into syllable units, as is the script, while another set was segmented into an equal number of word units. The sentence composed of word units was used as a baseline control for possible individual or group differences in memory. To illustrate this material with English examples, a sentence separated into words might be:

Momo/travelled/upcountry/yesterday.

The same sentence segmented into syllable units was:

Mo/mo/tra/velled/up/coun/try/yes/ter/day.

The listener was asked to repeat the sentence immediately after hearing it, and answer a comprehension question.

Results (TABLE 1) reveal a striking interaction between literacy group and task. First consider sentences containing word units. Literacy in every script enhanced performance on this task with all groups of literates, schooled and nonschooled, performing better than nonliterates. The possibility that literacy facilitates *oral* language comprehension skills is not self-evident, and results here are especially provocative since they suggest that such facilitative effects are common to literacies in scripts with quite different patterns of relationship to the spoken language (the Vai script maps syllables, for example, while the English alphabet maps phonemes).

Next, consider comprehension of sentences containing syllable units. With this material, the only group showing superior performance was that of Vai script readers whose tested reading proficiency was at an advanced level. Other literate groups dropped to the level of nonliterates. The performance of indi-

TABLE 1. Relationship Between Literacy and Oral Language Comprehension: Mean Scores on Auditory Integration Task[a]

Literacy Group	Word Sentences Perfectly Recalled (maximum 5)	Syllable Sentences Perfectly Recalled (maximum 5)
Nonliterate men	1.45	.90
Arabic literates		
Qur'anic only	2.50	1.00
Arabic language	2.60	1.10
Vai script literates		
Beginning	2.80	1.10
Advanced	2.85	2.40
English literates (students)	3.45	2.00

[a] Adapted from Scribner and Cole.[10]

viduals with English schooling is especially interesting: they turned in the best comprehension performance for word sentences, but they, too, dropped below advanced Vai script literates on the syllable sentence task.

Group levels of performance thus upheld the hypothesis that the specific processing requirements of the Vai script, as distinguished from those in other writing systems, fostered comprehension of syllabic speech. Through techniques of multiple regression, we subjected this outcome to a more stringent test, controlling for personal background factors. We also entered each person's score for word sentences as a control factor for memory and other task variables. In equations predicting comprehension of syllable sentences, we found that, among some twenty background factors, only one affected performance — advanced reading score in Vai script.

These results are the first derived from experimental studies to establish a formative role for literacy skills on comprehension and memory for spoken language. All Vai people in these studies were, of course, native speakers; no group had more or less experience listening to naturally spoken Vai than any other. Vai script readers, however, also hear their language in syllabic form during the reading process, and perhaps on that account, were better equipped to hear and understand Vai when it was presented in syllabic form during a purely auditory task. The skills involved were clearly script-specific.

Now let us turn to a study involving higher-order cognitive skills such as those required in composing and writing personal letters. Effective written communication requires a greater elaboration of meaning than does face to face oral communication. We thought it reasonable to expect that Vai script literates with extensive letter writing experience might have acquired special skills for composing well-organized and unambiguous messages. We tested this proposition with an instructional task that required the transmission of information in a well-structured form. We taught people to play a simple board game in which markers were moved to a finish line by a procedure similar to the throw of a die. After learning the game, each individual was asked to describe it to someone unfamiliar with it. In addition, we asked informants to dictate a letter explaining the game to someone far away who had never seen it before. Board games are popular among the Vai who play a game called "ludo" which has a similar racing format and is somewhat like parcheesi. We transcribed the instructions and coded them for the amount of game-related information they contained and for the presence of statements describing the materials of the game. On both these measures — information and description — men literate in the Vai script were far superior to nonliterates and were also superior to Qur'anic literates who lacked experience in letter-writing. When we analyzed outcomes using multiple regression techniques so that we could control for possible background differences among the groups, we secured strong effects for Vai script literacy. What is more, Vai script effects were strongest for literates who reported the most extensive letter-writing experiences.

We also analyzed instruction protocols to see whether they reflected characteristics of Vai literates' style of communication in their day-to-day letter-writing practices. Over the years Vai letters have evolved certain stylized formats. Here is an example:

This letter belongs to Pa Lamii in Vonzuan. My greeting to you, and my greeting to Mother.

This is your information. I am asking you to do me a favor. The people I called to saw my timber charged me $160.00. I paid them $120.00 and $40.00 still needed, but business is hard this time. I am therefore sending your child to you to please credit me amount of $40.00 to pay these people. Please do not let me down.

I stopped so far.

I am Moley Doma
Vaitown

The statements "This is your information. I am asking you to do me a favor" serve to contextualize or frame the communication. They tell the recipient what the communication is about and what information to expect. This aspect of an effective communication was well understood by Vai literates and clearly explained in the interviews. In one discussion on the characteristics of a good letter, a middle-aged farmer said: "You must first make the person to understand that you are informing him through words. Then he will give his attention there. It is the correct way of writing the Vai script."

Transcribed protocols of game instructions were analyzed for the presence or absence of this stylistic feature. Over a range of experimental conditions, we found that Vai script literates more commonly contextualized their instructions by beginning with a general characterization of the game in a manner analogous to the introduction of the topic in a personal letter. Here is an example of such an opening: "This is a game I am coming to tell you about where two people take a race and one of them wins." This stylistic consistency strengthens the case for considering the better performance of Vai script literates on this task to be the result of a generalization of skills they had acquired in their letter-writing practices.

In other studies, we uncovered specific effects associated with Qur'anic literacy and with literacy acquired through participation in English schooling.

The entire program of research and its pattern of findings can be summed up in the following statement: over and above a common core of decoding and encoding skills associated with all three literacies, we found specific processing skills related to the characteristics of particular writing systems and to the cognitive demands of particular reading and writing tasks. Literacy tasks characteristic of the classroom environment in English schools differed in certain respects from those in the daily environment of the Vai script literate and these in turn from those of the Qur'anic schoolboy or the Arabic scholar. Insofar as we could identify them, processing skills, whether primarily perceptual, linguistic, or cognitive, tended to reflect the functional requirements of well-practiced literacy tasks in each of these literacy domains.

IMPLICATIONS OF THE VAI RESEARCH

The skills associated with literacy in Vai country are not necessarily associated with everyday literacy practices in our society; there is a world of difference between the two settings. The general significance of this research, therefore, lies not so much in its specific findings as in the broader framework it suggests for understanding the interrelationship between social and psychological processes involved in literacy. We describe this framework as a practice approach to literacy.[b] "Practice" is used here to denote a recurrent set of goal-directed activities with some common object, carried out with a particular technology and involving the application of particular knowledge. A practice is a usual mode or method of doing something and cultural practices exist in all domains. Growing rice, for example, is an agricultural practice, sewing trousers is a craft practice, and writing letters is a literacy practice.

Literacy practices involve a common "object" — a written language. They employ a particular technology — an orthography and the conventions of written representation, as well as the mode of production and distribution of writing. They draw on particular domains of knowledge — information and concepts needed to read and write with understanding and to accomplish particular purposes. Recent historical and anthropological studies[21-29] support the observations of the Vai research that the literacy practices that arise in a given society are dependent on that society's history and structure. Societies differ in the functions they generate for literacy and in their perceptions of its instrumental and ideological values. Detailed comparative case studies also show that, as among the Vai, in most societies literacy has a plurality of functions even when only one writing system is in use. The more complex the society and the more developed the technologies for producing writing, the greater the variety of social functions which are mediated by written language — in our terms, the more diverse are the literacy practices within that society. Among the Vai it was possible to trace the connections between particular spheres of activity and kinds of literacy practices with great clarity because of the division of literacy work across three scripts which were differentially employed in various domains. Links between social functions of literacy and personal practices of literacy in our society are extraordinarily complex, but wherever there is a reader, there is an individual involved in the use of a social technology and socially created knowledge for purposes which have a social origin.

For sound scientific and educational reasons, a considerable amount of reading research concentrates on the individual reader as a unit of analysis. But ignoring the socially embedded nature of reading and reading skills limits the scope of this research, and undermines its applicability to educational programs.

One limitation is an underestimation of the context-dependent nature of reading skills. Reading research is almost wholly devoted to the study of a small set of reading tasks that typically occur in the classroom. Important as these are, and no one suggests that they are not, it is still the case that school-like literacy tasks are not necessarily representative of the many productive literacy practices encountered in daily life. A lack of ability to perform

[b] Scribner, S. Literacy as a cultural practice. Paper delivered at American Anthropological Association Annual Meeting, Houston, Texas, 1977.

school tasks may not preclude ability to perform others; school and nonschool literacies, Vai research suggests, do not exhaust each other. One implication is that reading research should be extended to a wider range of tasks in an effort to specify distinctive as well as common underlying processes in what people do when they read.

Failure to take into account the social nature of literacy practices also leads to an underestimation of the many learning opportunities for acquiring skills that arise outside of the classroom. The relationship between ability and performance, between can and do, is interactive, not a one-way street. As the Vai research suggests, participation in well-motivated reading and writing activities may promote the acquisition of certain skills, not merely reflect already formed skills. Although evidence for the formative role of particular literacy tasks on linguistic and cognitive skills is still only suggestive, what we know argues for more deliberate attention to the kind of reading and writing we ask students to do. If specific reading tasks invoke specific processing operations, pedagogy needs to take that fact into account. Treating reading as a single phenomenon rather than as a rich variety of activities with written language is not consonant with the research described here. On the other hand, a functional approach to reading, which values both its social meaning and personal significance, may contribute to our educational horizons as well as deepen our understanding of what Huey called the "most remarkable performance" in human history.

REFERENCES

1. HUEY, E. B. 1908. The Psychology and Pedagogy of Reading. Macmillan. New York, NY.
2. COLLINS, A. M., A. L. BROWN, J. L. MORGAN & W. F. BREWER. 1977. The analysis of reading tasks and texts. Technical Reports No. 43. Center for the Study of Reading. Champaign, IL.
3. GIBSON, E. J. & H. LEVIN. 1975. The Psychology of Reading. The M.I.T. Press. Cambridge, MA.
4. STICHT, T., Ed. 1975. Reading for Working: A Functional Literacy Anthology. Human Resources Research Organization. Alexandria, VA.
5. JUST, M. A. & P. A. CARPENTER. 1980. A theory of reading: From eye fixation to comprehension. Psychol. Rev. 87: 329–353.
6. FARNHAM-DIGGORY, S. 1984. Why reading? Devel. Rev. 4: 62–71.
7. RUMELHART, D. 1977. Toward an interactive model of reading. In Attention and Performance, VI. S. Dornie, Ed. Erlbaum. Hillsdale, NJ.
8. PIAGET, P. & B. INHELDER. 1969. The Psychology of the Child. Basic Books. New York, NY.
9. _____, 1979. The World of Literacy: Policy, Research and Action. International Development Research Centre. Ottawa, Canada.
10. SCRIBNER, S. & M. COLE. 1981. The Psychology of Literacy. Harvard University Press. Cambridge, MA.
11. PLATO. The Republic. Translated, with an introduction and notes by F. M. Cornford. 1945. Oxford University Press. London.
12. McLUHAN, M. 1962. The Gutenberg Galaxy. University of Toronto Press. Toronto, Canada.

13. McLuhan, M. 1965. Understanding Media: The Extensions of Man. McGraw-Hill Book Company. New York, NY.
14. Ong, W. J. 1970. The Presence of the Word. Simon and Shuster. New York, NY.
15. Ong, W. J. 1971. Rhetoric, Romance and Technology: Studies on the Interaction of Expression and Culture. Cornell University Press. Ithaca, NY.
16. Greenfield, P. 1972. Oral or written language: The consequences for cognitive development in Africa, the United States and England. Language & Speech 15: 169–178.
17. Greenfield, P. & J. Bruner. 1969. Culture and cognitive growth. *In* Handbook of Socialization Theory and Research. D. A. Goslin, Ed. Rand McNally. New York, NY.
18. Olson, D. R. 1977. From utterance to text: The bias of language in speech and writing. Harvard Ed. Rev. 47: 257–281.
19. Reder, S. & K. R. Green. 1979. Literacy as a functional component of social structure in an Alaska fishing village. Paper presented at the 78th Annual Meeting of the American Anthropological Association, Ohio.
20. Wagner, D. A. & A. Lotfi. 1983. Learning to read by "rote." *In* Literacy and Ethnicity. Special issue of the International Journal of the Sociology of Language 42(4).
21. Oxenham, J. 1980. Literacy, Reading, Writing and Social Organization. Routledge & Kegan Paul. London.
22. Cipolla, C. 1969. Literacy and Development in the West. Penguin. Baltimore, MD.
23. Laquer, T. W. 1976. The cultural origins of popular literacy in England. Oxford Rev. Ed. 2: 255–275.
24. Cressy, D. 1980. Literacy and the Social Order. Cambridge University Press. Cambridge.
25. Graff, H. J. 1979. The Literacy Myth. Literacy and Social Structure in the 19th Century City. Academic Press. New York, NY.
26. Stone, L. 1969. Literacy and education in England, 1640–1800. Past & Present 42: 61–139.
27. Goody, J., Ed. 1968. Literacy in Traditional Societies. Cambridge University Press. Cambridge.
28. Heath, S. B. 1980. The functions and uses of literacy. J. Commun. 30: 123–133.
29. Smith, M. R. S. 1982. An Ethnography of the Vai People. Ph.D. dissertation, Cambridge University.

A Structure and Meaning Based Classification of Lexical Categories[a]

DORIS AARONSON[b] AND STEVEN FERRES[c]

Department of Psychology
New York University
New York, New York 10003

In this paper a hierarchical organization for lexical categories is proposed. It is supported by both psychological and linguistic data and provides a framework for evaluating performance differences among reading tasks. Much of the past psychological research on lexical categories has been motivated primarily by linguistic criteria, and does not adequately account for encoding variations that occur with changes in cognitive task demands. In addition, most past work does not deal with an organizational system for lexical categories, but rather with individual categories: for example, nouns and verbs,[1-5] conjunctions,[6] prepositions,[7] and determiners.[8-10]

INTRODUCTION

Words as Units of Text

This paper deals with properties of words because they are important linguistic and cognitive units of text. Linguistically, a word can be defined as a "minimum free form" which is the union of a particular complex of sounds (phonology) with a particular meaning (semantics) capable of a particular grammatical employment (syntax).[11] Cognitively, words are an important unit in the perception, comprehension, and memory of text.[12,13] This paper focuses on the traditional lexical category or form class of words as defined in dictionaries (e.g., noun, verb), because that is an organizational level which is relatively word-specific. Alternatively, one might classify words according to functional role (e.g., subject, object), case role (actor, agent), or one of several types of propositional calculus (for example, see Kintsch[14]).

Recent work makes it clear that lexical, syntactic, and semantic attributes are not mutually exclusive, and indeed interact in important ways.[13,15-18] As discussed below, the various lexical categories contribute differentially to the syntax and semantics of the sentence, and to the cognitive processing of "structure" and "meaning" in text units larger than the word. Conversely, senten-

[a] This research was supported in part by United States Public Health Service Grant MH-16,496 from The National Institute of Mental Health and by an NYU Research Challenge Grant.

[b] Address for correspondence: Dr. Doris Aaronson, Department of Psychology, New York University, 6 Washington Place (Room 858), New York, New York 10003.
[c] Present address: 12 Church St., Ramsey, NJ 07446.

tial context differentially facilitates the coding of words in the various lexical categories. Although linguistic levels do interact, useful information can be gained from studying words in the various lexical categories either in isolation, or averaged over a large number of sentences having a wide variety of syntactic and semantic structures. The present paper takes this last approach and focuses primarily on the properties of lexical categories in an effort to expand on past research.[19-23] Below we put forth evidence that the lexical categories provide selective cues for syntactic and semantic processing. Thus, a theory of lexical organization is an important start toward understanding how linguistic information is used during various performance tasks, such as reading.

A Hierarchical Organization of Lexical Categories

Traditionally,[d] the lexical categories have been divided into content words and function words. However, such a gross partitioning is not sufficient to account for performance differences that occur when the very same words are read under different task demands. We will argue for an additional partitioning based on "meaning" and "structural" attributes, used when subjects code words within a sentence context. We use these terms as hypothetical constructs, with the goal of developing a psychological, rather than a strictly linguistic classification of lexical categories. In this context, the subject's cognitive processing of information from the various lexical categories may be based on "linguistic" as well as "verbal" information. For example, the coding of *structural* information from words may be based on properties such as their form class, and their syntactic (functional) role within the surface phrase structure, as well as their length in letters or syllables (for example, function words, which emphasize structure, are often shorter than content words), or their rhythmic value within the text (for example, function words are often unstressed). Processing *meaning* information from words may include processing their semantic attributes, their referential relation to other text components and to worldly entities, and their propositional involvement, as well as their familiarity or word frequency (content words with more selective or specific meaning often have lower frequency in the vocabulary), or their stress value within a covert acoustic representation (words that convey more meaning within a context often carry a heavier stress value).

---

[d] Although the content/function distinction is traditional, there is little agreement on details. On the basis of linguistic criteria, Fries[22] and Aborn and Rubenstein[19] place some pronouns, along with nouns, into a single subclass of content words, while Glanzer[23] and Fillenbaum *et al.*[21] consider all pronouns to be function words. Klein and Simmons[24] call non-*ly* adverbs function words, Fries calls adverbs of degree function words, while most researchers call all adverbs content words. On the basis of psychological data, there is also variability in word categorization. In a perception task, subjects generally matched content words with long tones and function words with short tones, but there were systematic inconsistencies.[25] In our own laboratory, subjects generally assigned content words to "key conceptual" and "supporting" roles, and function words to "relational" roles, but contextual and lexical factors interacted to yield a complex picture.

In sum, it is the theoretical orientation of the paper that the psychological processing of "structure" and "meaning" of words is based on an integration of various linguistic and verbal attributes. Thus, in addition to considering such stimulus attributes, we will examine subjective ratings of the more global psychological concepts of structure and meaning. We assume that there is not a strict structure (S) versus meaning (M) dichotomy, but rather, that words vary from one to another in their linguistic and verbal attributes, and thus in their *relative emphasis* on structure or meaning, for instance, as indexed by a ratio such as $S/(S+M)$. The three hypotheses below provide the basis for a "psycho-linguistic" organization of lexical categories based on the structure and meaning properties of words.

H1. Structure-Meaning Hypothesis

Lexical categories in English can be organized hierarchically on the basis of their relative contribution to the structure and meaning of a sentence (as diagrammed in FIGURE 1, and discussed below). That is, each category can be conceptualized in terms of a ratio, $S/(S+M)$, and the categories then form a hierarchy based on this ratio. First, the words can be divided into content words, whose primary role is to convey meaning (M), and function words, whose primary role is to signal the structural (S) organization of the sentence. Within this division both the content and function words can be further partitioned into subsets that differ in their relative emphasis on meaning or structure. The content words include a noun set (M) consisting of nouns, adjectives, and adverbs (denoted Adv(A)) which modify those adjectives, and a verb set (S) consisting of lexical verbs, auxiliary verbs, and those adverbs (denoted Adv(V)) which modify the verbs. The noun set carries much of the sentence's specific meaning, while the verb set structures the sentence into a subject and a predicate. The function words include a meaning subset of "definiteness" words (M), (that is, articles and pronouns) that delimit or substitute for nouns. Function words also include a structural subset of "organizational" words (S), (that is, conjunctions and prepositions) that provide cues to the upcoming clause and phrase units. In the results section, more details are presented on the above lexical categories, and also on the bottom-most level of function words in FIGURE 1.

The following points are important in considering FIGURE 1. (1) The theoretical organization is that of a *hierarchical* tree structure: the nodes in descending order have *directional* implications regarding the importance of successive divisions. For example, the tree structure does *not* imply that definiteness words (M) contribute more to meaning than verbs (S) do, because the higher levels of the tree structure classify definiteness words as function words (S) and verbs as content words (M). (2) We will be concerned primarily with a *comparison* of meaning (M) and structure (S) attributes *within* each nodal grouping, rather than with an absolute scale of either attribute that cuts across branches. For example, we will be concerned with proportional indicators, $S/(S+M)$, between the verb and noun set, which branch directly from the same node, rather than between the verb and definiteness set, having different immediately superior nodes.

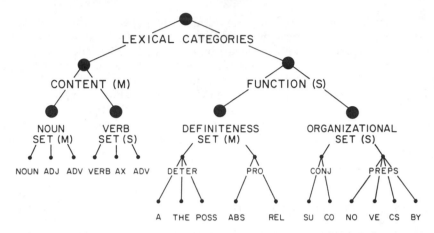

FIGURE 1. A hierarchical organization of lexical categories based on their emphasis on meaning (M) or structure (S). The lexical abbreviations in order are: ADJ = adjective; ADV = adverb for adjectives; AX = auxiliary verb; ADV = adverb for verbs; DETER = determiner; PRO = pronoun; CONJ = conjunction; PREPS = prepositions; POSS, ABS, REL = possessive, absolute, relative pronouns; SU, CO = subordinate, coordinate conjunctions; NO, VE, CS, BY = noun, verb, complex syntax and passive by prepositions.

(3) The hierarchical organization is assumed to concern only the top two levels of the diagram in FIGURE 1, down to the noun, verb, definiteness and organizational nodes. The lower subcategories are listed in FIGURE 1 (with disconnected branches and smaller nodes) in order to indicate the composition of the four sets of primary interest. Although simple structure-meaning trade-offs do not characterize some of the subcategories, it is important to consider these lower levels for two reasons. (a) A better understanding of the supercategories is obtained by knowing how the subcategories function. (b) The structure and meaning *attributes* of the subcategories do relate to the (reading time) RT data in systematic ways that are theoretically useful in understanding the reading process, as specified below in H3.

H2. Continuum Hypothesis

The psycholinguistic attributes of structure and meaning comprise conceptual scales on which ALL words or lexical categories can be located by empirical indices. Individual words and categories can be characterized (a) in terms of their importance, relative to other words, in conveying the structure and the meaning of sentences, and also (b) in terms of their own relative structure-versus-meaning emphasis (e.g., $S/(S+M)$).

Lexical Categories and Performance Tasks

Reading strategies vary depending on the memory and the comprehension demands of the reading situation. These performance demands, or retrieval requirements, influence both (1) the coding procedure, that is, the linguistic units, the direction, and the time course of coding; and (2) the resultant coded representation, that is, the linguistic level, the amount, and the classes of linguistic information that are preserved. For example, for the identical *New York Times* article, a student preparing for an exam in political science and a subway commuter preparing for a cocktail party would use different reading strategies and end up with different information or a different organization. The student would engage in left-to-right processing with prolonged pauses at words (S) initiating phrase-based coding or mnemonic "chunking" units. The commuter would pause at key content words (M) to integrate meaning across those phrase breaks.[26] These differences in cognitive processing when people read for different purposes provide the basis for the third hypothesis.

H3. Performance Task Hypothesis

The lexical categories, with their meaning and structure attributes, have differential importance for language processing in various types of reading tasks. (a) Categories and attributes which are more important for structural organization will be more important when reading for complete retention than for immediate comprehension of gist. (b) Categories and attributes which are more important for conveying meaning will be more important for comprehension than memory tasks. (c) Both task groups code the meaning attributes of words, but comprehension subjects spend little or no time explicitly coding structure.

Lexical Categories as Cues for Processing Structure

Supporting H1, empirical evidence suggests that people can use the S-categories in Figure 1 to help structure sentences into phrase units. The *verb* is scored as the most important sentential division in cluster analyses of recall data[27] and in subjective parsing data.[28] *Conjunctions* are coded differently in contexts where they conjoin sentences as opposed to phrases.[6] In developing syntactic coding strategies, Clark and Clark[12] suggest that people use *prepositions* as structural cues that a noun phrase has been initiated. Supporting H3, past research suggests that the above S-categories, which occur heavily at phrase onsets, provide important cues for a reading strategy that breaks up or "chunks" the sentence into memory-span sized phrase units. When memory is required, phrase boundary words are signalled by prolonged pauses in oral reading,[29,30] and increased eye fixations[31] and dwell times[32,33] in silent reading.

Lexical Categories as Cues for Processing Meaning

Supporting H1, past work shows that the M-categories are especially helpful in coding sentential meaning. When *nouns* are deleted, sentence comprehensibility drops markedly.[2] *Determiners* such as "a" and "the" influence whether or not people integrate the semantic information from one sentence to the next.[10,34] Anaphoric *pronouns* play an important role in aiding the semantic integration of sentence components.[35] Supporting H3, past work suggests that people use the M-categories (FIGURE 1) heavily in tasks emphasizing comprehension. That work is based on increased reading times when pronouns and nouns are used to integrate old and new semantic information,[36,37] on decreased reading times when predictable content words provide semantic facilitation,[38] and on improved comprehension performance when pronouns, definite articles, and nouns facilitate the formation of anaphoric relations.[10,37,39]

Stimulus Factors and Subject Strategies

Stimulus factors can induce or encourage particular reading strategies in addition to the strategy effects attributable to the task demands. For example, when the text itself is more highly constrained into units, a phrase-unit coding strategy, generally characteristic of memory tasks, is encouraged. This occurs more often when phrase units are explicitly marked with punctuation, when the acoustic stress pattern highlights the phrase units (as in some poetry), and when the semantic content (redundancy) of text is more constrained.[31,40] But when these factors are reduced, the reader will lean toward a strategy more characteristic of comprehension tasks. Thus, in many natural reading situations, the performance task demands interact with the linguistic attributes of the text to yield mixtures of the strategies hypothesized in H3. However, as a research tool, we used relatively extreme reading tasks to provide evidence on the range of strategies that is possible during reading.

Goals and Organizations of the Paper

Our goals for this paper are (a) to obtain a broad picture of the role of each individual lexical category in conveying linguistic information to the reader, and (b) to obtain an integrated view of a large number of lexical categories: their similarities, differences, and relationships to each other. To accomplish these goals we use four complementary sources of evidence: (1) subjective ratings of the linguistic attributes of words and sentences, (2) distributional analyses of the occurrence and co-occurrence of lexical categories in text, (3) subject-paced word-by-word reading times, and (4) reviews of the past research literature. Although there is not perfect agreement among these types of evidence, the consistency is usually good. Our theoretical ideas will focus on consistencies among these "converging techniques," no one being considered as primary. As past research literature is used as data to support the proposed theory, the traditional "results" and "discussion" sections have been combined. The section below explains the methods for the subjective ratings, the distributional analyses, and the reading time experiment. The results and discussion of those data in the following sections are organized in accord with the lexical hierarchy in FIGURE 1.

TABLE 1. Sample Stimulus Sentences

1a.	Because it had a prejudiced population /// Washington was burned // by the militants.
1b.	Only the lower economic section // of Washington /// was burned by the militants.
2a.	The waiter // serving the President /// made known his feelings // about foreign policy.
2b.	In a meeting with the cabinet /// the President made known // his feelings // about foreign policy.
3a.	The doctor // whose treatment // did cure the patient /// was able to continue // his work.
3b.	Because of the doctor's new cure /// the patient was able // to continue his work.
4a.	After many long hours of debate /// the housing bill was approved // by the legislature.
4b.	The candidate who strongly favored // the housing bill /// was approved // by the legislature.
5a.	Within all of the government /// only the office // of the President /// issued a statement // about the arms treaty.
5b.	Because he is the highest officer // in the country /// the President issued // a statement // about the arms treaty.

NOTE: Double and triple slashes indicate, respectively, "natural breaks" marked by 40–80% and 90–100% of the subjects.

METHODS

Stimulus Sentences

Forty-five pairs of sentences were constructed such that both sentences in a pair had identically worded second parts. Variations in the first part imposed different linguistic structures on the second part (for example, see the pairs in TABLE 1). These pairs permit us to assess differences in the rating data and reading times due to structural factors, such as phrase boundaries, separately from the particular words involved. Sentences within each pair were equated for number of syllables, and sentences from the two sets were equated for range (9 to 19) and mean (14.4) number of words. One member of each pair was presented in each half-session, and half-sessions were counterbalanced over subjects for the reading experiment and all of the rating experiments. The sentences were varied widely in syntactic structure, including clauses and phrases that varied in number, length, location, subject-rated complexity (three-point scale) and importance[e] of the individual words to their sentence (five-point scale). The semantic content was not constrained by any specific rules and was obtained primarily from newspapers and magazines. More detailed information about the stimulus words is provided in TABLES 2 and 3, which are discussed later. These stimuli were used for other purposes by Aaronson and Scarborough.[32,33]

[e] The data from the complexity and importance ratings will not be reported in the present paper. These ratings were done (1) to insure that sentence-complexity and word-importance were equated for the two counterbalanced subsets of stimuli, and thus for two half-sessions of practice and (2) to provide additional data for another research project.

TABLE 2. Sampling of Lexical Categories

Lexical Category	N for All Stimuli	N for S, M Ratings	SE for Structure	SE for Meaning	SE for S/(S+M)	N for RT Analyses	SE for Relative RTs (sec) Recall	Compre- hension
Content Words	662	93	.047	.059	.006	364	.005	.002
Verb set	172	45	.066	.106	.011	172	.008	.002
Verbs	89	15	.064	.084	.008	89	.012	.003
Auxiliary verbs	60	15	.070	.054	.008	60	.014	.003
Adverbs for verbs	23	15	.052	.085	.008	23	.017	.006
Noun set	490	48	.057	.054	.004	192	.005	.003
Nouns	302	15	.089	.043	.008	90	.007	.004
Adjectives	167	18	.048	.085	.008	81	.007	.004
Adverbs for adjective	21	15	.049	.089	.008	21	.011	.007
Function words	300	161	.022	.046	.004	300	.004	.002
Organizational set	107	61	.032	.058	.006	107	.006	.003
Subordinate conjunction	9	9	.052	.156	.011	9	.020	.008
Coordinate conjunction	8	8	.117	.122	.012	8	.034	.009
Noun prepositions	39	15	.054	.124	.012	39	.009	.005
Verb prepositions	30	14	.062	.075	.009	30	.009	.006
Complex syntax prepositions	13	11	.068	.140	.010	13	.019	.007
Passive by prepositions	8	4	.071	.129	.000	8	.032	.008
Definiteness set	193	100	.028	.066	.006	193	.006	.002
A, An	33	17	.054	.066	.008	33	.012	.005
The	109	36	.035	.038	.005	109	.009	.002
Absolute possessive pronoun	29	26	.044	.057	.006	29	.017	.004
Absolute nominal pronoun	7	7	.096	.165	.018	7	.012	.008
Relative possessive pronoun	6	6	.046	.051	.000	6	.020	.004
Relative nominal pronoun	9	8	.148	.127	.018	9	.016	.007

ABBREVIATIONS: N = sample size, S = structure, M = meaning, SE = standard error.
NOTE: SE values of "zero" indicate that actual values were beyond the third decimal place.

Stimulus Rating Procedures

To provide evidence for H1 and H2, and to provide a stimulus description for the reading experiment, ratings of word attributes and phrase breaks were obtained from undergraduates. Most psycholinguists do not use ratings from linguistically "naive" subjects, and some have told us that such subjects are not capable of classifying or describing English. Rather, stimuli are generally described or classified by the experimenter or by a trained linguist according to rules based on a currently popular linguistic theory. As psychologists, we were not convinced that current linguistic theories were adequate as psychological theories of language *processing*. Further, trained linguists often do not agree among themselves on which theory is best, or on the application of a given theory to describe specific bodies of text. Thus, in the traditions of psychophysics and psychometrics, we asked college subjects to rate the stimuli in various ways in order to supplement the other types of evidence described below. We suspect that college students do have a reasonable knowledge of English, especially when the data from many of them are averaged together.

Structure and Meaning Ratings

Twelve undergraduates provided five-point judgments of structure and meaning for samples of words in all eighteen lexical categories. The sample sizes in the total sentence set and in the structure and meaning rating experiment are in TABLE 2. Sampling guidelines were formulated to obtain sets of three underlined words to be rated in each of the 90 sentences. These guidelines were: (a) 15 words should be sampled in each of six content categories (one content word per sentence), (b) function words with small samples ($n \leqslant 15$) in the total sentence set should be sampled in their entirety, and (c) larger samples of function words should be sampled in proportion to their frequency in the total set. Due to constraints imposed by the particular sentences, a few minor variations were made in the guidelines, as observed in TABLE 2.

Instructions to the subjects. Each underlined word was rated separately for its contribution (1) to structure and (2) to meaning within its particular sentence. The rating instructions were designed to be unrestrictive and theoretically neutral, as illustrated by the following excerpt: "Words in sentences play two roles in helping you understand the sentence. They contribute to the meaning and they provide structural information to help you organize the context into ideas. Most words contribute to both meaning and structural aspects. But any particular word might contribute more or less to either type of information than other words do. How much a particular word contributes to structure or to meaning depends on many things, including: (a) the particular *word* itself; (b) its local and total sentence *context*; as well as (c) the knowledge or orientation of the *reader*. We would like you to rate some of the words in 90 sentences according to how much you think each particular word contributes to structure and to meaning. You will have a five-point scale for indicating each of these attributes separately for each word in its particular context. There are no right or wrong answers . . ."

General information on the mathematical properties of the ratings is presented here, so that readers can more easily interpret the data when broken up by lexical category in the results section.

Validity and reliability. Since the psychological variables of structure and meaning should reflect in part the linguistic attributes of syntax and semantics, a partial validity check can be based on relations between the ratings and linguistic properties of the stimuli. In accord with the hierarchial organization, function words can be checked for syntactic attributes and content words for semantic attributes. Thus, structure ratings were compared for the same class of words when located at phrase boundaries ("high" syntax) and within phrases ("low" syntax), on the basis of standard phrase structure grammar.[41] A function word category, possessive pronouns, had a large enough sample size at both locations to provide such a test. Nine "high" and seventeen "low" syntax possessive pronouns received average "structure" ratings of 3.1 and 2.9, respectively (t test: $p < 0.05$), supporting the supposition that a positive relationship exists between structure and syntax. Analogously, nouns and adjectives were examined that were located either in the main sentence ("high" semantic value within the sentence context) or in a relative or subordinate clause ("low" semantic value). The 20 "high" semantic words had average meaning ratings of 4.2 and the 10 "low" semantic words had average meaning ratings of 4.0 (t test: $p < 0.05$), furnishing evidence for a positive relationship between meaning and semantic value within the sentence context. Although the sample sizes of the various lexical categories that were rated are generally too small to be split up for extensive linguistic comparisons, the above tests provide some evidence that naive subjects base their ratings in part on linguistic attributes. In addition, however, the results sections for each lexical category provide evidence that the subjective ratings generally vary as one would expect, in relation to linguistic attributes. For example, content words are rated higher on meaning than on structure, and higher on meaning than are the function words.

The standard errors (SEs) in TABLE 2 provide a partial check on the reliability of the structure and meaning ratings. In general these SEs are small in relation to the means (FIGURES 3, 5, and 8): for most categories, SEs are 1%–2% of the mean rating value, and all are less than 5% of the mean rating value.

Independence and range. As structure and meaning were both rated by the same subjects, one might be concerned that rating one attribute could influence rating the other. An examination of correlation coefficients suggests that this is not a problem. The average Pearson correlation of structure and meaning ratings, taken over subjects, is positive but not significant, $r = 0.12$. Further, for each individual lexical category, correlations taken over subjects were generally small positive values. For 15 of the 18 categories $0 \leqslant r \leqslant .3$. In contrast, correlations of structure and meaning taken over items were negative for 13 out of 18 lexical categories, with an average of $r = -0.13$. Thus, there was a positive correlation between structure and meaning from one subject to another, but a negative correlation from one item to another.

Therefore, the word and category effects based on item data cannot be attributed to subject response biases created by the within-subjects design.

Let us note one further property of the ratings: the two scales differ somewhat in sensitivity. The highest and lowest averaged meaning ratings for particular categories are 4.239 for nouns and 1.961 for "the," yielding a range of 2.278 scale points. The highest and lowest averaged values for structure are 3.478 for verbs and 2.528 for adverbs that modify adjectives, yielding a range of 0.95. To obtain a sensitivity index these values can be compared to the standard errors. The overall SE for meaning, 0.0507, is larger than that for structure, 0.0311. A "sensitivity ratio" of the range divided by the SE yields 44.93 for meaning and 30.55 for structure. Thus, the meaning scale is almost 50% more sensitive than the structure scale. However, these data do not permit one to decide whether there are true stimulus differences in these attributes, or whether subjects were using the rating scales differently for the attributes.

Function Word Ratings

To provide supplementary data for two lexical classes, eight undergraduates (who did not serve in any other experiments in this series) gave five-point subjective judgments of articles and prepositions respectively on two linguistic dimensions: definiteness and organizational attributes. Subjects rated one word of each kind, underlined respectively in red or blue in one sentence at a time. The rating instructions provided only a general conceptual framework, as illustrated by the following excerpts. *Definiteness*: "Some function words limit, specify, individualize, or give definiteness to substantive words in a sentence . . . Rate how precisely the word specifies or limits its associated content word for the particular sentence context in which it occurs." *Organization*: "Some function words help us to organize the words of a sentence into meaningful groups that go together . . . Rate how useful the word is as an organizational aid for the particular sentence context in which it occurs."

As in the structure/meaning ratings, subjects in the definiteness/organization experiment had further instructions on the use of the scales, defined anchor points along the scale, and example sentences. Pilot work, and correlation and validity checks were done to insure that the instructions were interpreted appropriately by the subjects based on the psychological, linguistic, and mathematical scaling criteria.

Phrase Boundary Ratings

Ten additional undergraduates drew lines where "natural divisions" within the sentence occurred. As a validity check, the location of these subjective phrase boundaries agreed 98% of the time with standard syntactic definitions,[41] and "major" constituent breaks were marked more frequently than "minor" ones. For the data presented below we accepted as phrase breaks those points marked by at least 40% of the subjects (see TABLE 1).

Newspaper and Magazine Text Ratings

We performed statistical analyses of newspaper and magazine text (1) to support more general conclusions about lexical distributions and (2) to check whether the 90 stimulus sentences have linguistic properties similar to those of naturally occurring text. The literature dealing with analyses of writing style[42] suggests that individual authors have strong systematic biases in their use of and distributions of function words. Thus, we sampled small amounts, two or three paragraphs, from each of eighteen different authors. We used letters to the editor, signed columns and news articles from the *Southampton Press* (October 12, 1978) (a weekly newspaper) and the *Pennsylvania Gazette* (May 1978) (a monthly magazine).

The samples included slightly more than 4,600 words (about 500 sentences). We used this text to score, for example, co-occurrence relationships between articles and nouns; verbs, auxiliaries and adverbs; and nouns, adjectives, and their adverbs. Further details will be described when the particular data are presented.

RT Procedure

College subjects viewed sentences displayed one word at a time in the center of a computer screen. The subjects pressed a key when they wanted to begin a trial and each time they wanted to read another word in the sentence for that trial. The previous word was removed with the appearance of each new word and the computer recorded the reading time (RT) for the previous word in msec. Two groups of twenty-four subjects each performed different tasks after viewing a sentence. RECALL subjects attempted to write down the entire sentence verbatim on a prepared response sheet. COMPREHENSION subjects responded to a 3–7-word YES/NO statement about the sentence. Both groups viewed the same 6 practice and 90 experimental sentences during a one-hour session.

Statistical Analyses

The statistical analyses generally involved binomial and χ^2 test for frequency data, and F- and t-tests for rating scale and reading time data. To facilitate interpretation of the results, sample sizes (i.e., df + 1) for the lexical categories, and standard errors for the structure and meaning ratings and the RT data are displayed in TABLE 2. These will not be presented separately with each statistical test. The statistics for the subjective rating and phrase marking procedures, as well as the reading times used item rather than subject error terms because (1) that is an appropriate way to supplement the text distribution data which could only be based on items, (2) we were concerned about generalizing to other language samples (cf. Clark[43]), and (3) item variance was generally larger than subject variance. Limitations of our computer facilities prevented running both item and subject analyses.

RESULTS AND DISCUSSION

The results and discussion will be organized in terms of the hierarchical tree diagram in FIGURE 1. For each level in the tree, the structure and meaning attributes of the given class will be considered in terms of past literature, linguistic distributional data, and subjective ratings to provide evidence for H1 and H2. Further, the word-by-word reading time (RT) data for content words and function words will be considered at the ends of those respective sections to provide evidence for H3.

Content versus Function Words

Subject Ratings

The uppermost branching in FIGURE 1, dividing the content and function words, is supported by both the rating and the phrase break data. Averaging the ratings over the subcategories shows that the content words, (C), are rated higher on meaning, M, and lower on structure, S, than are the function words, (F). The scale values are: M(C) = 3.8, S(C) = 2.9; M(F) = 2.6, S(F) = 3.1 (Interaction F-test: $p < 0.0001$; all main effects: $p < 0.05$). The percent of the total meaning plus structure rating devoted to structure (i.e., S/(S+M)) is 43.3% for content words and 53.8% for function words (t-test: $p < 0.0001$). Thus, the subjective ratings support H1 in partitioning the lexical categories into a content set emphasizing meaning and a function set emphasizing structure. Ratings for the 18 individual subcategories are in FIGURES 3, 5, and 8, and will be discussed later, when each particular subcategory is considered in detail.

Phrase-Break Data

TABLE 3 is based on subject judgments of "natural divisions" in the sentence. These data show that function words are located more frequently at the start than at the end of subjectively marked phrases: start(F) = 100%, end(F) = 0%. This is an ideal location for a cue to structural organization. Words that start a grammatical unit cue the reader that a new constituent is beginning, that it is of a particular linguistic type, and that the previous unit has ended. Words ending phrase units are often ambiguous structural cues, as an additional word or so can usually provide an appropriate continuation (for example, The teenage boy cleaned the bedroom/throughly/ yesterday). Past research shows that recall subjects use these phrase-structure cues to aid their "memory-chunking" patterns.[30,32,33,44]

Although individual subcategories vary, TABLE 3 shows that content words occur more often at the end than the beginning of subjectively marked phrases: start(C) = 38%, end(C) = 62% (t-test: $p < 0.0001$). This is an ideal place for the reader to pause to integrate the semantic content of a phrase. Past research shows that comprehension subjects often do their semantic integration at the ends of phrases, clauses, and sentences.[32,45]

TABLE 3. Proportion of Words at Various Sentence Locations

	S/PB	E/PB	S/T	E/T	N/T
Content Words	.378	.622	.171	.332	.497
Verb Set	.607	.393	.395	.239	.366
Verbs	.517	.483	.348	.326	.326
Auxiliary verbs	.897	.103	.583	.067	.350
Adverbs for verbs	.200	.800	.087	.348	.565
Noun set	.297	.703	.092	.365	.543
Nouns	.161	.839	.106	.553	.341
Adjectives	.454	.545	.060	.072	.868
Adverbs for adjectives	1.000	.000	.143	.000	.857
Function Words	1.000	.000	.350	.000	.650
Organizational set	1.000	.000	.523	.000	.477
Subordinate conjunction	1.000	.000	.778	.000	.222
Coordinate conjunction	1.000	.000	.500	.000	.500
Noun prepositions	1.000	.000	.538	.000	.462
Verb prepositions	1.000	.000	.367	.000	.633
Complex syntax prepositions	1.000	.000	.538	.000	.462
Passive by prepositions	1.000	.000	.750	.000	.250
Definiteness set	1.000	.000	.254	.000	.746
A, an	1.000	.000	.091	.000	.909
The	1.000	.000	.229	.000	.771
Absolute possessive pronoun	1.000	.000	.241	.000	.759
Absolute nominal pronoun	–	–	.000	.000	1.000
Relative possessive pronoun	1.000	.000	1.000	.000	.000
Relative nominal pronoun	1.000	.000	.889	.000	.111

NOTE: S, E and N are, respectively, the number of words at the start, end and nonphrase break locations. PB and T are the number of words at phrase breaks and the total number of words in each lexical category. The set averages are weighted (by sample size) category averages.

This interaction between lexical categories (function, content) and phrase locations (start, end) is significant (t-test on difference scores: $p < 0.0001$). Thus, the phrase-break data, as well as the structure and meaning ratings, support H1 for the topmost branching point in the hierarchical organization of lexical categories. The following sections will examine in detail the lower branches of this organization. First the content words will be considered and then the function words.

Content Words

Past Literature

As indicated at the second level of the tree in FIGURE 1, past research provides evidence for splitting the content words into a verb set emphasizing structure more and meaning less than the noun set (H1). According to many theories of syntax,[41,46] the verb is the keystone of the sentence organization. It relates the sentential subject to the object, or to a predicate complement. In fact, the verb often tells the reader how many major sentence components to expect, and their syntactic (functional) role. For example, "*slap*" is a two-argument verb that signals the reader that the sentence contains two important nouns, a subject and an object. "*Sleep*" is a one-argument verb, and "*put*" is a three-argument verb. Psychological cluster-analyses of words in sentences, based on a variety of paradigms, including subjective parsings of visible text[28,47] as well as recall of memorized text,[27,48] show substantial agreement with the main points of linguistic theory. The verb is the focal point for sentence organization; empirically it is the highest point in the word cluster.

Consistent with H1, Glanzer's[23] research suggests that the noun set carries more specific semantic information than the verb set. In a word association task, he found faster RTs to produce associations to nouns than to verbs, and to adjectives than to adverbs. But he found fewer different associations to nouns than to verbs, and to adjectives than to adverbs. These results suggest that the noun set has strong, readily available, specific and reliable connections to other words. In contrast, the verb set has weak and less readily available, but generalized connections to a larger variety of words. Finally, partly on account of strength of semantic associations, paired-associate recall accuracy was higher for nouns than verbs, and for adjectives than adverbs.

Distributional Data

Supporting the division of content words into two lexical sets, FIGURE 2a shows that the locations of verbs and nouns over the sentence are quite different (χ^2-test: $p < 0.02$). In order to form a single distribution for sentences of various lengths, we "Vincentized" (that is, proportionalized) the serial positions along the x axis. Verbs show a peaked distribution over sentence positions, with the mean of the distribution near the middle of the sentence.

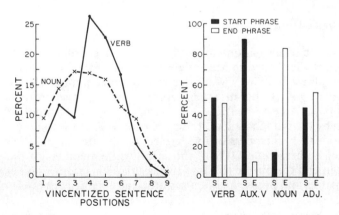

FIGURE 2. *Left*: Distributions of verbs and nouns over Vincentized sentence positions. *Right*: The percent of phrase boundary words that start (S) or end (E) a phrase for verb and noun set categories.

This centralized location of the verb[f] would be ideal for its role as an organizational keystone interrelating the subject noun phrase and the predicate object or complement. On the average, this central position divides the sentence into two approximately equal parts in terms of semantic propositions, syntactic constituents, and number of words. For a large proportion of sentences, this division would result in two strings, each within the short-term memory span (especially when considering linguistic redundancy). In contrast, nouns have a broader distribution over the sentence. The wider and more even distribution of nouns over serial positions would be appropriate for conveying sentential meaning. The reader can encounter one major idea or meaning unit at a time and code it adequately before the next is reached. Distributional data for the magazine text showed similar patterns. On the basis of Vincent tenths, the mean location for verbs was more central than for nouns, 48.0% of the way into the sentences versus 58%, and the spread for verbs was smaller, SD = 27% versus 31%.

Rating Data

The rating data in FIGURE 3 provide psychological evidence that the verb and noun sets contribute differentially to the structure and meaning of the sentence. The verb set was rated higher on structure than the noun set (S(V) = 3.2, S(N) = 2.8) but lower on meaning (M(V) = 3.7, M(N) = 3.9). (Interaction F-test: $p < 0.0001$; all main effects, $p < 0.05$). The data in FIGURE 3c are the proportions of the combined structure plus meaning values that were given to structure, S/(S+M). Again the verb set is higher than the noun set (%S(V) = 46, %S(N) = 41; t test: $p < 0.001$). Note that both sets were rated higher on meaning than structure, which is appropriate for content words. A problem for the theory is that auxiliary verbs are rated substantially lower on meaning than are other members of the verb set.

Phrase Break Data

The distributions of content words at subjectively marked phrase breaks also support the Structure-Meaning Hypothesis, H1. FIGURE 2b shows the percent of phrase boundary words that start or end a phrase. This graph omits both types of adverbs because their sample sizes at phrase breaks were small (Adv(V) = 10; Adv(A) = 3). Adverbs occur mostly in the middle of phrases, as shown by the data in TABLE 3 (also see sample sizes for total text in TABLE 2). In FIGURE 2b, members of the verb set more often signal the start than the end of a phrase unit (71% of the cases) while members of the noun set more often end the phrase (69% of the cases). This interaction between lexical categories and phrase location is statistically significant (t test on differ-

---

[f] Because the present research was done with lexical categories in English sentences, one must be cautious in generalizing to other languages. For example, in German the verb is often at the end of the sentence, and data on *psychological* processing may suggest that German verbs contribute less to structure and more to meaning than English verbs do.

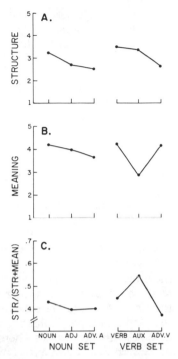

FIGURE 3. Means of subjective ratings for **(A)** structure, **(B)** meaning, and **(C)** the proportion of the total structure plus meaning rating devoted to structure for six categories of content words.

ence scores: $p < 0.0001$). It is analogous to the interaction of phrase location with content (M) and function (S) words discussed earlier. Thus, the two panels of FIGURE 2 show sentential and phrase information that complement one another. Verbs are central (both position-wise and conceptually) to the total sentence organization, and they cue the onset of phrases. Nouns are more widely distributed, and they terminate a phrase or idea unit.

The rating and phrase-break data also support the Continuum Hypothesis, H2, for content words. These data do not show a sharp bimodal split between the verb and noun sets. Rather, both types of data are at intermediate positions relative to the possible range on their respective scales. Although both classes of content words contribute to both structure and meaning, the verb set conveys more structure and less meaning than the noun set.

Ordering of Content Words

In accord with H2, the categories within the noun and verb sets can be arranged in the left to right order of FIGURE 1 based on both meaning and structure criteria. First, past literature in psychology and linguistics provides evidence that the noun and verb are each at the head of their set based on both meaning and structure criteria.[27,28,41,47,49] Second, the present data support this "head" position. The ratings in FIGURE 3 show that the noun and the verb are each higher with respect to both structure and meaning than the other two categories in their respective sets. Also, the phrase-break data in the right-most column of TABLE 3 show that the noun and the verb each occur at subjectively marked phrase boundaries (start plus end) more often than do the other two categories in their respective sets. Given these head positions, lexical distance data (TABLE 4) along with the rating and phrase-break data can be used to order the remaining two categories in each set. The data on lexical distance in TABLE 4 support the left-to-right ordering in FIGURE 1 for "modifier" categories in relation to the head word in each set. Word pairs that are closer and have more stable and predictable orderings in the surface structure of sentences should more often share subjective linguistic relations.[13,27,28,47] Such relations should in turn lead to more consistent patterns of cognitive processing and hence to more consistent reading time patterns.

To provide a lexical distance measure, a score of 1 was assigned to two words in adjacent serial positions; a score of 2 was assigned if one word intervened, and so forth. Thus, the distance and range scores in TABLE 4 are absolute distances, regardless of direction. The "Positional Ordering" column in TABLE 4 indicates the percentage of cases in which the word pairs were in the order specified in the left-most column. For example, in the stimulus sentences adverbs preceded their verbs 44% of the time (and followed 56% of the time). All data are based on the total samples available in the text, but the samples for particular rows are not identical. For example, Aux.V-Adv(V) includes only those cases where a given verb was associated with both an auxiliary verb and an adverb. Obviously not all verbs fit this pattern.

Within the framework of H2, the continuum hypothesis, the *distance* and the *positional ordering* data in TABLE 4 suggest that the verb set be ordered as follows: verb, auxiliary verb and then adverb(V). The data for both the stimuli and the magazine text agree[g] in showing that the verbs are closer to their auxiliaries than to their adverbs. Also, for both sets of data, position relations were more stable between the verb and its auxiliary (100%) than between the verb and its adverb (44%). Somewhat analogously, the noun set should be ordered: noun, adjective, and then adverb(A). Adjectives almost always precede their nouns (the exceptions are predicate adjectives), and adverbs almost always precede their adjectives. Adjectives are closest to the noun and adverbs are almost twice as far from the related noun.

The subjective *rating* data in FIGURE 3 in general lend support to this within-set ordering. But the fact that the meaning rating for auxiliaries is low represents a deviation from the expected monotonic order suggested by the other four indicators (S, S/S+M, position and phrase-break data). Finally, the *phrase-break* data in TABLE 3 support the within-set ordering for the modifying categories. Auxiliaries occur more often at the beginnings of

---

[g] The ordinal relationships among the cells in TABLE 4 show strong agreement between the stimuli and the magazine text. The absolute numbers obviously differ because of idiosyncracies in the particular texts. The linguistic details of newspaper and magazine text may not be typical of all text, and the stimuli were constrained by the experimental design and controls on sentence and phrase length, matching sentence pairs, and so forth.

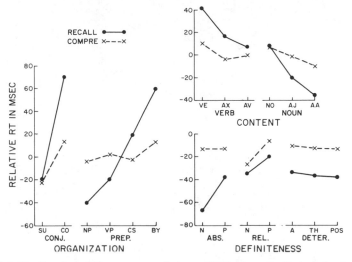

FIGURE 4. Reading time difference scores between RTs for a particular lexical category and the mean word-by-word RTs for their sentences for four lexical sets. Ordered abbreviations: VE = verb; AX = auxiliary; AV = adverb for verb; NO = noun; AJ = adjective; AA = adverb for adjective; CONJ = conjunction; SU = subordinate; CO = coordinate; PREP = preposition; NP = noun preposition; VP = verb preposition; CS = complex syntax preposition; BY = passive by; ABS = absolute pronoun; REL = relative pronoun; N = nominal; P = possessive; DETER = determiner; A = a, an; TH = the; POS = possessive. The rel RTs are obtained from subjects who read for subsequent recall (*solid lines*) or comprehension (*dashed lines*) of the sentences (from A&F [b]).

phrases and less often at the ends in comparison to adverbs(V). This supports ordering the auxiliary next to the verb in providing structural cues. Adjectives occur more often at the ends of phrases and less often at the beginnings in comparison to adverbs(A). This supports ordering the adjective next to the noun in providing a stopping place to integrate meaning over the phrase unit.

Reading Time Data for Content Words

The reading times (RTs), averaged over all lexical categories, were 580 and 400 msec/word respectively for recall and comprehension subjects. However, our focus here is not on these absolute RTs but rather, on RT *patterns* among the various lexical categories. For each task group, the RT patterns indicate which lexical categories are read slower or faster than average. To index such patterns, the *y* axes in FIGURE 4 are difference scores:[h] the RT difference be-

---

[h] Analyses using ratios produced trends identical to those using difference scores. The data on ratios, practice effects, individual differences, RT correlations among lexical categories, and complete statistical analyses are presented in Aaronson and Ferres.[50] A mathematical model to predict the RT data based on stimulus attributes and subject strategies is presented in Aaronson and Ferres.[51] We discuss in the present paper only the RT data directly relevant to H3.

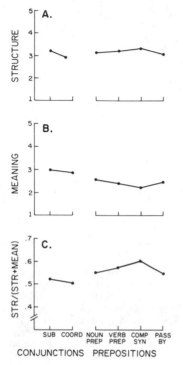

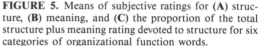

FIGURE 5. Means of subjective ratings for **(A)** structure, **(B)** meaning, and **(C)** the proportion of the total structure plus meaning rating devoted to structure for six categories of organizational function words.

tween each word and the mean for its sentence, to be called "relative RT" or "rel RT." Words read slower than average (for example, the verb set) have positive rel RTs, and those read faster than average (for example, the definiteness set) have negative rel RTs.

The graph in the upper right of FIGURE 4 compares the data for the two task groups for the verb and noun sets (main effects of sets, F-test: $p < 0.05$). Recall subjects spend relatively more of their time on the verb set (S) and relatively less of their time on the noun set (M) in comparison to comprehension subjects. This interaction between performance tasks and lexical categories is statistically significant (F-test: $p < 0.001$), and provides strong support for the Performance Task Hypothesis, H3.

In sum, the data for content words provide evidence for two subsets, with the verb set emphasizing structure more and meaning less than the noun set (H1). Furthermore, the data from several sources together provide evidence for an ordinal arrangement of the three categories within each set, (H2), although there are problems with some aspects of the data (such as meaning ratings for auxiliaries). Finally, the RT data suggest that the verb and noun sets have differential importances for the two task groups. But once again, we stress two points. (1) We are not suggesting a dichotomy between structure and meaning, nor that verbs convey only structure and nouns only meaning. (2) We are suggesting a relative emphasis, both in terms of linguistic attributes, (H2), and in terms of performance tasks, (H3). The data and theoretical comments on the noun and verb sets must be placed in perspective, that is, in relation to the function words. The noun and verb sets are content words, and as such, both convey more semantic information than other lexical categories. The past literature provides evidence on the strong semantic role played by verbs.[12,13,35]

Function Words

Both the rating and the phrase-break data support the division of the function set into an organizational set emphasizing structure more and meaning less than the definiteness set (H1). More organizational than definiteness words signal the onset of a phrase unit (TABLE 3), 52% versus 25% (t test: $p < 0.005$). Averaged over all subcategories, organizational words contribute slightly more to structure than definiteness words do: for S/(S+M), organizational words = 0.56 and definiteness words = 0.53 (FIGURES 5 and 8).

Organizational Set

This set consists of conjunctions and prepositions, which often initiate major surface structure changes that are followed by important meaning units. A conjunction may introduce a clause with its own subject and predicate, and prepositions generally precede noun phrases. Although the primary role of the organizational set concerns structure, its contributions to meaning will also be evaluated in order (1) to provide a more complete psycholinguistic description of the particular subcategories and (2) to provide a basis for comparison to other lexical sets on meaning attributes.

Conjunctions

Attempts to order the two types of conjunctions, subordinates and coordinates, relatively to each other (H2) proved equivocal. As discussed below, the data on means will suggest that subordinates (for example, after, where, when, although, because, that) contribute more to structure than do coordinates (for example, and, or, but) but the data on variances will suggest the opposite.

Structural Attributes

Means. Three weak trends together suggest that subordinates contribute more to sentence structure than do coordinates. But the variance data suggest the reverse structural ordering for conjunctions. First, the subject raters (FIGURE 5) gave a higher structure score to subordinates (3.2) than to coordinates (2.9) (t test: $p < 0.05$). And, the percentage of the total rating devoted to structure, S/(S+M), gives subordinates (52%) a slight edge over coordinates (51%) (t test: p = ns). Second, the percentage of words located at subjective phrase breaks (TABLE 3) is higher for subordinates (78%) than for coordinates

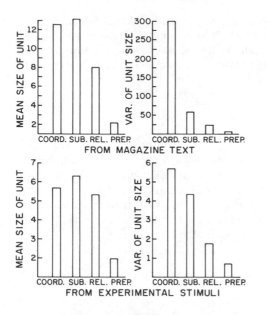

FIGURE 6. Mean and variance of unit size for coordinate and subordinate conjunctions, relative pronouns, and prepositions, based on stimulus and magazine counts of the number of words in the domain of each function word.

(50%) (binominal test: $p < 0.10$). Third, for both the stimulus sentences and the magazine text, the unit size of the conjunction's domain (unit size scored by DA, FIGURE 6) is larger for subordinates than for coordinates by about ½ word (t tests: stimuli, p = ns; magazine text, p = ns).

Variability. Coordinates can join a variety of linguistic contexts, including parallel constituents of any syntactic structure, while the syntax of subordinate clauses is more restricted and predictable. The subordinate immediately precedes and thus "cues" its domain, but a coordinate splits its domain in two, often with little prior contextual warning. Chomsky[41] has commented on the greater variability in syntactic structure associated with the coordinate along with its split or multiple branching property. He stated (p. 196): "It has sometimes been claimed that the traditional coordinated structures are necessarily right-recursive (Yngve, 1960) or left-recursive (Harman, 1963).[i] These conclusions seem to me equally unacceptable . . . In fact, there is no grammatical motivation for any internal structure, . . . Notice that there are cases where further structure might be justified, . . . but the issue is rather whether it is always necessary . . . In these cases all known syntactic, semantic, phonetic, and perceptual considerations converge in support of the traditional view that these constructions are typically coordinating (multiple-branching)."

It is possible that lexical categories occurring in a variable set of structural patterns will provide a more important aid to organizing the sentence than those whose patterns are more consistent and predictable from prior context. Thus, three types of structural variability data are relevant. First, for the subjective ratings, the variance for structure is more than four times

---

[i] References 52 and 53 in this paper.

greater for coordinates than for subordinates (0.096 versus 0.022, F-test: p < 0.05), while the variance for meaning is about twice as large for subordinates (0.194 versus 0.104). Second, the binominal variance for being located at a phrase break or not is 1.3 times greater for coordinates than for subordinates. Third, the variance for the number of words in the coordinate's domain (unit size, FIGURE 6) is 1.3 times larger for coordinates than subordinates in the stimuli, and 5 times larger in the magazine text (F-test: $p < 0.01$). Although F-ratios for the conjunctions generally do not reach statistical significance because of the small sample size of items (n(sub) = 9, n(coord) = 8), variances on three qualitively different types of data replicate this result. The joint probability associated with these replications is beyond the 0.01 significance level. Further, these trends are opposite to the usual statistical pattern in data, of variances being monotonically related to their means.[62]

Meaning Attributes

Past literature. The subordinates are more important than the coordinates in conveying meaning. First, for the magazine text and for 500 sentences studied by Aborn and Rubenstein[19] subordinates, as a linguistic class, occur (as linguistic "tokens") about 50% more often than coordinates. This is in part because they have over twice as many individual members (that is, linguistic "types"), with little semantic overlap. For example, subordinates signal spatial information (where), temporal information (when), causal information (because), and conditional information (if, unless).[54]

Coordinates such as "and," "or," and "but" are more general or universal logical operators, where the semantic evaluation of the string lies far more in the conjoined components than in the conjunctions themselves.[13,55] However, the coordinates do assume subtle gradations of meaning, depending on their context. For example, Jeremy[6] has illustrated the semantic attributes of coordinates by showing that subjects use sentential coordinates to describe pairs of events that are temporally sequential or spatially separate, but phrasal coordinates for events that are simultaneous or in the same location.

Rating data. In accordance with the magazine word-frequency data and the past literature, our subjects gave meaning ratings that were slightly higher for subordinates (2.97) than for coordinates (2.87). But, within the framework of H1, both categories of function words were rated lower on meaning than on structure (FIGURE 5).

Prepositions

In comparison with other lexical categories, prepositions provide an important contribution to sentence organization, (H1). The four subcategories of prepositions vary with respect to their structural role, and they can be ordered for structure in roughly the same way using several different approaches, (H2).

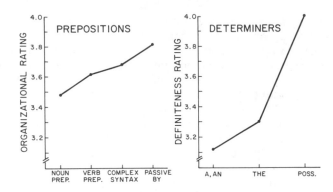

FIGURE 7. Mean subject ratings for usefulness of prepositions in organizing sentences (*left*) and for definiteness of determiners in modifying content words (*right*).

Structural Attributes

Past literature. On the basis of their sphere of linguistic influence and differences between the surface and deep structure, four types of prepositions[13,54] would be ranked from least to most structure as follows. First, "noun prepositions" generally cue local modification for the adjacent *prior* noun (for example, "a *picnic in* the woods"). "Verb prepositions," which modify the immediately *prior* verb (for example, "*burned to* the ground"), would fall second. As verbs have a broader organizational range over the sentence context than nouns do, so would their prepositional modifier phrases. Third, "complex syntax" prepositions, by definition, are structurally removed from their associated content word (for example, "*save* his crops *from* the freeze"), and they are often clausal or sentential modifiers in the deep structure. Finally, the "passive by" (for example, "was censured *by* the senator") signals a reorganization of the entire sentence.

Rating data. The data from both rating experiments show that prepositions are high on structural attributes. In the five-point organizational rating study (FIGURE 7) all preposition categories attained mean scores well above the middle of the scale. Further, the ordering of prepositions from least to most useful as "organizational aids" matches the above ordering based on linguistic notions (F-test: $p < 0.05$). The structure and $S/(S+M)$ ratings in FIGURE 5 are both above the middle of the scale, and they also agree with the above ordering except for "by." However, that data point should be replicated, as the sample size for "by" in that rating study was only four.

Phrase break data. The important contribution of prepositions to structuring the sentence is illustrated by the high rate (in comparison to other categories) at which they fall at subjectively marked phrase breaks (55%), and by the fact that 100% of those prepositions initiate rather than terminate a phrase unit (TABLE 3). The ordering of preposition categories based on these phrase break data does not strictly match that put forth above. But it does place the pair of simple modifier categories (noun and verb prepositions) before the structurally more complex pair on the basis of linguistic theory ("complex" and "by" prepositions).

Meaning Attributes

Past literature. Although the primary role of prepositions is in the structural organization of the sentence,[12] they contribute to meaning (H2), as do all other lexical categories. First, prepositions themselves carry some small amount of meaning. Context, however, is often required for an unambiguous semantic interpretation, as many prepositions have multiple meanings.[13] Prepositional meanings include spatial (in, on, at, near, under, over), temporal (before, after, during), directional (from, to), manner and instrumental (with, against) attributes. Second, prepositions contribute to meaning through their role in cueing the reader that an upcoming meaning unit will modify and be integrated with an earlier content word.[54]

Rating data. The subject ratings (FIGURE 5) provide some information on the meaning attributes of prepositions. Three points are of interest. First, as a group, prepositions have a lower absolute meaning rating than any other group of lexical categories (although the determiners are a close second). However, they are rated just below the middle of the five-point scale, clearly denoting a semantic contribution for the subject raters. Second, the ordering among the four preposition categories provided by these ratings is inverse to that based on structure. This is consistent with the trade-off between structure and meaning suggested by H1. (Note that the rating for "by" is again not consistent with the monotonic ordering expected for prepositions.) Third, averaged over the four categories, preposition ratings are 43% meaning and 57% structure. Thus, even on a relative basis, they rank lower on meaning than any other set of lexical categories. This supports their placement under the double set of S-nodes in the theoretical hierarchy of FIGURE 1.

Distributional data. In general, the frequency of occurrence of lexical categories is directly related to their contribution to meaning and inversely related to their contribution to structure. For example, on the basis of Aborn and Rubenstein's[19] data, content and function words comprised respectively 60% and 40% of their corpus. In their data, subordinates occurred 50% more often than coordinates: 0.77% versus 0.51%. This trend also holds for prepositions in our own stimuli and in the 4600 words of magazine text. For noun, verb, complex and "by" prepositions the frequencies were 39, 30, 13, 8 and 203, 100, 65, and 25 respectively in the stimuli and in the magazine text. This is again consistent with the structure-based ordering put forth above, and with the structure/meaning tradeoff of H1.

Reading Time Data for Organizational Words

An examination of rel RTs for the two function word sets at the second level of the hierarchical tree (FIGURE 1) provides further tests of the Performance Task Hypothesis, H3. The data for the organizational set are on the left of

FIGURE 4, and those for the definiteness set are at the lower right. Although the organizational set is read more slowly than the definiteness set (F-test: $p < 0.002$), the rel RT interaction between these lexical sets and the task groups is consistent with H3. Recall subjects spend relatively more of their time on the organizational set (S) and relatively less of their time on the definiteness set (M) in comparison to comprehension subjects. The interaction between performance groups and lexical categories reaches a marginal significance level (F-test: $p < 0.07$).

Next, let us examine the organizational set in more detail, first the conjunctions and then the prepositions. On the basis of the evidence relevant to H1, we tentatively suggested that coordinates emphasize structure more and meaning less than subordinates. Consistent with that view, the rel RTs for conjunctions show an interaction between lexical categories and task groups that supports H3 (F-test: $p < 0.08$). Rel RTs for the more structurally oriented coordinates are 58 msec longer for recall than for comprehension subjects (t test: $p < 0.025$), but subordinate rel RTs are about the same for both task groups.

Finally, consider the rel RTs for the four types of prepositions. Again, there is an interaction between task groups and lexical categories that supports H3 (F-test: $p < 0.001$). For recall subjects, rel RTs increase with the structural importance of prepositions (F-test: $p < 0.001$). Recall subjects have shorter rel RTs than comprehension subjects for prepositions that are structurally less important, that is, the noun and verb prepositions which serve as adjectival and adverbial modifiers. But these recall subjects have longer rel RTs than comprehension subjects for prepositions that signal a reorganization of the surface structure, that is, complex syntax prepositions and "passive by" prepositions. In contrast, comprehension subjects show a rather flat rel RT profile across all prepositional categories (lexical category effects for comprehension only: F-test: $p < 0.30$). Their rel RT increase from noun prepositions to "by" is about 20 msec in contrast to about 100 msec for recall subjects (t test: $p < 0.001$).

In sum, four different approaches provided evidence that the conjunctions and prepositions contribute substantially to structuring the sentence (H1). More cautiously, the prepositions, and possibly the conjunctions, might be rank-ordered along a structural dimension (H2). Within this context, the RT data suggest that recall and comprehension subjects differ in their coding of structure and meaning for the subcategories of organizational words (H3). Within the larger domain of function words, the "organizational" classes contribute more to structure than the complementary classes of "definiteness" words described below.

Definiteness Set

The determiners and pronouns are labeled M in the second level of the hierarchy because of their close association with the nouns. But, as function words, definiteness words contribute more to structure than to meaning as indicated by their superordinate node in the tree and by the empirical data below.

Determiners

Meaning Attributes

Past literature. The traditional linguistic literature discusses determiners as noun modifiers. The indefinite articles ("a", "an") refer to "any" member of a given noun class, while the definite articles ("the", and with our addition, possessives) refer to a specific member. We have tentatively added possessive pronouns (for example, hers, his) to this set as they also are short, high-frequency, low-content modifiers that do in fact provide definiteness restrictions for a following noun. The recent literature discusses overlap among these semantic divisions and finer gradations within them. For example, Burton-Roberts[56] discusses four different kinds of indefinite articles: the specific indefinite ("*A* man was in the garden last night"), the nonspecific indefinite ("I'm going to buy *a* loaf of bread"), the generic indefinite ("*A* whale is a mammal"), and the attributive indefinite ("John is *a* scientist").

The determiners contribute in other ways to meaning. One way lies in their anaphoric or remote referencing properties. The first mention of a noun in context is referenced with "a". Subsequent references to that noun are preceded by "the" or by a possessive pronoun if one wants to relate the second instance back to the original.[34] An example is: "An old truck crashed on 69th Street. The truck killed four people." P. de Villiers[10] showed that "the" induces subjects to integrate recent and prior context and to perceive a set of sentences as a unified story, while "a" does not. Further, determiners influence the meaning of adjectives as well as nouns, for example, in the sentence "There's (a/the) most unusual bird in the cage."[9] The modifiers following "a" mean "remarkable," but when following "the" they imply superlative. These authors also show that the acoustic stress pattern interacts with the determiner in conveying meaning.

Rating data. The five-point "definiteness" rating experiment described earlier provides evidence that the "definiteness" attribute has psychological validity. In accord with (H2), the data in FIGURE 7 show that subject raters order the determiners from least to most definite in the same way as linguistic theory would: "a", "the", and possessive (F-test: $p < 0.01$).

The "meaning" ratings from our subjects (FIGURE 8, left) provide an index of the semantic contribution of determiners to the general sentence context (H1), and they provide additional evidence for H2. First, note that the upward slope of the meaning curve is similar to the data in FIGURE 7 for definiteness (F-test: $p < 0.001$). Although both ratings used a five-point scale, values for the specific semantic attribute of definiteness fell in the top half of the scale, but values for a more general contribution to meaning within the total sentence context more often fell in the bottom half. The more general rating contrasts this function word category with the content words whose meaning ratings consistently fell in the top half of the scale (FIGURE 3).

Structural Attributes

Past literature. As function words, determiners also play a syntactic role in that they initiate and explicitly cue a noun phrase. The structural force of "the" was illustrated by Bond and Gray[28] when they obtained different subjective phrase groupings depending on whether or not "the" preceded a noun: "children who/are happy and gay" and "the children/who are happy and gay."

Phrase break data. For our own stimuli, about 15% of the subjectively marked phrase breaks were initiated by a determiner, and the percentage of times that each type of determiner occurred at a marked phrase break, rather than at other syntactic locations, increased with the definiteness rating for that category: 9% ("a", "an"), 23% ("the"), 24% (possessive) (*t* test, a versus the: $p < 0.03$).

Distributional data. The determiners do more than cue the reader that a noun phrase has begun; they also signal information about the length and lexical composition of the noun phrase. Distributional statistics for our stimuli showed that the stronger determiners, "the" and possessive, are more often directly followed by their noun, in 66% and 59% of the cases respectively. But the indefinite "a, an" immediately precedes its noun only 48% of the time, as it often has one or more intervening adjectives before the noun (*t* test, "a" versus "the": $p < 0.03$). Perhaps "the" and possessive (with their anaphoric referents) serve to delimit the terminal noun more precisely than "a" can do alone. For the 4600 words of magazine text, 54%, 67%, and 77% of the time, "a, an," and "the" and possessive, respectively, are directly followed by their noun with no intervening adjectives (χ^2: $p < 0.01$), following the same ordering as in FIGURE 7.

Rating data. The subjective ratings in FIGURE 8 provide a more general assessment of the structural contribution of determiners. There are several points to note. First, as function words, their scale value for structure is higher than that for meaning for two out of three categories. This yields a score for S/(S+M) above 50% and above that for content words. But, there is little discrimination among the three classes of determiners on the structure scale, in contrast to the strong upward slope for definiteness and meaning ratings. Within the framework of H2, determiners contribute more to structure than to meaning, but their subtle gradations of meaning are important to the sentence context.

Pronouns

In accord with standard dictionaries and grammar texts, pronouns can be divided into "relative" (for example, "who", "whose") and "absolute" (for want of a better term, for example, "he", "his"), with the relatives contributing more to structure. Although not indicated in FIGURE 1, data will be provided separately for pronouns subdivided into "possessive" (for example, "his", "whose") and "nominal" (for example, "he", "who"). Thus, "absolute possessives" are considered as members of both the pronouns and the determiners.

Meaning Attributes

Past literature. Pronouns substitute for or modify nouns. Their anaphoric referencing feature aids integration of the meaning of their own phrase unit with that of their associated noun. Glanzer's[23] work provides evidence for the integrative role of pronouns. Although pronouns are recalled less well than nouns in isolation, they are recalled better than nouns when surrounded by context. Thus, pronouns could provide a linking or integrating function that nouns could not. Corroborating those results, better recall is obtained in the Peterson and Peterson paradigm for sentences containing more pronouns than nouns,[57,58] and probe recall scores are better for sentences containing a pronoun than a noun as subject, object or both.[39] Further, in determining sentence meaning the anaphoric pronoun interacts with the semantic features of verbs,[35] and with acoustic stress patterns.[59] Thus, past literature provides evidence that definiteness function words make important contributions to meaning, supporting both their M-designation at the second level in the lexical hierarchy (FIGURE 1), and the Structure-Meaning Hypothesis, H1.

Rating data. The subjective ratings in FIGURE 8 provide further information on the contribution of pronouns to meaning. Three points stand out. First, the pronouns as a group have the highest meaning ratings of all the function word classes. Second, as a set of function words, their overall meaning ratings are lower than those for both sets of content words. Third, the highest meaning value within the pronouns is obtained by the absolute nominal ("he," "she"). Of all the pronouns, this one shares the most features with the nouns, as it can stand freely as the subject or object of an independent clause. The other pronouns are noun modifiers and/or parts of dependent clauses.

Structural Attributes

Rating data. The structural ratings for pronouns in FIGURE 8 are higher than those for determiners and about equal to those for prepositions. But, the relative percentage of their total rating devoted to structure, S/S+M, is 50%, lower than that for all other groups of function words. A second point observed in the percentage structure graph is that the values are higher for relative than for absolute pronouns, for example, higher for "who" than "he" and higher for "whose" than "his." Indeed this is expected for words that cue an upcoming clause.

Phrase break data. The subjective phrase-break data (TABLE 3) for pronouns are strongly bimodal. The frequency of occurrence of absolute pronouns at phrase breaks is lower, and the frequency for relatives is higher than for any other set of lexical categories. This ordering of pronouns is consistent with the S/(S+M) data. Further, it suggests that the relative pronouns share some features with the organizational words. FIGURE 6 shows that the size and variance of the phrase unit domain for the relatives are somewhere between the values for the two subclasses of organizational words.

Reading Time Data for Definiteness Words

The RT data for definiteness words (FIGURE 4) show two results that are consistent with the Performance Task Hypothesis (H3). First, the rel RTs for

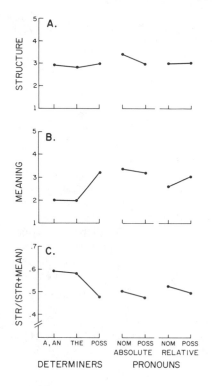

FIGURE 8. Means of subjective ratings for **(A)** structure, **(B)** meaning, and **(C)** the proportion of the total structure plus meaning rating devoted to structure for six categories of definiteness function words.

comprehension are above those for recall at every point, for both determiners (F-test: $p < 0.001$) and pronouns (F-test: $p < 0.04$). As determiners are noun delimiters, and pronouns are noun substitutes, these results are consistent with the noun set data where comprehension rel RTs are greater than recall rel RTs. As mentioned earlier, these trends for definiteness words (M) are opposite to those for organizational words (S), where the average rel RT is greater for recall than for comprehension subjects.

Second, the pronoun graph shows an interaction between task groups and the absolute-relative aspect that is consistent with the other task-x-category interactions. Recall subjects spend less time coding absolute pronouns than relatives, which introduce clauses with their own subjects and predicates. But comprehension rel RTs do not differ for these two structurally different pronoun types. The 40 msec difference between task groups for absolute pronouns is statistically significant (*t* test: $p < 0.01$), but the task difference for relative pronouns is not, again supporting H3.

In sum, the rating data, the phrase break data and past research together yield evidence (a) that, in general, the definiteness set provides an important contribution to the sentence structure, in comparison to the content words, and (b) that, as a group, definiteness words contribute more to meaning than do the organizational function words. This supports their position in the hierarchy with an S-label for the first node and an M-label for the second. Consistently with this mixed S/M position, rel RTs for recall subjects are sensitive to the structural attributes of pronouns (S), but the general task effects show similarities to those for the noun set (M).

Lexical Categories and Reading Deficiencies

Recent reviews of individual differences in reading[60] and of linguistic and cognitive factors in dyslexia[61] show that most researchers have been oriented toward single-factor theories. But there is little agreement on what that "critical" factor is, with studies implicating visual code formation, letter discrimination, letter sequencing, use of orthographic regularity, spelling-to-sound mappings, phonological recoding, morphological coding, memory for word order, semantic memory, short-term memory, identification of syntactic relations, prediction from syntactic and semantic context, semantic integration, and use of syntax in mnemonic coding. With reasonable research projects implicating all of these factors, it is likely that (a) many reading deficiencies are multi-determined, and/or (b) there are many different types of reading deficiencies being classified together.

The present volume is addressed both to reading processes and reading disabilities. Although the present research was conducted with normal college readers, it has implications for the notion of *multifactor theories* of normal reading and of reading deficiencies. In particular, reading is *not* a single performance task, and researchers should not be looking for *the* theory of reading or of reading disability. Rather, we read for many different goals: for example, searching for key words, skimming for essence, reading for gist, reading for special topical information, leisure reading, reading in depth, or studying for exams. The present research shows that the various lexical categories play differential roles, depending on the reading task, and on the reading strategy used for the given task. Some tasks and strategies emphasize structural coding while others emphasize meaning. Indeed, a reader equipped for the variety of natural reading tasks in everyday life must have (1) a wide range of linguistic and cognitive skills, and (2) the ability to use the particular skills or strategies appropriate for the given reading task. Thus, we suggest (a) that some reading deficiencies may occur because the reader does not select and integrate multiple skills in an optimal way for each given reading task, and (b) many past research projects cannot assess the complexities of a multidimensional situation because they are wedded to a single or a few restricted research paradigms.

CONCLUSIONS

Within the framework of the *Continuum Hypothesis* (H2), the structural and meaning attributes of 18 lexical categories were examined. Subjective ratings on these dimensions, along with the extent to which categories cue the onset of a phrase unit or provide a terminal point for semantic integration, permit us to compare and rank the various lexical categories relative to one another. These data, plus distributional statistics and special-purpose ratings are gener-

TABLE 4. Descriptive Statistics on Lexical Distances and Positions

Lexical Category	90 Stimulus Sentences			Newspaper and Magazine Text		
	Absolute Distance	Distance Range	Positional Ordering	Absolute Distance	Distance Range	Positional Ordering
Verb set						
Auxiliary verb – Verb	1.16	1-2	100%	1.38	1-2	100%
Auxiliary verb – Adverb (V)	1.10	1-2	90%	1.94	1-12	84%
Adverb (V) – Verb	1.43	1-4	44%	1.72	1-11	62%
Noun set						
Adjective – Noun	1.63	1-8	88%	1.26	1-10	98%
Adverb (A) – Adjective	1.10	1-3	97%	1.16	1-3	100%
Adverb (A) – Noun	2.90	2-7	57%	2.46	2-9	97%

ally consistent with each other, although the data on auxiliary verbs, conjunctions, and "by" provide some minor problems. The simultaneous application of several different empirical approaches yields natural reliability information. Together these data provide a picture of the relative contributions to sentential structure and meaning for the individual lexical categories.

Further, the data support the *Structure-Meaning Hypothesis* (H1), in that they are consistent with the hierarchical organization of FIGURE 1. The summary data in TABLE 5 show that function words, (S), more frequently cue the start of a phrase unit and have higher structural ratings than do content words, (M). Within these major branches, the data show a greater contribution to structure for the verb set, (M, S), than the noun set (M, M), and for the organizational set, (S, S), than the definiteness set (S, M).

The Pearson correlations in TABLE 5 between the subjective structure and meaning ratings provide a summary statistic useful in evaluating H1. For the two branches on which both hierarchical levels have identical labels, there is a negative correlation between structure and meaning. Those organizational words (S, S) which contribute more to structure also contribute correspondingly less to meaning (r(S, M) = −0.34, p = 0.01). Those members of the noun set (M, M) which contribute more to meaning also contribute correspondingly less to structure (r(S, M) = −0.18, p = 0.11, one-tail test). Categories on the two "mixture" branches that are biased toward structure on one level and toward meaning on the other, do not show this trade-off. Although the separate correlational values for the 18 lexical categories are not large (−0.58 to +0.41), their distribution is systematic. All of the nine correlations for the categories with identical labels at both hierarchical levels (noun and organizational sets) are negative, but five of the nine correlations for the other two sets are positive (Mann-Whitney U-test: noun & organizational versus verb & definiteness sets, U = 14; 67, p < 0.02).

In sum, the lexical categories have a systematic hierarchical organization based on stimulus attributes that are important for linguistic performance tasks. Further, both past literature, and the present RT data support the *Performance Task Hypothesis*. Lexical categories that contribute more to structuring the sentence are reflected more strongly in the performance data when we read for faithful retention of the text than for comprehension of gist. Those with a larger role in sentence meaning are weighted more heavily in compre-

TABLE 5. Summary Indices for Lexical Categories

	Content (M)		Function (S)	
	Verb (M,S)	Noun (M,M)	Org. (S,S)	Def. (S,M)
% Begin Phrase	40%	9%	52%	25%
% Structure	46%	41%	56%	53%
r(S, M)	− .01	− .18	− .34	+ .04

NOTE: Row 1 is the percent of all words in a category that are the first word of a subjectively marked phrase. Row 2 is the percent of the combined structure plus meaning ratings devoted to structure. Row 3 is the Pearson correlation between structure and meaning ratings for words within each lexical set.

henion than in memory tasks. When we read for different purposes, we use the various lexical categories differentially in our coding of linguistic information.

SUMMARY

A hierarchical organization for lexical categories is proposed based on the relative contribution of words to the structure and meaning of text. Function words primarily signal the sentential structure while conent words primarily convey its meaning. But within these traditional categories, further divisions can be made that have psycholinguistic importance. For example, within the content words, verbs emphasize structure more than nouns do, and within the function words, pronouns emphasize meaning more than prepositions do. The hierarchical organization is supported by subjective ratings of sentences and by distributional analyses of printed text. Further, the time spent reading the various categories depends on the performance demands. Structural information is more important when reading for retention than for comprehension of gist. But meaning is more important for comprehension than for retention tasks.

ACKNOWLEDGMENTS

We thank Nancy Bowles, Tom Carr, Miriam Divinsky, Beth Fischer, Murray Glanzer, Margaret Jean Intons-Peterson, Robert Sherak, and Mary Vanderwart for helpful comments.

REFERENCES

1. HEALY, A. & G. MILLER. 1970. The verb as the main determinant of sentence meaning. Psychonom. Sci. **20**: 372.
2. HEALY, A. & G. MILLER. 1971. The relative contribution of nouns and verbs to sentence acceptability and comprehensibility. Psychonom. Sci. **24**: 94–96.
3. HUTTENLOCHER, J. & F. LUI. 1979. The semantic organization of some simple nouns and verbs. J. Verb. Learn. Verb. Behav. **18**: 141–162.
4. RAEBURN, V. P. 1979. The role of the verb in sentence memory. Mem. Cognit. **7**: 133–140.
5. REYNOLDS, A. G. & P. W. FLAGG. 1976. Recognition memory for elements of sentences. Mem. Cognit. **4**: 422–432.
6. JEREMY, R. J. 1978. Use of coordinate sentences with the conjunction *and* for describing temporal and locative relations between events. J. Psycholing. Res. **7**: 135–150.
7. AARONSON, M., D. BERTOLUCCI, J. PHILLIPS & D. AARONSON. 1978. Preschool preposition test: Developmental screening for Head Start. Proceedings of AERA, ERIC Document #ED 164585.
8. HEALY, A. 1980. Proofreading errors on the word *the*: New evidence on reading units. J. Exp. Psychol. Hum. Percept. Perform. **6**: 45–57.
9. RANDO, E. & D. J. NAPOLI. 1978. Definites in *There*-sentences. Language **54**: 300–313.

10. DEVILLIERS, P. A. 1974. Imagery and theme in recall of connected discourse. J. Exp. Psychol. **103**: 263–268.
11. LYONS, J. 1968. Introduction to Theoretical Linguistics. Cambridge University Press. London.
12. CLARK, H. H. & E. V. CLARK. 1977. Psychology and Language. Harcourt Brace Jovanovich. New York, NY.
13. MILLER, G. A. & P. N JOHNSON-LAIRD. 1976. Language and Perception. Harvard University Press. Cambridge, MA.
14. KINTSCH, W. 1974. The Representation of Meaning in Memory. Erlbaum. Hillsdale, NJ.
15. BOCK, J. K. 1982. Toward a cognitive psychology of syntax: Information processing contributions to sentence formulation Psychol. Rev. **89**: 1–47.
16. BRESNAN, J. 1978. A realistic transformational grammar. *In* Linguistic Theory and Psychological Reality. M. Halle, J. Bresnan, & G. A. Miller, Eds. MIT press. Cambridge, MA.
17. GAZDAR, G. 1979. Constitutent structures. Unpublished manuscript, Cognitive Studies Programme, School of Social Sciences, University of Sussex, England.
18. LYONS, J. 1977. Semantics, Vol. 2. Cambridge University Press. London.
19. ABORN, M. & H. RUBENSTEIN. 1956. Word-class distribution in sentences of fixed length. Language **32**: 666–674.
20. ABORN, M., H. RUBENSTEIN & T. D. STERLING. 1959. Sources of contextual constraint upon words in sentences. J. Exp. Psychol. **57**: 171–180.
21. FILLENBAUM, S., L. V. JONES & A. RAPOPORT. 1963. The predictability of words and their grammatical classes as a function of rate of detection from a speech transcript. J. Verb. Learn. Verb. Behav. **2**: 186–194.
22. FRIES, C. C. 1952. The Structure of English. Harcourt Brace. New York, NY.
23. GLANZER, M. 1962. Grammatical category: A rote learning and word association analysis. J. Verb. Learn. Verb. Behav. **1**: 31–41.
24. KLEIN, S. & R. F. SIMMONS. 1961. Automated analysis and coding of English grammar for information processing systems. Systems Development Corp., Rep. SP-490, Santa Monica, CA.
25. HAMILL, B. W. 1976. A linguistic correlate of sentential rhythmic patterns. J. Exp. Psychol. Hum. Percept. Perform. **2**: 71–79.
26. AARONSON, D. 1976. Performance theories for sentence coding: Some qualitative observations. J. Exp. Psychol. Hum. Percept. Perform. **2**: 42–55.
27. LEVELT, W. J. M. 1970. Hierarchial chunking in sentence processing. Percept. Psychophys. **8**: 99–103.
28. BOND, Z. S. & J. GRAY. 1973. Subjective phrase structure: An empirical investigation. J. Psycholing. Res. **2**: 259–266.
29. O'CONNELL, D. C. & S. KOWAL. 1972. Cross-linguistic and rate phenomena in adults and adolescents. J. Psychol. Res. **1**: 155–164.
30. WILKES, A. L. & R. A. KENNEDY. 1969. Relationship between pausing and retrieval latency in sentences of varying grammatical form. J. Exp. Psychol. **79**: 241–245.
31. GIBSON, E. J. & H. LEVIN. 1975. The Psychology of Reading. MIT Press. Cambridge, MA.
32. AARONSON, D. & H. S. SCARBOROUGH. 1976. Performance theories for sentence coding: Some quantitative evidence. J. Exp. Psychol. Hum. Percept. Perform. **2**: 56–70.
33. AARONSON, D. & H. S. SCARBOROUGH. 1977. Performance theories for sentence coding: Some quantitative models. J. Verb. Learn. Verb. Behav. **16**: 277–303.
34. IRWIN, D. E., J. V. BOCK & K. E. STANOVICH. 1982. Effects of information structure cues on visual word processing. J. Verb. Learn. Verb. Behav. **21**: 307–325.

35. CARAMAZZA, A., E. GROBER & C. GARVEY. 1977. Comprehension of anaphoric pronouns. J. Verb. Learn. Verb. Behav. **16**: 601–609.
36. CARPENTER, P. A. & M. A. JUST. 1977. Integrative processes in comprehension. *In* Basic Processes in Reading: Perception and Comprehension. D. LaBerge & S. J. Samuels, Eds. Erlbaum. Hillsdale, NJ.
37. LESGOLD, A. M., S. F. ROTH & M. E. CURTIS. 1979. Foregrounding effects in discourse comprehension. J. Verb. Learn. Verb. Behav. **18**: 291–308.
38. FOSS, D. J., R. K. CIRILO & M. A. BLANK. 1979. Semantic facilitation and lexical access during sentence processing: An investigation of individual differences. Mem. Cognit. **5**: 346–353.
39. LESGOLD, A. M. 1972. Pronominalization: A device for unifying sentences in memory. J. Verb. Learn. Verb. Behav. **11**: 316–323.
40. MORAY, N. & A. TAYLOR. 1958. The effect of redundancy in shadowing one of two dichotic messages. Lang. Speech **1**: 102–109.
41. CHOMSKY, N. 1965. Aspects of the Theory of Syntax. MIT Press. Cambridge, MA.
42. MOSTELLER, F. & D. L. WALLACE. 1977. Deciding authorship. *In* Statistics: A Guide to Political and Social Issues. J. M. Tanur *et al.,* Eds. Holden-Day. San Francisco, CA.
43. CLARK, H. H. 1973. The language-as-fixed-effect fallacy: A critique of language statistics in psychological research. J. Verb. Learn. Verb. Behav. **12**: 335–359.
44. JARVELLA, R. J. 1971. Syntactic processing of connected speech. J. Verb. Learn. Verb. Behav. **10**: 409–416.
45. MITCHELL, D. C. & D. W. GREEN. 1978. The effects of context and content on immediate processing in reading. Q. J. Exp. Psychol. **30**: 609–636.
46. COOPER, W. E. & J. PACCIA-COOPER. 1980. Syntax and Speech. Harvard University Press. Cambridge, MA.
47. MARTIN, E. 1970. Toward an analysis of subjective phrase structure. Psychol. Bull. **74**: 153–166.
48. KINTSCH, W. & J. KEENAN. 1973. Reading rate and retention as a function of the number of propositions in the basic structure of sentences. Cognit. Psychol. **5**: 257–274.
49. KOUTSOUDAS, A. 1966. Writing Transformational Grammars: An Introduction. McGraw-Hill. New York, NY.
50. AARONSON, D. & S. FERRES. 1983. Lexical categories and reading tasks. J. Exp. Psychol. Hum. Percept. Perform. **9**: 675–699.
51. AARONSON, D. & S. FERRES. 1983. A model for coding lexical categories during reading. J. Exp. Psychol. Hum. Percept. Perform. **9**: 700–725.
52. YNGVE, V. 1960. A model and a hypothesis for language structure. Proc. Am. Philos. Soc. **104**: 444–466.
53. HARMAN, G. H. 1963. Generative grammars without transformational rules: A defense of phrase structure. Language **39**: 597–616.
54. GOVE, P. B., Ed. 1976. Webster's Third New International Dictionary. G & C Merriam. Springfield, MA.
55. BENDIX, E. H. 1966. Componential Analysis of General Vocabulary: The Semantic Structure of a Set of Verbs in English, Hindi, and Japanese. Mouton. The Hague.
56. BURTON-ROBERTS, N. 1976. On the generic indefinite article. Language **52**: 427–448.
57. BEATTY, J. & J. BORREE. 1976. Effects of word class on the recall of sentences. J. Verb. Learn. Verb. Behav. **10**: 604–607.
58. MARTIN E. & D. A. WALTER. 1969. Subject uncertainty and word-class effects in short-term memory for sentences. J. Exp. Psychol **80**: 47–51.

59. MARATSOS, M. P. 1973. The effects of stress on the understanding of pronominal co-reference in children. J. Psycholing. Res. **2**: 1–8.
60. CARR, T. H. 1981. Building theories of reading ability: On the relation between individual differences in cognitive skills and reading comprehension. Cognition **9**: 73–113.
61. VELLUTINO, F. R. 1978. Toward an understanding of dyslexia: Psychological factors in specific reading disability. *In* Dyslexia: An Appraisal of Current Knowledge. A. L. Benton & D. Pearl, Eds. Oxford University Press. New York, NY.
62. WINER, B. J. 1962. Statistical Principles in Experimental Design. McGraw-Hill. New York, NY.

The Reading of Content and Noncontent Words by Dyslexics[a]

MARION BLANK AND CAROL BRUSKIN

Department of Psychiatry
Columbia University
New York, New York 10032

INTRODUCTION

Automatic decoding is a major component of fluent reading. Until automaticity is achieved, the reader must concentrate on decoding the written word, leaving little or no attention to spare for the vital task of comprehension.[1] Samuels[2] has offered a model outlining the acquisition of automaticity. Of critical importance to his model is the fact that full automaticity is not a word-by-word identification process, but rather entails the grouping of words into larger units such as phrases, clauses, and sentences.

When words are "chunked" into these larger units, the reader's experience is one of perceiving meaningful ideas (for instance, "the boy," "has been seen," "all of them," and so on). While the semantic, or meaning, aspect may be the one most salient to the reader, there is another, often overlooked, dimension according to which the chunking may take place. This dimension is related more to the syntactic aspects of language and involves the grouping of words into what has commonly been termed content and noncontent categories. For example, the phrase "the boy" contains the referential notion of a particular individual, but this idea is conveyed through two words, the noncontent word "the" and the content word "boy."

As is so commonly the case in a domain as complex as language, the boundaries between content and noncontent words are not firm. It is partly for this reason that a variety of terms has been used to designate this distinction. They have included contentive versus functor,[3] open- versus closed-class[4] and context-independent versus context-dependent.[5] Regardless of the multiple terminology, the categories of *content*, *open-class*, *contentive*, and *context-independent* generally refer to nouns, verbs, and adjectives — words that carry most of the representational meaning. By contrast, the categories of *noncontent*, *closed-class*, *functro*, and *context-dependent* generally include prepositions, conjunctions, and auxiliary verbs — words that primarily serve the syntactic function of organizing the content words into meaningful segments.

The distinction between content and noncontent words is vital in language processing, and there is evidence that the individual language user treats these words as representing distinctly different categories from early life. For ex-

[a] This research was supported by Grant HD-12278-04 from the National Institute of Child Health and Development.

59

ample, the earliest utterances of the young child consist mainly of content words.[3,6,7] As described by Brown,[3] in the first stage of language acquisition ". . . nouns, verbs and adjectives are . . . used frequently . . . while inflections, auxiliaries, prepositions, articles, and the copula are used seldom or not at all" (p. 249). However, in the second stage, a dramatic change occurs in that ". . . a set of little words and inflections begins to appear. . . . All these, like an intricate sort of ivy, begin to grow up between and upon the major construction blocks, the nouns and verbs, to which Stage I is largely limited" (p. 249). The restriction to content words in Stage I and the expansion to noncontent words in Stage II suggests that, even at a very early age, human beings sense and respond to the differences between the two groups of words.

There is also evidence that, despite their relatively early appearance in children's utterances, noncontent words are less accessible or less available to conscious analysis.[8] For example, Egido[9] tested pre-school children's ability to differentiate words (both content and noncontent) from non-words. Whereas the children readily and accurately identified content words as real words, they inconsistently classified the noncontent words, sometimes identifying them as words and sometimes as nonwords. Comparable results were obtained in a study by Ehri,[10] where she required kindergarten and first-grade children to learn content and noncontent words as paired associates to nonsense figures. The kindergarten children showed no mastery of the noncontent words, and the first-grade children found the noncontent words more difficult than the nouns or adjectives.

Such differential performance with respect to content and noncontent words is relevant to the "chunking" process described earlier. These meaningful word groups most often contain content and noncontent words. Hence, implicit in the idea of chunking is that there must be a merging of the less accessible (noncontent) with the more accessible (content) words. This merging occurs in both oral and written language.

In oral language, a number of distinct cues exist to facilitate the process. They include supralinguistic features such as prosody, gestures, and pauses, which all help to mark the phrasal structures. In written language, however, such cues are largely absent. As a result, acquisition of reading fluency requires the child to ". . . transfer from a system in which prosodic marking plays a major role in identifying syntactic phrases (i.e., oral language) to a system in which the phrases go largely unmarked graphically (i.e., written language). The child must learn to compensate somehow for the lack of overt graphic marking of many syntactic units."[11] (p. 181).

The child's task is even more difficult than the above quote would indicate. Not only are the supralinguistic cues minimally marked for the reader, but the manner in which words are presented on a printed page conflicts with the implicit knowledge which the child has learned from oral (everyday) language. For example, in a *spoken phrase* such as "the boy," the two words are not of equal weight: "boy" is stressed, and thus stands out as more salient than "the." Further, temporal factors clearly indicate a single semantic unit. By contrast, in the silence of the *printed page*, both words occupy equal amounts of space (3 letters each) and are separated by equal intervals. They thereby might tend to be processed by early and disabled readers as if they are to receive equal "psychological" weight. In other words, written text requires children to set aside their expectations regarding syntactic "chunking" gained in oral language and requires them to learn a new set of rules.

These comments suggest that mastery of noncontent words in written language may be particularly difficult for children. They also suggest that the relative ease with which this mastery is achieved will relate to the development of reading skill.[12] Evidence exists to support this hypothesis. Teachers commonly report ". . . some of the most troublesome words for beginning and disabled readers are the three-, four-, and five-letter words that make up the bulk of English prose. They are often referred to as 'demons', a label which reflects the almost universal difficulty they cause children . . . most of the demons fit a linguistic category called 'function words,'"[13] (p. 136).

RESEARCH WITH NORMAL READERS

Our previous research has shown that differential performance with respect to content and noncontent words is both (a) related to level of reading skill and (b) continues well into the school years.[14,15] These findings derive from a study of third- and fifth-grade children who were required to read and spell a list of words. The words were matched for frequency of appearance in text at grade level[16] and number of syllables. Analyses of latencies to read the words revealed that, at both grades, noncontent words took significantly longer than content words. Further, when the children were divided into three levels of reading proficiency (i.e., high, average, and low), it was found that (1) the best readers, *regardless of grade*, exhibited little difference in latency between the two categories, (2) the average readers exhibited a small, but significant, difference with the noncontent words taking longer to identify, and (3) the least skilled—albeit still normal readers—exhibited the greatest difference. The effects of word class were evident, not only in latency measures, but also in the errors made in reading and spelling. More noncontent words were misread and misspelled than were content words. Again, this pattern was most marked in the performance of the least skilled readers.

THE PRESENT RESEARCH:
DYSLEXIC READERS

In the research just described, the children ranged across several levels of reading proficiency; nonetheless, they were all within normal range. If the content/noncontent distinction was as important as we suspected, its effect would also be found—probably in most extreme form—in children who were experiencing difficulty in the acquisition of reading, that is, in dyslexic children. Accordingly, this is the issue we have chosen to investigate and report in the current research.

Before proceeding, it seems necessary to define the term "dyslexia," since it is one that has often aroused controversy.[17] Despite this controversy the label is in many ways preferable to the wide variety of terms that are com-

TABLE 1. Words in Isolation

Nouns	Verbs	Noncontent Words
man	make	these
sound	walk	could
boy	went	than
bird	play	why
house	put	has
mother	follow	very
children	happen	because
window	carry	without
worm	bounce	whose
newspaper	remember	however
finger	compare	during
fence	climb	since
blanket	forget	rather
grandfather	disappear	possible
river	begin	also
bath	yell	thus

monly used in this area (e.g., "poor readers," "disabled readers," "retarded readers," and so forth). These latter terms contain essentially no information about the children other than that they are not achieving at grade level. By contrast, the definition of dyslexia set forth by the World Federation of Neurology[18] indicates that there has been an assessment of intelligence and that the reading failure represents a low level of attainment relative to the child's intellectual capability. In the present study, the children were categorized as dyslexic if both verbal and performance IQs were above 95, and if they had achieved a reading quotient of less than .85 based on the formula:

$$\frac{\text{Reading Age (Gilmore Accuracy Score)} \times 100}{\text{Chronological Age} \times \text{Full Scale IQ (WISC-R)}}.$$

The sample of children in the current work consists of 16 dyslexic boys, all of whom were reading on a much lower level than their age, grade, and intellectual ability would lead one to predict. (Their mean reading grade was 2.0, their mean grade was 5.7, their mean chronological age was 11.2 years, and their mean full scale IQ was 108.)

The task given to these children was similar to that described above, but it was expanded to include an important feature which was not studied in the previous work. Specifically, the stimuli presented to the normal readers in the research cited above involved only the reading aloud of words in isolation, and while this task yielded interesting effects of word class, the phenomenon is truly relevant only if it can be shown to exist in the actual reading process, that is, in the reading of connected text. In order to assess this, the children were given two tasks: (1) they were asked to read aloud words in isolation: the same words read by the third graders in the previous study were used, since this list was the most appropriate to their reading level (TABLE 1); and (2) they were asked to read words in context. The Gilmore Oral Reading

FORM C-1

The girl has a cat.
The girl is Mary.
The cat is Puff.
^the Puff is gray.
Father is in the yard.
Father works hard.

FORM C-3

Mary is just twelve years old.
Her brother Dick is fourteen.
They both go to the same school.
Mary is in Grade Seven.
She likes her class in cooking.
Dick is now in Grade Nine.
Although he enjoys all his school work,
Dick likes the work in art class best.

FORM C-5

Summers are exciting for Mary and Dick. For two years Dick has attended a Boy Scout camp. The camp is located beside a sparkling mountain lake, where the boys enjoy healthy outdoor living. Among numerous activities, the boys improve their swimming, sometimes go sailing, and—most important— go on extended camping trips. Dick hopes to return to camp this coming summer. Last July Mary was thrilled when she attended a Girl Scout day camp for two weeks. She remembers the swimming instruction, the nature study, and especially the campfires. Mary will probably attend overnight Scout camp for the first time this next summer.

FIGURE 1. Passages 1, 3, and 5 from the Gilmore Oral Reading Test showing typical errors made by the children. A circle (e.g., ⓐ) denotes an omitted word; a caret (e.g., ^) denotes an inserted word; a diagonal line through a word (e.g., numerous) denotes a mispronunciation; a horizontal line through a word (e.g. the) denotes a substitution.

Test[19] was used for the latter purpose. In this test, a child is given a number of passages of increasing levels of difficulty and is required to read aloud until he reaches the passage in which he makes ten or more errors. FIGURE 1 shows a partial set of passages read by the children and the types of errors made by the dyslexic children in the sample. The measures used to assess performance on the words in isolation were (1) latency to read the words, and (2) accuracy of identification. Performance on the words in context was assessed by accuracy only.

RESULTS

Reading of Words in Isolation

Latency

The pattern of response times for the content (nouns and verbs) and noncontent words is shown in TABLE 2. The latencies were measured using a voice-key which gave a measure of the time from the onset of the stimulus to the child's vocal response. A 3 × 2 repeated measures analysis of variance (with word class and number of syllables as factors) indicated that word class was significant ($F = 20.35$; $df = 2/15$; $p < 0.001$). As assessed by the Duncan's Multiple Range Test, noncontent words took significantly longer to read than either nouns or verbs ($p = 0.05$), while the latter two categories (i.e., content words) did not differ from each other. Not surprisingly, the children took longer to read the multisyllable words than the single syllable words ($F = 12.59$; $df = 1/15$; $p < 0.001$). There was, however, no interaction between word class and number of syllables, indicating that the latency differential was maintained for both single and multisyllable words.

Errors

An analysis was also carried out on the number of errors made in reading words in isolation. As before, these results were calculated on the basis of word class and number of syllables. The reader will note that the error rate is quite low, since the words were selected to be those which are common in third grade (i.e., for 8–9 year old normal readers). (Remember that the dyslexics averaged over 11 years of age.) In terms of the single syllable words, there were a greater number of errors on the noncontent words than on the nouns or verbs. In a total of 37 errors, 22 were made on the noncontent words, 8 were made on the nouns, and 7 on the verbs (see TABLE 2). Thus, even though only 33% of the words were in the noncontent category, 59% of the errors were made on these words.

The analysis of errors on the multisyllable words yielded somewhat different results. First, there were fewer errors in the reading of the multisyllable words than in the single syllable words. This rather surprising result may be due to the children's attending more fully to the longer words and their

TABLE 2. Responses to Words in Isolation and in Context

(a) Latencies (in seconds) to Words in Isolation

	Nouns	Verbs	Noncontent Words
Single syllable words	1.28[a]	1.31	1.49
	.18	.19	.32
Multisyllable words	1.37	1.44	1.53
	.23	.22	.35

(b) Total Number of Errors to Words in Isolation

	Nouns	Verbs	Noncontent Words
Single syllable words	8	7	22
Multisyllable words	10	5	2

(c) Total Number of Errors to Words in Context

	Content	Noncontent
Single syllable words	28	79/13[b]
Multisyllable words	66	14/19

[a] The upper number represents the mean, the lower number the standard deviation.
[b] The first number represents errors on whole words, the second on bound morphemes (e.g., noncontent morphemes attached to content words such as wash*ing*).

being more careful in reading them. The pattern of errors was also different from that observed for the single syllable words. Of a total of 16 errors, 10 were made on the verbs, 5 on the noncontent words, and only 1 noun was misread. This would suggest that, for some reason, the noncontent multisyllable words do not cause as much difficulty in terms of error, although they clearly do so in terms of latency.

Reading of Words in Context

The Gilmore Oral Reading Test,[18] which served as the material for the reading of connected text, is scored for a wide variety of errors, including repetitions, hesitations, and self-corrections. For the present purpose of studying the reading of connected text, we were interested only in the words that the children misread, failed to read, or inserted into the text. The results indicated that there were fewer such errors in the reading of contextual material than in the reading of isolated words. It could not be determined whether this result was due to the differential difficulty of the words in the two tasks, or whether contextual reading leads to fewer errors than does the reading of words in isolation, as reported by Krieger.[20] Nevertheless, the results still revealed more errors on noncontent words and bound morphemes than on content words. A total of 120 errors were made on the single syllable words in the first six passages. Of these, 92 errors were on the noncontent words and bound morphemes, but only 28 were on the content words. Given that there is a differential frequency for the two word classes (973 content words versus

1619 noncontent words read by the children), one might attribute the results to that factor alone. However, a χ^2 analysis taking this factor into account indicated that the error difference was significant ($\chi^2 = 10.02$, $p < 0.01$).

The error pattern is even more striking when one considers the issue of differential frequency in print. It is well established that frequency affects readability, in that greater frequency is associated with better performance.[21] This factor was controlled for the words presented in isolation, where the words were matched for frequency across word class. In normal text, however, the noncontent words are generally of far greater frequency than the content words and, hence, should have an advantage *vis à vis* word recognition. Nevertheless, the noncontent words still proved more difficult.

The pattern of errors on multisyllable words is somewhat harder to discern. There were only three multisyllable noncontent words in the texts completed by the children. These appeared 38 times in the passages read. Nevertheless, the results mirror those of the single syllable words: of the 204 instances of noncontent words and bound morphemes, there were a total of 33 errors, or an error rate of 16%. By contrast, of the 735 instances of multisyllable content words, there was a total of only 66 errors, or an error rate of 9%. As tested by χ^2, this difference is significant ($\chi^2 = 8.02$; $p < 0.01$).

IMPLICATIONS FOR THE READING PROCESS

The present research is clearly of an exploratory nature. We chose to use a seminaturalistic approach rather than to tightly control all the potentially relevant variables (e.g., grapheme-phoneme correspondence in the content and noncontent categories, having identical words in the isolation and connected text conditions, and so on). Therefore, the results should be interpreted with caution and be seen as a first step in exploring an important domain of language. Nonetheless, even in this preliminary form, the results raise a number of interesting ideas that are consonant with established literature, and these we will explore below.

One issue of interest derives from the idea that initially stimulated this research, namely, the role of word class in fluent word identification. The results we found parallel those of a study by Aaron,[22] where it was found that dyslexic children omitted, substituted, or added noncontent words more often than words from other form classes. The consequence for their reading of text was that "errors invariably resulted in agrammatic sentences. . ." (p. 27). The Aaron finding is particularly important because it serves to highlight the role that noncontent words play in natural text. More than half the words on any page of print are from the noncontent domain. As a result, the children are constantly required to deal with a group of words that (a) cause them confusion and difficulty, and (b) result in their being faced with incomprehensible agrammatic sentences.

In evaluating the findings of the present research, it is important to recognize that both tasks (words in isolation and words in text) required the children to say the words out loud. It has been suggested that the word identification difficulties of the poor reader may be most marked when they are required to *articulate* words.[23,24] As a result, it is possible that the effect shown in the present research would be muted or altered were the tasks to have required silent rather than oral reading.

The difficulties displayed by children who are experiencing problems in mastering written language (e.g., dyslexics) have interesting parallels in the difficulties displayed by children who are experiencing problems in mastering oral language (e.g., autistic children). For example, it has been shown that even when autistic children are using relatively complex grammatical structures in their speech, their use of noncontent words and morphemes is inferior to that of other children who are at a comparable level of language ability.[25] The discrepant performance with respect to word class is also seen in the language of Broca's aphasics who have lesions in the anterior portion of the left hemisphere. These patients focus on content words in speech and omit most of the noncontent words and bound morphemes.[26] *Thus, the content/noncontent distinction seems to reflect a common dimension subserving adequate functioning in both oral and written language.*

While the effects of word class are clearly discernible, the source of these effects is little understood. One promising explanation has been offered from studies using the visual hemifield paradigm.[27] In that research, it was found that presentation of both classes of words to the left visual field (right hemisphere) resulted in poor, but equal, levels of accuracy in word identification. By contrast, when the words were presented to the right visual field (left hemisphere), accuracy increased, although not in a uniform manner. Performance on the content words was significantly better than performance on the noncontent words. These results led Bradley and Garrett[27] to suggest that there may be differential access for content and noncontent words in the left hemisphere, whereas the same mechanism serves to access both word classes in the right hemisphere.

Some support for this hypothesis is available in studies of "deep dyslexics." These are a subgroup of adult alexics who have left hemisphere damage and show a complex set of symptoms in reading, including particular difficulties in identifying noncontent words.[28,29,30] Their difficulties are aptly illustrated in the performance of a French dyslexic: in French, the word *car* can serve different semantic/syntactic roles. When it serves as a noun, it means "vehicle" or "bus"; when it serves as a conjunction it means "because." A sentence was created in which the word was used in its two different roles: "Le car ralentit car le moteur chauffe," which translates into "the bus stops because the motor overheats." Strikingly, the patient was able to read the word when it functioned as a noun (*bus*) but not when it functioned as a noncontent word (*because*).[31]

Although it has not yet been considered, the discussion of the content/noncontent distinction clearly has bearing on the teaching of reading, in particular, the teaching of decoding. In the main, the teaching of word identification has focused on helping the child achieve grapheme-phoneme correspondences. As has been commonly noted, many of the noncontent words do not lend themselves to the grapheme-phoneme correspondences which the children are taught (e.g., "are", "be", "whose", "could", and so on). In addition, in conveying to the children the idea that the same set of grapheme-phoneme correspondences is applicable to all words, the teaching runs *counter* both to the reality of our language and to the definite sense of differentiation that children possess about the two classes of words. The children may not be, and probably are not, conscious of their behavior, but the evidence from both spoken and written language indicates that they perceive and respond to content and noncontent words as separate groups. Therefore, rather than teaching (implicitly or explicitly) that a set of common rules applies to all words, it would seem reasonable and useful to capitalize on the distinction that the children already possess and teach the two classes of words as distinct categories.

A program based on these principles has been outlined by the present investigators,[14] in which the two classes of words are taught separately. For the content words, grapheme-phoneme correspondences are stressed, while other analytic procedures are used for the noncontent words. In addition, emphasis is placed on helping the children realize the role that this latter group of words plays in structuring language into meaningful units. The program has been used with children displaying a variety of reading difficulties, and it has shown promising results. Further, it has the value of showing the way in which advances in our basic knowledge of language can be used to enhance the teaching of the vital skills involved in literacy.

REFERENCES

1. LeBerge, D. & S. J. Samuels. 1974. Toward a theory of automatic information processing in reading. Cognitive Psychol. **6**: 293–323.
2. Samuels, S. J. 1979. The method of repeated readings. Reading Teacher : 403–409.
3. Brown, R. 1973. A First Language. Harvard University Press. Cambridge, MA.
4. Thorne, J. F., P. Bratley & H. Dewar. 1968. The syntactic analysis of English by machine. *In* Machine Intelligence, Vol. 3. D. Michie, Ed. American Elsevier, New York, NY.
5. Ehri, L. C. 1975. Word consciousness in readers and pre-readers. J. Ed. Psychol. **67**: 204–212.
6. Bloom, L. & M. Lahey. 1978. Language Development and Language Disorders. John Wiley & Sons. New York, NY.
7. deVilliers, J. G. & P. M. deVilliers. 1973. A cross-sectional study of the development of grammatical morphemes in child speech. J. Psycholing. Res. **2**: 267–278.
8. Luria, A. R. 1982. Language and Cognition. J. V. Wertsch, Ed. John Wiley & Sons. New York, NY.
9. Egido, C. 1981. Invisibility of closed class words in children's word judgements. Unpublished paper.
10. Ehri, L. C. 1976. Word learning in beginning readers: Effects of form class and defining contexts. J. Ed. Psychol. **68**: 832–842.
11. Schreiber, P. A. 1980. On the acquisition of reading fluency. J. Reading Behav. **XII**: 177–186.

12. Cunningham, P. M. 1980. Teaching *were*, *with*, *what*, and other four letter words. Reading Teacher (Nov.) : 160–163.

13. Jolly, H. B., Jr. 1981. Teaching basic function words. Reading Teacher **35**: 136–140.

14. Blank, M. & C. Bruskin. 1982. Sentences and non-content words: Missing ingredients in reading instruction. Ann. Dyslexia **32**: 103–121.

15. Bruskin, C. & M. Blank. 1984. The effects of word class on children's reading and spelling. Brain & Language **21**: 219–232.

16. Carroll, J. B., P. Davies & B. Richman. 1971. Word Frequency Book. American Heritage. New York, NY.

17. Rutter, M. 1978. Prevalence and types of dyslexia. *In* Dyslexia: An Appraisal of Current Knowledge. A. L. Benton & D. Pearl, Eds. Oxford University Press. New York, NY.

18. Critchley, M. 1970. Developmental Dyslexia. Charles C Thomas. Springfield, IL.

19. Gilmore, J. V. & E. C. Gilmore. 1968. Gilmore Oral Reading Test. Harcourt, Brace & Jovanovich. New York, NY.

20. Krieger, V. K. 1981. A hierarchy of "confusable" high frequency words in isolation and context. Learning Disab. Q. **4**: 131–138.

21. Gibson, E. J. & H. Levin. 1975. The Psychology of Reading. M.I.T. Press. Cambridge, MA.

22. Aaron, P. G. 1982. The neuropsychology of developmental dyslexia. *In* Reading Disorders: Varieties and Treatments. P. G. Aaron & R. N. Malatesha, Eds. Academic Press. New York, NY.

23. Denckla, M. B. & R. G. Rudel. 1976. Rapid automatized naming (R.A.N.): Dyslexia differentiated from other learning disabilities. Neuropsychologia **14**: 471–479.

24. Wolf, M. 1980. The word retrieval process and reading in children and aphasics. *In* Children's Language, Vol. 3. K. Nelson, Ed. Gardner Press. New York, NY.

25. Bartolucci, G., S. J. Pierce & D. Streiner. 1980. Cross-sectional studies of grammatical morphemes in autistic and mentally retarded children. J. Autism Devel. Dis. **10**: 39–49.

26. Marin, O. S. M., E. M. Saffran & M. F. Schwartz. 1976. Dissociations of language in aphasia: Implications for normal function. Ann. N.Y. Acad. Sci. **280**: 868–884.

27. Bradley, D. C. & M. F. Garrett. 1981. Hemisphere differences in recognition of function and content words. Massachusetts Institute of Technology. Unpublished manuscript.

28. Shallice T. & E. K. Warrington. 1975. Word recognition in a phonemic dyslexic patient. Q. J. Exp. Psychol. **27**: 187–199.

29. Patterson, K. E. 1981. Neuropsychological approaches to the study of reading. Br. J. Psychol. **72**: 151–174.

30. Coltheart, M. 1980. Deep dyslexia: A right-hemisphere hypothesis. *In* Deep Dyslexia. M. Coltheart, K. Patterson & J. C. Marshall, Eds. Routledge and Kegan Paul. London.

31. De Loche, G. & X. Seron. 1981. Part of speech and phonological form implied in written-word comprehension: Evidence from homograph disambiguation by normal and aphasic subjects. Brain & Language **13**: 250–258.

Timing Analysis of Coding and Articulation Processes in Dyslexia

SAMUEL W. ANDERSON,[a,b] FRANCES NASH PODWALL,[c]
AND JOSEPH JAFFE[a]

[a]Department of Communication Sciences
New York State Psychiatric Institute, and
College of Physicians & Surgeons of
Columbia University New York, New York 10032

[c]Division of Special Education
Board of Education of the City of New York
Brooklyn, New York 11201

For several years now, evidence has been accumulating in support of the hypothesis that developmental dyslexia is often an "aphasic" phenomenon of the anomic variety.[1-5] More than a decade of work has established that a test of naming is the best predictor of reading progress.[6,7] It is especially interesting that the deficit is clearly manifested when the names of items must be *spoken* rapidly under time pressure.

This requirement for rapid, repetitive serial responses to overlearned stimuli has been dubbed an "automatized" naming task.[8,9] It is argued that since reading requires instantaneous evocation of linguistic (auditory) associations by visual stimuli, and that the process must be so automatic as to occur without awareness, it must be linguistic-auditory, rather than visual, factors that are of prime importance in most cases of reading failure.

Perhaps most interesting is the general finding that the naming deficit itself is greatest, not for naming letters or numerals, but for the names of "use objects" (FIGURE 1); the deficit is also quite large on color names. The total time required to scan and name 50 items is greater for either objects or colors than for letters or numerals, both in dyslexic subjects and age-matched controls,[10] so that, at least among primary school subjects, dyslexic children require extra time to perform all four subtests, even though two of them employ lexical symbols as stimuli and two do not. Our study has replicated this result, and has gone on to employ computer processing of the time structure of spoken responses in order to identify cognitive and articulatory components of processing time for the Rapid Automatized Naming (RAN) test of Denckla and Rudel among both dyslexic and normal schoolchildren.

Evidence in support of other hypotheses as to the nature of the deficit in dyslexia is equivocal at the present time, although recent careful work by Leisman has systematically excluded eye movement speed,[11] preprogramming of eye movements,[12] and visual perceptual localization,[13] all of which were found to function normally in dyslexic children. But although no visual-

[b] Address for correspondence: Dr. Samuel W. Anderson, 722 West 168th Street, New York, New York 10032.

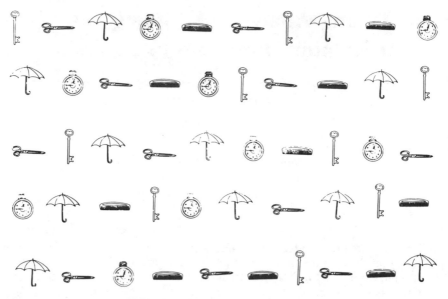

FIGURE 1. The RAN use object subtest.

perceptual deficit was found by Morrison *et al.*[14] in a tachistoscopic task, these authors report *memory encoding* deficits in 12-year-old dyslexic children for "automatized" stimuli (letters), and also for geometric forms and "abstract" forms. From this result, they concluded that dyslexia is traceable to a "basic information processing deficiency" (p. 77) that is not restricted to verbal materials.

Unlike the RAN test, Morrison's task did not employ spoken responses, so that the importance of lexical labelling of his stimuli in memory encoding could not be assessed from the data. Subsequently, Liberman *et al.*[15] challenged the inference that naming does not facilitate memory, even for the "abstract" forms employed by Morrison and associates. We believe that it is time to examine spoken responses in detail, and to attempt a determination of just what aspect of the dyslexic's performance requires the extra time in rapid automatized naming. If visual search, targetting, and image perception times are apparently quite normal in many cases, we are led to assume that there are negligible differences between dyslexic and normal subjects in stimulus registration time. Remaining are response-related sources of delay: (*a*) differences in hesitation time (pausing) between spoken names; (*b*) differences in syllabic articulation time for uttering the spoken names; (*c*) differences in frequency of pausing due to clustering of names together without intervening hesitations; and (*d*) interactions between the first three patterns.

From the results of many speech studies it is not clear that there is any single, obvious relation between the length of a pause and the amount of preparation time required for the subsequent vocalization,[16] at least among adult subjects with no language impairment of any kind. Other studies indicate

FIGURE 2. The RAN numeral subtest.

that vowel lengths in a polysyllabic vocalization (phrase) vary according to the amount of preplanning required.[17] Gould and Boies[18] propose modelling preparation time as an information processing concept: Verbal output cannot exceed an overall rate limit imposed by preparation time, so that a need for increased preparation time will yield more pauses, longer pauses, slower word articulation rate, or some combination of these (p. 1146). A design was constructed to weigh the relative importance of each of them.

MATERIALS

The Rapid Automatized Naming (RAN) test consists of four 11″ × 14″ cards (subtests), each containing an array of five items repeated in random sequence so as to total 50 stimuli per card. (FIGURES 1, 2, and 3 are reduced copies of three of the cards). The four sets of stimuli are:
   A. Use objects-pictures (comb, key, scissors, umbrella, watch) (FIGURE 1).
   B. Colors (black, blue, green, red, yellow) (not shown).
   C. Numbers (2,4,6,7,9) (FIGURE 2).
   D. Letters (a,d,o,p,s) (FIGURE 3).
Stimuli are arranged in grids on the cards as shown.

PROCEDURE

The four RAN subtests are administered, in counterbalanced order, to the children individually, with only the child and the examiner present in a quiet room. Each session was tape recorded using a Sony TC-45 cassette recorder with ECM-16 lapel microphone placed within 6 inches of the mouth. (The

FIGURE 3. The RAN letter subtest.

microphone was not always clipped to lapel or collar since children did not always wear clothing that permitted attachment to it within the critical distance of 6 inches. In many cases, the child was asked to wear a specially prepared vest that permitted correct microphone placement.)

Initially, the child is asked to name the first five items on a card (which always constitute the set of five alternatives on that subtest) in order to establish that they are familiar to him, and that he can articulate the names intelligibly. (Use of semantic variants, such as "clock" for "watch," is corrected, but if a child can give no name for an item at all, the subtest is not given.) Following this preliminary procedure, the child is instructed to name all the pictures on the card as accurately and as fast as he can, beginning after the words "get ready, get set, go!" The examiner times the performance with a stopwatch, starting with the child's first response. Although not required for our analysis, stopwatch timing is retained as a standard visible reminder of the importance of speed in performing the task. The examiner monitors the child's performance to assure that all items on the card are named.

SUBJECTS

The RAN test was first administered to six dyslexic males—two children at each of three age levels (8, 9, and 10 years). All were under treatment for their reading difficulty at the Child Development Clinic at Long Island Jewish–Hillside Medical Center in Queens, New York. The criterion for the diagnosis of dyslexia was a tested reading level at two or more years below appropriate grade level for age. No subject was receiving any drug, either acutely or chronically, at the time of testing. All had scores of at least 90 on either the verbal or performance subtests of the WISC. No clinically significant articulation defect was found among these children.

The RAN test was then given to six control subjects obtained from the Ramsey, New Jersey public schools. These were matched pairwise with respect to age, sex, and full scale WISC level. All control subjects had reading scores that were at or above expected grade level for age. The tape recorded data were brought back to our laboratory for processing.

COMPUTER ANALYSIS

As the tape-recorded subtests are played back, the computer samples the acoustic level every 400 μsec after low-pass filtering. The entire subtest performance was digitized and segmented by a DEC PDP/12 computer, converting it to digit sequences on magnetic tape. This tape was then read into an IBM 360/44 mainframe to obtain speech unit frequencies, mean durations, standard deviations, and coefficients of variation. The speech units obtained are: *pauses* (silent gaps ≥ 200 msec); *vocalizations* (speech segments composed of at least one vowel and containing no pauses; and *vowels* (vocalic segments ⩾ 60 msec in duration). These statistics were finally evaluated

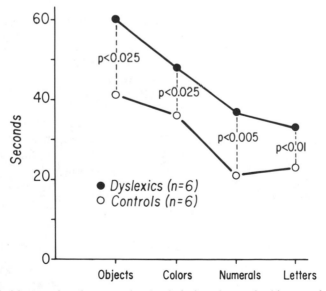

FIGURE 4. Mean total performance time by dyslexic and control subjects on the four RAN subtests.

to construct timing profiles by use of the BMD 07M Stepwise Discriminant Analysis. (Technical details of signal processing are found in Anderson and Jaffe[19] and those of statistical analysis, in Dixon.[20])

RESULTS

As is seen in FIGURE 4, the total time scores, both for the dyslexic and for the normal children on all four subtests, are comparable to those obtained by Denckla and Rudel.[10] Total time means between groups are all significant by paired t test (one-tailed): for objects, $p < 0.025$; for colors, $p < 0.025$; for numbers $p < 0.005$, and for letters $p < 0.01$.

FIGURE 5 shows the results of separately accumulated silent time and speaking time for each subtest, expressed as the mean difference between time values for dyslexics and controls. Because the dyslexic children require more Pause Time, Vocalization Time, and Vowel Time, the differentials are all positive, and are significant by paired t-test for every subtest. Pause Time (silent time) is computed by summing together all pauses in a RAN performance; Vocalization Time (speaking time) is the sum of the times required by all the vocalizations in the performance. Therefore, of course, Pause Time + Vocalization Time = Total Time. Similarly, Vocalization Time is parsed into Vowel Time and its complement (transyllabic time). Only Vowel Time is considered here, however, because the mean *differential* Vocalization Time (dyslexic minus control) is seen to be almost exactly equal to the differential Vowel Time (FIGURE 5).

Because all the RAN performances were essentially error-free, differential Vowel Time can be interpreted as a difference in syllabic articulation rate, since it is well known that the rate of speaking in English is almost perfectly indexed by mean vowel length (see Anderson[17] for a review). Thus, we are led to the general conclusion that the dyslexics as a group were slower not only because they paused more, but also because they articulated more slowly as well. Apart from the results on the colors subtest (about which we believe there is reason to find that our results are atypical[d]), Pause Time differences are responsible for between two-thirds and three-quarters of the Total Time differences between the groups as a whole.

Analysis of the phonetic structures of the subtests (TABLE 1) indicates that the very long vowels seen in both groups on color-naming are associated with an unusually large number of transitions (80) between vowels and semivowels (y,w) or vowels and laterals (l,r) among the names *black, blue, green, red, yellow,* just as syllabic type predicts. At the other end of the scale is the list of numbers, with only 30 transitions and the shortest mean vowel length for both groups.

---

[d] On the colors subtest, the normal (but not the dyslexic) subjects found it difficult to believe or remember that our poorly photographed "red" stimulus should not be called "orange," so that several children alternated, somewhat hesitantly, between these two names for one color. For subsequent work with the RAN we have standardized the colors subtest with Munsell chips selected with the concurrence of Dr. Rita Rudel.

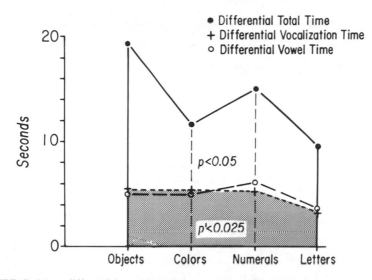

FIGURE 5. Mean differential cumulative times between dyslexic and control subjects taken up by pauses, vocalizations, and vowels on four RAN subtests. Differential time = dyslexic time − control time. p = confidence level for differential pause time; p' = confidence level for differential vocalization time.

Other phonetic frequency effects appear to be absent, with the number of vowels and the number of consonants having no apparent effect on the speech of either group.

The Gould and Boies model of cognitive preparation for speech[18] was adapted as a general information-processing rate measure, encompassing any source of delay not imposed by the articulatory upper limit of speaking rate.

TABLE 1. Phonetic Frequencies in Repeating Name Lists of the Four Ran Subtests and Measured Mean Vowel Lengths in Dyslexic and Control Subjects

Subtest	No. of Consonants	No. of Vowels[a]	No. of l,r,w,y Transitions	Vowel Length (msec)	
Objects	65	61	52	284	(dyslexics)
				210	(controls)
Colors	55	50	80	397	(dyslexics)
				306	(controls)
Numerals	55	50	30	257	(dyslexics)
				197	(controls)
Letters	30	50	61	282	(dyslexics)
				204	(controls)

[a] The vowel count omits all reduced vowels, that is, vowels on syllables that are completely unstressed. By this criterion, all names in the entire RAN test, with one exception, receive a vowel count of one. The exception is the object name "umbrella," which contains two full vowels and one reduced one; since it occurs eleven times on the object list, that list contains a total of 61 vowels.

TABLE 2. Proportion of Mean Estimated Preparation Time Allocated to Pause Time

Group	Objects	Colors	Numbers	Letters
Dyslexic	0.979	0.787	0.972	0.940
Control	0.972	0.820	0.795	0.873

Thus, "preparation time" includes nonarticulatory limits on speaking rate, such as perceptual attention span, lexical retrieval lag, and the time required for motor programming of speech units prior to their execcution. The following calculation was performed for each subject to estimate his mean preparation time for each subtest:

Preparation Time = (Pause Time + Vocalization Time − Nv / AR_{max}), where

Nv = number of vowels uttered in a subtest performance
and
AR_{max} = Articulation Rate, in vowels per second, on the subject's fastest subtest.

According to this formula, each subject prepares entirely during pauses on his fastest subtest. TABLE 2 reveals that the means for each group show very little preparation time during speech (even on the colors subtest, upon which no subject achieved his maximum articulation rate). It is worth noting that only on the colors subtest, where a known cognitive difficulty selectively impaired the performance of the normal controls, did the normal subjects have a relatively greater proportion of preparation time devoted to pausing. However, values seen in TABLE 2 are never far below 80%; even on the numbers and letters tasks they are high in spite of the fact that these subtests are performed most quickly.

The uniformly high values in TABLE 2 led us to reexamine the Gould and Boies analysis, to wit, the assumption that each subject articulates at his maximum possible speed on his fastest subtest. First, observe that since the demand characteristics are not unique for any subtest, it seems likely that if speaking is slowed due to cognitive preparation on three of the subtests, then it is also slowed to some extent of the fourth. Second, it can be inferred that if no subject has an articulatory deficit, and since $Nv \approx 50$ for all subtest performances, the term $Nv/AR_{max} \approx K$, where K is an ideal constant for all subjects and subtests. Because K is unknown, it cannot be used to recalculate the values in TABLE 2; but since *Differential* Preparation Time

TABLE 3. Differential Slowing Due to Pausing as Proportion of Total Slowing in Dyslexia

Objects	Colors	Numbers	Letters
0.719	0.539	0.674	0.661

(DPT) equals (Dyslexic Pause Time + Dyslexic Vocalization Time − K) − (Control Pause Time + Control Vocalization Time − K),

the unknown K term term drops out of this estimate of relative slowing in dyslexia, which is now attributed to increased preparation time alone.

Thus, the ratios of Differential Pause Time to Differential Total Time obtained from FIGURE 5 yield the values in TABLE 3, which estimate, for each subtest, the proportion of extra preparation time required by dyslexics that is due to increased pausing.

A comparison of TABLE 3 and FIGURE 5 shows that in three of four subtest, the extra total time needed by the dyslexic subjects was distributed in nearly the same proportions among pause and vocalization times: about 70 and 30%, respectively. As for colors, the discrepancy is due to a relatively greater amount of pause time among controls, in spite the fact that their pause was predictably shorter. (The extra time can be traced to more frequent pausing on the part of the controls, apparently due to the artifactual reason discussed above.)

We cannot use the DPT technique to solve for the separate preparation times; but if we assume that extra time required by dyslexic subjects is simply allocated in the same proportions as all preparation time, then an estimate of 0.7 would replace the values around 0.9 in TABLE 2, with correspondingly still lower values for the control subjects on the most automatized subtests (numbers and letters).

TABLE 4 summarizes the set of statistics obtained from the computer analysis. It is noteworthy that mean vocalization length was longer for dyslexics in the high cognitive load subtests (objects and colors), while it was longer for the normal controls in the low cognitive load subtests (numbers and letters). This can be accounted for by the higher degree of clustering (vowels per vocalization) on the part of controls in performing the latter subtests. Although differences in mean vowel length are found in every test to account for differences in total vocalization time, the vowels tend to become shorter as they are clustered together in longer vocalizations, that is, shortening is indexed by the measure of clustering (a phenomenon that is usually observed in phonetics). Except for colors, it would appear that differential slowing is apportioned about 70% to pausing and 30% to vowels, independently of clustering and of cognitive load.

As suggested by the results of Stark and Tallal,[19] we attempted to find a constant differential vowel length between control and dyslexic subjects that, if weighted by the number of postvocalic consonants in each subtest, would account for the measured mean vowel differentials for that subtest in TABLE 1:

C = (N / n) (Dyslexic Vowel Length − Control Vowel Length),

where N = number of vowels in the subtest and n = number of postvocalic (stop) consonants in the subtest. It immediately becomes clear that, for these data, this hypothesis is not plausible. This can be seen most easily in the case of stops: The numbers subtest shows a differential mean vowel of 60 msec in duration (which is the smallest of the four, to be sure), but is totally devoid of postvocalic stops. If we modify the hypothesis to state that dyslexic

TABLE 4. Mean Values for Seven Selected Speech Statistics Used in the Construction of Performance Timing Profiles that Discriminate Dyslexic and Control Subjects on all Four Subtests of the Rapid Automatized Naming Test

Speech Statistic	Objects		Colors		Numerals		Letters	
	Dyslexic	Control	Dyslexic	Control	Dyslexic	Control	Dyslexic	Control
Mean vocalization duration (sec)	.843	.404	.635	.452	.506	.670	.534	.606
Mean pause duration (sec)	.821	.588	.704	.506	.575	.440	.562	.428
Standard deviation of pause duration	.646	.299	.412	.307	.369	.207	.324	.248
Coefficient of variation, vocalization duration	.518	.639	.680	.720	.794	.684	.798	.953
Mean vowel duration (sec)	.284	.210	.397	.306	.257	.197	.282	.204
Vowels per vocalization	1.45	1.58	1.46	1.33	1.64	2.23	1.62	2.18
Total subtest time (sec)	60.387	41.013	47.647	35.803	36.920	20.747	32.968	23.180

TABLE 5. Speech Timing Profiles Derived from Dyslexic and Nondyslexic Classification Functions (BMD 07M)[a] in Four Ran Subtests

Speech Statistic	Profile Weights			
	Objects	Colors	Numerals	Letters
Mean vocalization duration (sec)	549	-38	-81	-17
Mean pause duration (sec)	-254	18	9	90
Standard deviation of pause duration	72	-137	48	-30
Coefficient of variation, vocalization duration	-297	-11	25	18
Mean vowel duration (sec)	-651	53	151	331
Vowels per vocalization	-16	77	29	-24
Total subtest time (sec)	2	2	0	-2
Constant	158	-138	-73	-13

[a] Discriminant function is expressed as $D = \Sigma W_i \times S_i + \text{constant}$ for each subtest, where W_i is the ith profile weight and S_i is the ith speech statistic. A positive value for D classifies a subject as dyslexic, a negative value as nondyslexic.

vowels are differentially prolonged by a constant whenever followed by *any* consonant, the fit is no better. The reason for this is again evident from TABLE 1: the differentials are quite similar, yet the numbers of consonants in the various subtests differ by as much as a factor of two. The results do show a tendency for subtest mean vowel lengths to rank according to the numbers of laterals and glides, but this can be predicted from phonetics, and is seen, as expected, independently in the two groups.

Finally, stepwise discriminant analysis (BMD 07M) was performed on speech unit statistics obtained from speech signal processing. A minimum of seven units was found necessary to correctly classify all subjects on the objects subtest, fewer for the others. The seven statistics are given in TABLE 4, and the profile weights in TABLE 5 were obtained by subtracting the coefficients for the normal classification function from corresponding dyslexic coefficients. A positive value of D, calculated from the profile weights as indicated at the bottom of TABLE 5, is obtained for every dyslexic subject but for none of the controls on all four subtests. The size of N in this study precludes the inference that the multiple discriminator profiles are reliable; however, the *single* parameter vowel length does correctly classify all subjects in both groups on the letters subtest. Although differences in this parameter are often under one-tenth of a second on the average, its sensitivity to age difference as well as diagnosis appears to be at least as great as the conventional RAN measure of total time. Since it is known in phonetics that prolongation of vowels is a correlate of more frequent pausing, longer vowels are an especially sensitive marker, not just of slowing during the vowels themselves, but of extra pause time contributed by the *numerosity* of pauses (rather than pause length). As is seen in TABLE 6, both vowel length and total time vary more with age among dyslexic than among normal subjects, a suggestion from this pilot study that is worth following up systemically.

DISCUSSION

The conclusions to be drawn from these results appear to be five:

1. Dyslexic children require more time to perform the RAN test because of *both* greater vocalization time *and* pause time requirements.

2. The objects subtest, reliably known to require the most extra time, shows, the widest distribution of slowed speech parameters, involving vocalizations, pauses and vowels.

TABLE 6. Mean Durations of Vowels, Pauses, and Total Times in Letters Subtest (Seconds)

Age (yr)	Dyslexic Subjects			Normal Subjects		
	Vowel	Pause	Total Time	Vowel	Pause	Total Time
8	.310	.650	41.30	.218	.461	24.43
9	.285	.581	31.60	.190	.394	23.46
10	.250	.457	26.00	.205	.430	21.65

3. Dyslexics show longer mean vowels on all subtests, and this unit alone is sufficient to classify all subjects correctly on the letters subtest. A direct correlation between vowel lengthening and increased frequency of pausing is a probable basis for the power of vowel length to identify dyslexics on highly "automatized" naming tests.

4. No systematic tendency was found for dyslexic children to prolong vowels *only* within specific phonetic contexts, such as in preconsonantal position. It is possible that lengthening is maximized in certain phonetic contexts, but vowel prolongation was found to occur quite generally.

5. Differences in cognitive preparation time were consistent across three of the four subtests, indicating that dyslexic subjects perform the RAN more slowly because of a need for extra cognitive time rather than a need to articulate slowly.

It may be questioned whether our assumption of a single ideal maximum articulation rate is validly applied to all subtest performances in view of their quite different phonetic and semantic demands. But it should be emphasized that our minimum vocalic criterion of 60-msec duration selects only vowels receiving syllabic stress (see footnote to TABLE 1), and that such vowels in normal spontaneous speech have been found to occur at very constant rates.[20] Alteration of word rate in English is known to have relatively little effect on stressed syllable rate.

To be sure, an unassailable resolution of this issue would require ascertaining whether the RAN subtests are, in fact, differentially rate-limited on the basis of their articulatory demands alone, and whether dyslexics have relatively more or less articulatory difficulty in terms of those demands. In this study, we have concerned ourselves only with a comparison between two extant hypotheses about dysphasic phenomena in developmental dyslexia; in terms of the models employed to compare them, the weight of evidence is quite clear.

There is some recent evidence suggesting that the primary psychophysiological deficit in dyslexia may be nothing but slowed simple reaction time, especially to visually presented stimuli, regardless of whether either stimulus or response does or does not involved speech or language.[23] While we have seen that other factors indeed contribute to information-processing rate in the RAN, our results are not inconsistent with this view.

We conclude that the extra time required by dyslexics to perform the RAN test is distributed across the subtest performances as the children observe the stimuli and prepare to name the items in rapid succession. It is this preparation task, which occurs partly during pausing and partly during vocalizing, rather than the task of articulating the names, that is the primary source of naming difficulty in these children.

SUMMARY

Several investigators[6,7,10] have found that the time required to perform serial naming tasks is a good predictor of dyslexia in children. Protracted overall time scores, such as are reported for the Rapid Automatized Naming (RAN) test of Denckla and Rudel,[24] are, by themselves, insufficient to determine the extent to which the performance deficit is cognitive in nature, or is the articulatory consequence of an inability master the quickly changing acoustic formant patterns associated with consonants, as proposed by Tallal.[21,25]

We administered the RAN test to matched groups of dyslexic and normal control children, aged 8 to 11 years. Measurement of speech signal durations was performed by computer. We applied the Gould and Boies[18] algorithm for extracting cognitive preparation time to these data, resulting in a partition of overall RAN test score into coding time and articulation time components. Differential performances between the groups on RAN subtests were examined for effects of postvocalic consonants and semantic load.

It was found that both vocalization time and pause time means were significantly longer for the dyslexics on each of the four RAN subtests: objects, colors, numbers, letters. The Gould and Boies analysis showed very little preparation time during speech in both groups, attributing virtually all coding time to pauses, although reanalysis suggested somewhat less. Increased vowel length among the dyslexics occurred on all subtests, but was not maximized on subtests with more numerous postvocalic consonants.

Vowel time differences between groups accounted for nearly all of the differences in vocalization time. Profiles were constructed on speech measures which, for each subtest, correctly identified each subject with his group. On the letters subtest it was found that vowel duration alone achieved a perfect discrimination between the dyslexic and control subjects.

ACKNOWLEDGMENTS

We gratefully acknowledge the assistance of Dr. Rachel Gittelman, Director of the Child Development Clinic at Long Island Jewish–Hillside Medical Center, and of Dr. Larry Ashley, Assistant Superintendant of Schools, Ramsey, New Jersey for help in carrying out these studies.

REFERENCES

1. MATTIS S., J. FRENCH & I. RAPIN. 1975. Dyslexia in children and young adults. Dev. Med. Child Neurol. 17: 150–163.
2. BODER, E. 1971. Developmental dyslexia: Prevailing diagnostic concepts and a new diagnostic approach through patterns of reading and spelling. In H. Myklebust, Ed. Progress in Learning Disabilities, Vol. 11.
3. DENCKLA, M. B. 1973. Recent research in dyslexia. Paper presented at Mt. Sinai Symposium on Dyslexia, February 1973.
4. CRITCHLEY, M. 1970. The Dyslexic Child. Charles C Thomas. Springfield, IL.
5. RUDEL, R. G., M. B. DENCKLA & M. BROMAN. 1978. Rapid silent response to repeated target symbols by dyslexic and nondyslexic children. Brain & Lang. 6: 52–62.
6. DeHIRSCH, K., J. JANSKY & W. S. LANGFORD. 1966. Predicting Reading Failure. Harper & Row. New York, NY.
7. JANSKY, J. & K. DeHIRSCH. 1973. Preventing Reading Failure. Harper & Row. New York, NY.

8. DENCKLA, M. B. & F. P. BOWEN. 1973. Dyslexia after left occipito-temporal lobectomy: A case report. Cortex **9**: 321–328.
9. EAKIN, S. & V. I. DOUGLAS. 1971. "Automatization" and oral reading problems in children. J. Learn. Dis. **4**: 31–38.
10. DENCKLA, M. B. & R. G. RUDEL. 1976. Rapid "automatized" naming (R.A.N.): Dyslexia differentiated from other learning disabilities. Neuropsychologia **14**: 471–479.
11. LEISMAN, G. & J. SCHWARTZ. 1978. Aetological factors in dyslexia. I: Saccadic eye movement control. Percept. Motor Skills **47**: 403–407.
12. LEISMAN, G., M. ASHKENAZI, L. SPRUNG & J. SCHWARTZ. 1978. Aetological factors in dyslexia. II: Oculomotor programming. Percept. Motor Skills **47**: 667–672.
13. LEISMAN, G. 1978. Aetiological factors in dyslexia. III: Oculomotor factors in visual perceptual response efficiency. Percept. Motor Skills **47**: 675–678.
14. MORRISON, F. J., B. GIORDANI & J. NAGY. 1977. Reading disability: An information processing analysis. Science **196**(4285): 77–79.
15. LIBERMAN, I., L. S. MARK & D. SHANKWEILER. 1978. Reading disability: Methodological problems in information processing analysis. Science **200**(4343): 801–802.
16. JAFFE, J., L. J. GERSTMAN & S. BRESKIN. 1972. Random generation of apparent speech rhythms. Lang. & Speech **15**: 68–71.
17. ANDERSON, S. W. 1975. Ballistic control of rhythmic articulatory movements in natural speech. *In* D. R. Aaronson & R. W. Rieber, Eds. Developmental Psycholinguistics and Communication Disorders. Ann. N. Y. Acad. Sci. **263**: 236–243.
18. GOULD, J. D. & S. J. BOIES. 1978. Writing, dictating and speaking letters. Science **201**: 1145–1147.
19. ANDERSON, S. W. & J. JAFFE. 1972. The definition, detection and timing of vocalic syllables in speech signals. Sci. Rep. No. 12, Department of Communication Sciences, New York State Psychiatric Institute.
20. DIXON, W. J., Ed. 1970. BMD Biomedical Computer Programs. University of California Press. Berkeley, CA.
21. STARK, R. E. & P. TALLAL. 1979. Analysis of stop consonant production errors in developmentally dysphasic children. J. Acoust. Soc. Am. **66**(6): 1703–1712.
22. ANDERSON, S. W. & F. N. PODWALL. 1977. Scalar timing control in spontaneous speech. J. Acoust. Soc. Am. **62**(Suppl. No. 1): S64.
23. BROMAN, M., R. G. RUDEL, E. HELFGOTT & J. KRIEGER. 1984. Inter- and intrahemispheric processing of visual and auditory stimuli by dyslexic children and normal readers. Int. J. Neuroscience. In press.
24. DENCKLA, M. B. & R. G. RUDEL. 1974. Rapid "automatized" naming of pictured objects, colors, letters and numbers by normal children. Cortx **10**: 186–202.
25. TALLAL, P., R. E. STARK, C. KALLMAN & D. MELLITS. 1980. Developmental dysphasia: Relation between acoustic processing deficits and verbal processing. Neuropsychologia **18**: 273–283.

ADDITIONAL REFERENCES NOT CITED IN THE TEXT

ANDERSON, S. W., & J. JAFFE. 1976. Speech timing characteristics on normal native speakers of English in New York City. Sci. Rep. No. 16, Department of Communication Sciences, New York State Psychiatric Institute.
BRESKIN, S., L. J. GERSTMAN & J. JAFFE. 1971. Methods for quantifying on-off speech patterns under delayed auditory feedback. J. Psycholing. Res. **1**: 89–98.
DENCKLA, M. B. 1972. Color-naming in dyslexic boys. Cortex **8**: 164–176.
DENCKLA, M. B. 1972. Performance on color task in kindergarten children. Cortex

8: 177–190.

JAFFE, J., S. W. ANDERSON & R. W. RIEBER. 1973. Research and clinical approaches to disorders of speech rate. J. Commun. Dis. **6:** 225–246.

JAFFE, J. & S. BRESKIN. 1970. Further consequences of a Markov model of speech rhythms. Computers & Biomed. Res. **3** (2): 174–177.

JAFFE, J., S. BRESKIN & L. J. GERSTMAN. 1970. Range of sequential constraint in monologue rhythms. Psychon. Sci. **19** (4): 233.

JAFFE, J. & S. FELDSTEIN. 1970. Rhythms of Dialogue. Academic Press. New York, NY.

PODWALL, F. N. 1976. How do speakers parse time? Parameters of rhythmic temporal patterning in natural speech of normal speakers, former stutterers and stutterers. Doctoral dissertation, The City University of New York.

RIEBER, R. W., S. BRESKIN & J. JAFFE. 1972. Pause time and phonation time in stuttering and cluttering. J. Psycholing. Res. **1:** 149–154.

SIEGEL, S. 1956. Nonparametric Statistics for the Behavioral Sciences. McGraw-Hill New York, NY.

Comparisons among EEG, Hair Minerals and Diet Predictions of Reading Performance in Children[a]

R. W. THATCHER, R. McALASTER,

M. L. LESTER, AND D. S. CANTOR

Applied Neuroscience Institute
Department of Human Ecology
University of Maryland Eastern Shore
Princess Anne, Maryland 21853

INTRODUCTION

Theoretical models of reading disability range from simple models in which reading disability is a unitary disorder resulting from a single antecedent condition[1] to models involving more than one type of reading disability and more than one antecedent condition, with complex interrelationships among both types of factors.[2,3] Recently, the more complex models of reading disability have prevailed as guides for research, with emphasis on developmental and environmental factors as contributors to reading disabilities.[4] In general, reading acquisition is viewed as a complex process involving a number of component skills which emerge in the course of development and that the different forms of reading disability may be associated with different patterns of deficiency in the component skills. The efficacy of these component skills may be influenced by the effects of maturational factors on brain physiology and/or ecological factors which influence brain function and consequent cognitive performance.

The ecological factors which have been of primary interest among researchers and have been shown to affect brain physiology and consequent cognitive performance and brain function can now be readily assessed by the use of computerized analyses of resting-state EEG.[7,17] In the present paper, we will attempt to examine nutrition (with a special emphasis on refined carbohydrate intake), hair trace elements, and measures of EEG as they may be related to the reading ability of school-age children. A careful examination of each of these variables as they are independently related to reading ability and as they interact with each other represents the first stage of developing a causal model of ecological factors which play a role in child development in general and in reading ability in particular.

In the present study, assessments of reading ability will be restricted to the Wide Range Achievement Test for reading performance in school-age children. The present study is a part of a larger effort to relate ecological vari-

[a] This study was supported by Grants from USDA SEA/CR HRD0200 and NIH-MBS (RR08079-0951) (R. W. T., principal investigator).

ables to child development. Analyses of this expanded and more complete data base is in progress and will be presented elsewhere.

METHODS

Subjects

A total of 184 children (100 males) aged 5 to 16 participated in the study. The subjects were recruited through newspaper advertisements and the cooperation of the Somerset County Board of Education. All children were students in the State of Maryland public school system. Ninety-seven percent of the children lived in rural communities with populations less than 25,000. Each child was paid $10.00 for participating.

Dietary Assessment

A 24-hour dietary recall was recorded for each child. Children, together with their accompanying parent or guardian, were interviewed. Protocols similar to those developed by Frank et al.[8] were used; a graduated series of bowls, glasses and cups was used to help the child specify, as accurately as possible, volume amounts of foods and beverages consumed.

For each 24-hour recall record, amounts for the following categories of diet composition were determined: (a) total calories, (b) calories from refined sucrose and snack foods, (c) carbohydrate content in grams and (d) protein content in grams. In order to obtain composition values for all food items in the sample diets, several sources of tabulated values for food composition were used.[9-12] Foods were categorized as "refined high sucrose and snack food" if the conventional use of the refined food was judged to be for dessert or snack, or if it was known that a dominant ingredient in the food was sugar (as in certain pre-sweetened cereals). Six food groupings which accounted for 95% of these high sucrose and snack foods are listed in order of their predominance of occurrence in the present sample: I. carbonated sodas and sweetened beverages; II. sugar, candy and sweet toppings; III. cookies, cakes, pastries and pies; IV. ice creams and popsicles; V. sugar cereals; and VI. salty and caramel snacks.

Psychometric Measures

An eight-item short form of the Wechsler Intelligence Scale for Children (WISC-1972) was administered to the children aged 6–16, and the corresponding subtests of the Wechsler Pre-school and Primary Scale of Intelligence (WPPSI) to the 5-year-old children.[13] The items were: information, arithmetic, vocabulary, digit span (sentences for the WPPSI), picture completion, block design, coding (animal house for the WPPSI), and mazes. From the scores on these subtests conventional measures of full-scale, verbal and performance IQ were derived. In addition, the Wide Range Achievement Test

(WRAT) was administered to evaluate the three primary areas of school achievement (reading, spelling and arithmetic).[14] Level I was administered to children aged 5 to 11; Level II was administered to children aged 12 and older.

Hair Analysis

Hair samples were taken from the nape of the neck, as close to the scalp as possible. A minimum quantity of 0.2 g was obtained. The samples were labelled, placed in a plastic sack, and sent to the Food and Drug Administration (FDA) Division of Nutrition laboratory in Washington, D.C. for analysis. From each hair sample, 1-cm lengths of hair (approximately 0.1 gm) were washed with 10-ml portions of hexane, alcohol and deionized water. The samples were dried overnight and then wet-ashed with a mixture containing 1.5 ml concentrated HNO_3 and 0.75 ml of H_2O_2 (30%). After drying overnight, the residue was diluted to a known volume with deionized water. The method of induction-coupled argon plasma (ICAP) spectroscopy (Jerrel-Ash Model 975 ICAP Atom-Comp Spectrometer) was used to analyze hair minerals. The hair minerals included nine essential minerals (Ca, Cr, Cu, Fe, Mg, Mn, Na, P, and Zn) and two toxic metals (Cd and Pb). Hair data were obtained for 140 of the children.

Electrophysiological Data Analyses

Grass silver disk electrodes were applied to the 19 scalp sites of the International 10/20 system.[15] A transorbital eye channel (electro-oculogram or EOG) was used to measure eye movements. All scalp recordings were referenced to linked ear lobes. Amplifier bandwidths were nominally 0.5 to 30 Hz, the outputs being 3 dB down at these frequencies. The EEG activity was digitized online by a PDP 11/03 data-acquisition system. An on-line artifact rejection routine was used which excluded segments of EEG if the voltage in any channel exceeded a preset limit determined at the beginning of each session to be typical of the subject's resting EEG and EOG.

One minute of eyes-closed artifact-free EEG was obtained at a digitization rate of 100 Hz with the subject's eyes closed. The EEG segments were analyzed by a PDP 11/70 computer and plotted by a Versatec printer/plotter. Each subject's EEG was then visually examined and edited to eliminate any artifacts that may have passed through the on-line artifact rejection process.

A two-dimensional recursive filter analysis was performed on the edited EEG samples for the following frequency bands: delta (1.5 to 3.5 Hz), theta (3.5 to 7.0 Hz), alpha (7.0 to 13 Hz) and beta (13 to 22 Hz). Coherence (that is, the ratio of the square of the cross spectrum to the product of the autospectrum[16] was computed for each frequency band for seven interhemisphere electrode pairs (01/02, P3/P4, T5/T6, T3/T4, C3/C4, F3/F4 and F7/F8; $4 \times 7 = 28$ variables). Amplitude asymmetry measures were computed from the absolute power ($uv*uv^2$) in each frequency band for the same interhemisphere electrode pairs as for coherence. The formula for amplitude asymmetry was ([(left − right)/(left + right)]/2) for all interhemisphere comparisons. Detailed presentation of these measures are provided by Dixon and Brown.[18]

Statistical Analyses

BMDP Biomedical Statistical Programs[19] were used for all analyses. Distributions and descriptive statistics were computed for each variable, using BMDP2D and BMDP7D programs. These measures included histograms, arithmetic means, standard deviations, variance, skewness, kurtosis and the coefficient of variation. After appropriate transformations[5,18] these analyses revealed that all variables approximated the normal distribution. As part of the data screening procedures, polynomial regression (BMDP5R) analyses were conducted with WRAT reading scores regressed on each of the independent variables. These analyses indicated which of the independent variables were systematically related to WRAT reading scores and whether the relationships were linear or nonlinear. Stepwise multiple regression analyses (BMDP2R) were then performed with WRAT reading scores as the dependent variable with age forced into the equation at the first step. In this way, entry of subsequent variables occurred independently of age.

A heuristic procedure was used to categorize the variables and compare their ability to account for the WRAT reading scores while adjusting for intercorrelations (multicollinearity). The procedure involved first analyzing each data category separately (for example, EEG, Trace Elements, and Diet) in order to determine which variables were the most strongly predictive of WRAT reading scores. Once these variables were identified, they were then combined into a final stepwise regression analysis which adjusted for intercorrelations between independent variables and computed the best linear fit of the data. In order to increase the power and reliability of the analyses, at least a 5:1 ratio of subjects to variables was maintained for all analyses.

RESULTS

Population Description

The present population of children had a mean full scale IQ of 109.21 and a standard deviation of 16.37 with a range of scores from 64 to 150. This population of children also had a mean WRAT reading score of 111.97 and a standard deviation of 17.07 with a range of scores from 58 to 156. These scores were normally distributed, with skewness, kurtosis, and the coefficient of variation within acceptable limits. The full scale IQ distribution is presented to allow for comparisons of the present population to other studies. In the analyses to follow, however, only WRAT reading scores will be analyzed.

EEG and Reading Ability

A stepwise regression analysis (BMDP2R) was used to test for a relationship between the various EEG variables in combination, after adjusting for the covariance of age. Because of the large number of EEG variables (96) it was not possible to include all of the EEG variables in one analysis. Consequently, separate regression analyses were performed on different subsets of the EEG data. The subsets were: relative power (32 variables), total power and power ratios (32 variables), interhemispheric coherence (16 variables), and amplitude asymmetry (16 variables). In each of these analyses the dependent variable was WRAT reading scores. FIGURE 1 summarizes the results of these analyses. The abscissa represents the number of steps in the regression equation before the entry of an individual variable failed to be significant at the $p < 0.05$ level. The ordinate represents the percent variance of the reading scores accounted for by each EEG variable set.

As can be seen in FIGURE 1, the EEG coherence measures accounted for the largest amount of variance (14.59%), amplitude asymmetries the next largest amount of variance (3.49%) and relative power the next largest amount (2.68%). None of the total power and power ratio variables were significant. In order to assess the combined associative power of the EEG variables, a stepwise regression analysis was performed with age entered first as a covariant and then the six significant coherence, amplitude-asymmetry and relative-power variables as determined by the previous regression analyses. After excluding age, the combined percent variance was 17% ($r = -0.2405$, $F = 8.235$, df $= 6/146$, $p < 0.001$).

Hair Minerals and Reading Ability

FIGURE 2 shows the results of a stepwise regression analysis (BMDP2R), in which age was entered first as a covariant, followed by the eleven trace elements. The abscissa and ordinates are the same as in FIGURE 1 except that the independent variables are trace elements and not EEG variables, and only a single regression analysis was performed. It can be seen in FIGURE 2 that only two trace elements (zinc and cadmium) were significantly related to reading performance and the total variance accounted for was 11.24% (cadmium: partial $r = -0.2592$, df $= 1/137$, $F = 9.87$, $p < 0.005$; zinc: partial

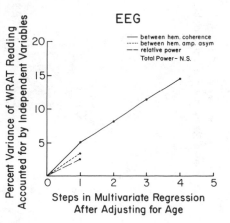

FIGURE 1. Ability of EEG variables to predict reading achievement scores. Abscissa is the number of steps in a stepwise regression analysis, after adjusting for age, in which individual EEG variates were significantly ($p < .05$) associated with reading achievement. The ordinate is the percent variance of WRAT reading achievement scores which is accounted for by the independent variables. Separate stepwise regression analyses were performed for each EEG variate type (i.e., interhemispheric coherence, interhemispheric amplitude asymmetry, relative power and total power).

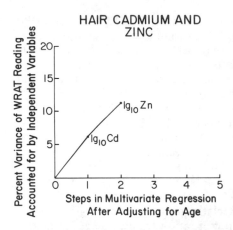

FIGURE 2. Ability of trace element variables to predict reading achievement scores. Abscissa is the number of steps in a stepwise regression analysis, after adjusting for age, in which individual trace element variates were significantly ($p < .05$) associated with reading achievement. The ordinate is the percent variance of WRAT reading achievement scores which is accounted for by the independent variables. After adjusting for the intercorrelation of the eleven trace elements only cadmium and zinc were significantly associated with reading achievement.

$r = 0.2397$, df $= 1/136$, $F = 8.29$, $p < 0.005$). It is interesting that the sign of the partial correlation coefficient was negative for cadmium ($r = -0.2592$ and positive for zinc ($r = 0.2397$). This is indicative of a reciprocal relationship between these two trace elements. That is, the greater the concentration of hair zinc, the higher the reading performance, while the greater the concentration of hair cadmium, the lower the reading performance.

Diet and Reading Performance

In order to control for age difference in the total caloric intake, the ratio of total calories to the calories derived from refined carbohydrate intake was computed for each child. This variable represents the proportion of refined foods in the child's diet. The results of the stepwise regression analysis (BMDP2R) with reading scores as the dependent variable and dietary measures as the independent variables after regressing out the effects of age is shown in FIGURE 3. It can be seen that only the proportion of refined foods in the

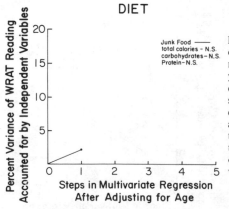

Junk Food ——
total calories – N.S.
carbohydrates – N.S.
Protein – N.S.

FIGURE 3. Ability of dietary variables to predict reading achievement scores. Abscissa is the number of steps in a stepwise regression analysis, after adjusting for age, in which individual dietary variates were significantly ($p < .05$) associated with reading achievement. The ordinate is the percent variance of WRAT reading achievement scores which is accounted for by the independent variables. After adjusting for the intercorrelation of the four dietary variables only the proportion of consumed junk food was significant.

TABLE 1. Stepwise Regression of Nutrition, EEG, and Hair Trace Elements and Their Combined Ability to Predict Reading Achievement

Independent Variable	Partial Correlation Coefficient	Increment in r Square	F	df[a]	Probability
T3 delta power	− .2519	6.59	7.06	1/92	.01
Hair cadmium	− .3198	6.80	7.83	1/91	.01
F3/F4 delta Coh.	.2279	3.46	4.12	1/90	.05
Hair zinc	.1970	2.93	3.59	1/89	.07
Junk calories	− .1164	0.98	1.21	1/88	.81

[a] Decreasing degrees of freedom reflect the step of entry into the regression equation. The degrees of freedom represent the pairwise deletion procedure of BMDP where each case must have all variables before entry.

diet was significantly related to reading performance and accounted for 2.59% of the reading score variance (partial $r = -0.1609$, df $= 1/132$, F $= 5.11$, $p < 0.025$).

Combined Diet, EEG and Hair Mineral Analyses

Each of the three variable classes (that is, EEG, nutrition, and trace elements) have been shown to be significantly associated with reading achievement with different degrees of associative strength. A final stepwise regression analysis was conducted in order to assess the overall strength of association between the combined variables and reading achievement, after adjusting for all intercorrelations. As in the previous analyses, age was entered first, followed by the variables which were significantly associated in the previous analyses. TABLE 1 shows the results of this analysis for the variables entered after age had been regressed out.

The partial correlation coefficients reveal the strength and direction of association and show that relative EEG power in the delta band in the temporal region and the concentration of cadmium were negatively correlated with reading achievement (that is, an increase in cadmium concentration or an increase in EEG slow waves was associated with decreased reading achievement), while frontal coherence and the concentration of zinc were positively correlated with reading achievement (that is, an increase in frontal coherence or zinc hair concentration was associated with increased reading achievement). The percent variance accounted for was 20.76% for the combination of variables.

To further explore the usefulness of these measures, a discriminant analysis (BMDP7M) was performed in which the above variables were entered as predictors to discriminate between high (standardized WRAT reading scores equal to or greater than 120) and low (standard reading scores equal to or less than 89) reading performers. In order to adjust for unequal *n*s, the PRIORS option in BMDP was used.

TABLE 2 shows the results of this analysis for both the direct classification

TABLE 2. Results of Discriminate Analyses between High and Low Reading Achievers Using Nutritional, EEG and Trace Element Variates

		Number of Cases Classified into Groups:	
Group	% Correct	Low	High
Direct Classification Matrix			
Low	100.0	7	0
High	90.9	2	20
Total	93.1		
Jackknifed Classification Matrix			
Low	71.4	5	2
High	77.3	5	17
Total	75.9		

matrix and the jackknife replication matrix. The direct classification yielded a classification accuracy of 93.1%. The more reliable leave-one-out replication (i.e., jackknife replication) showed that 75.9% of the children were accurately classified as either high or low reading achievers.

DISCUSSION

The results of the present study indicate that a variety of environmental, nutritional and neurophysiological factors may contribute to reading performance in children. Specifically, EEG measures of relative power and interhemispheric coherence, hair mineral concentrations, and refined carbohydrate intake were all significantly related to reading achievement in the present study. These findings are consistent with the view that reading is a performance which may be influenced by a variety of environmental, nutritional and physiological factors. Because of space limitations and our desire to statistically control age, the present paper did not analyze age-dependent processes. The latter are important, since different reading subskills may develop at different rates and exhibit different responses to environmental and nutritional agents at different ages. Detailed age analyses designed to investigate the latter issues are in progress.

As with all correlation analyses, no causal linkage between the independent variables studied here and reading achievement can be made. Only particular directions and strengths of associations were revealed by these analyses. In this respect, it is noteworthy that the strength of association with reading achievement scores was greatest for the EEG (15% of the variance), next for hair trace-element concentrations (12% of the variance) and then next for the proportion of junk food calories consumed by the children (2.4% of the variance). Of these variables, the strongest association between reading performance and EEG was with interhemispheric coherence, between reading performance and hair trace elements it was with cadmium, and between reading performance and nutrition it was with the proportion of the total caloric intake attributable to "junk food." Multivariate regression analyses, in which the intercorrelations between these variables were adjusted, showed that in combination these variables accounted for 20.76% of the variance of reading performance and could discriminate between high and low reading achievers with about a 76% accuracy.

Thus, while not all of the variance is accounted for by these variables, nonetheless a significant proportion of the variance is related to the environmental, nutritional and physiological measures studied. The results of these analyses also appear to have some physiological relevance. For example, increased delta activity in the temporal regions is related to diminished reading scores. This would be expected since the temporal cortex is fundamentally involved in language processing and short term memory. The finding of a negative relationship between reading scores and hair cadmium concentrations is also consistent with the known deleterious effects of this metallic toxin on neurophysiological processes[17] and verbal IQ.[5] Finally, the observed positive relationships between increased frontal coherence and reading scores and increased hair zinc concentrations and reading scores further emphasizes the multivariate relationship between reading ability and ecological factors and helps identify factors which may promote optimal brain development.

The variables of this study are measures related to general physiological aspects of children which seem to be associated with reading performance. Most models and studies of the reading process focus on psychological, educational, and learned aspects of reading. Often the adequacy of the physiological substrate to support these processes is taken for granted or at the other extreme the brain structures themselves are hypothesized to be abnormal. This study indicates that there may be an optimum physiological state for acquiring and/or maintaining reading skills. Furthermore, the functional state of even a "normal" brain may be influenced by ecologically determined variables such as body mineral status and diet. This does not diminish the importance of psychological and educational factors in the study of reading, but instead emphasizes that the physiological and the psychological go together and that deficiencies in the physiological domain may thwart whatever a behavioral approach may attempt to accomplish.

Further research in this area is needed; more specifically, the parameters defining an optimum state for reading skill acquisition and performance in terms of brain function, mineral status, and nutrition, must be determined.

ACKNOWLEDGMENTS

We gratefully acknowledge the assistance of Sheila Ignasias and Lang Anderson in the collection of psychometric measures, Dr. Barbara Harland for assistance with hair analysis, Dr. Lilly Lord and Anne Bennet for help in collection of dietary recalls, and Dr. Richard Horst, Judy Leasure, Faye Leatherbury and Rebecca Walker for assistance in various aspects of the study. We also thank Neurometrics, Inc. for the use of EEG acquisition and analysis software.

REFERENCES

1. GUTHRIE, J. T. 1973. Models of reading and reading disability. J. Educ. Psychol. **65**: 9–18.
2. APPLEBEE, A. N. 1971. Research in reading retardation: Two critical problems. J. Child Psychol. Psychiat. **12**: 91–113.
3. WIENER, M. & W. CROMER. 1967. Reading and reading difficulty: A conceptual analysis. Harvard Educ. Rev. **37**: 620–643.
4. DOEHRING, D. G. 1976. Evaluation of two models of reading disability. *In* The Neuropsychology of Learning Disorders. R. M. Knights & D. J. Bakker, Eds. University Park Press. Baltimore, MD.
5. THATCHER, R. W., M. L. LESTER, R. MCALASTER & R. HORST. 1982. Effects of low levels of cadmium and lead on cognitive functioning in children. Arch. Environ. Health **37**: 159–166.
6. THATCHER, R. W., M. L. LESTER, R. MCALASTER & R. HORST. 1982. Intelligence and lead toxins in rural children. J. Learn. Dis. **37**(3): 159–166.
7. TUCKER, D. M. & H. H. SANDSTEAD. 1981. Spectral electroencephalographic correlates of iron status: Tired blood revisited. Physiol. Behav. **26**: 439–449.
8. FRANK, G. C., G. S. BERENSON, P. E. SCHILLING & M. C. MOORE MC. 1977. Adapting the 24-hr. recall for epidemiologic studies of school children. J. Am Diet. Assoc. **71**: 26–31.
9. KIRSCHMANN, J. D. 1979. Nutrition Almanac: 200–233. McGraw-Hill. New York, NY.
10. KRAUS, B. 1979. Calories and Carbohydrates. Signet. New York, NY.
11. KRAUS, B. 1980. Calorie Guide to Brand Names and Basic Foods. Signet. New York, NY.
12. CONSUMER GUIDE. 1974. The Brand Name Food Game. Signet, New York, NY.
13. WECHSLER, D. 1974. Wechsler Intelligence Scale for Children — Revised. The Psychological Corporation. New York, NY.
14. JASTAK, J. F. & S. JASTAK. 1978. Wide Range Achievement Test Manual. Jastak Associates, Inc. Wilmington, DE.
15. JASPER, H. H. 1958. The ten-twenty electrode system of the International Federation. Electroenceph. Clin. Neurophysiol. **10**: 371–375.
16. OTNES, R. K. & L. ENOCHSON, 1972. Digital Time Series of Analysis. John Wiley. New York, NY.
17. THATCHER, R. W., R. MCALASTER & M. L. LESTER. 1984. Evoked potentials related to hair cadmium and lead. *In* Brain and Information. R. Karrer, D. Cohen & P. Tueting, Eds. Ann. N.Y. Acad. Sci. **425**: 384–390.
18. JOHN, E. R., L. PRICHEP, H. AHN, P. EASTON, J. FRIDMAN & H. KAYE. 1983. Neurometric evaluation of cognitive dysfunctions and neurological disorders in children. Prog. Neurobiol. **21**: 239–290.
19. DIXON, W. & M. BROWN. 1979. Biomedical Computer Programs, P-Series. University of California Press. Los Angeles, CA.

The Impact of Phonemic Processing Instruction on the Reading Achievement of Reading-Disabled Children

ELLIS RICHARDSON

Nathan Kline Institute for Psychiatric Research
Orangeburg, New York 10962

Unfortunately, after many years of research on the problem, we are still at a stage where developmental dyslexia must be defined in terms of discrepancy and exclusion—the discrepancy between reading achievement and expectation, and the exclusion of children whose discrepancy may be attributed to other causes (for example, lack of opportunity, mental retardation, or severe emotional disturbance).[1] Other than speculation that developmental dyslexia is due to some subtle form of brain disorder, we have so little positive evidence regarding its etiology that a clinical diagnosis based on discrepancy and exclusion is about the best we can do at the time.

DYSLEXIC SYNDROMES

In the past few years, significant progress has been made in the identification of the underlying causes of developmental dyslexia. Several studies have provided evidence which suggests that developmental dyslexia is not a single syndrome. For example, Mattis, French, and Rapin[2] have identified at least three separate syndromes which seem to be associated exclusively with developmental dyslexia, as opposed to being simply symptomatic of more general brain disorder. These are: (a) language disorder, (b) articulatory and graphomotor discoordination, and (c) visual-perceptual disorder. Decker and DeFries[3] provide data which delineate four distinct subtypes of children with reading problems and relate their results to those reported by Mattis and his associates.

In a widely cited clinical investigation of developmental dyslexia, Boder[4] classified dyslexic children into three categories: (a) dysphonetic, (b) dyseidetic, and (c) mixed dysphonetic-dyseidetic. The dysphonetic children evidence difficulty in learning to use letter-sounds in decoding while the dyseidetic have difficulty storing and retrieving whole word associations. The remarkable point about Boder's study is that 63% of her sample were diagnosed dysphonetic while an additional 22% were classified dysphonetic-dyseidetic. In other words, among a sample of children with severe reading problems, about 85% evidenced difficulty with phoneme-grapheme processing.

PHONEMIC PROCESSING DEFICITS

From Boder's research we might speculate that difficulty in apprehending and processing the component phonemes of the spoken language might be characteristic of children with reading disorders. In fact, this would seem to be the case. A number of recent studies have shown that a deficiency in the ability to process phonemic information (that is, phonetic segmentation, sound blending and auditory closure) is associated with reading difficulties.[5-11] In fact, Vellutino[12] cites numerous investigators who have offered results that suggest that the source of many reading-disabled children's problems lie in a lack of awareness of the linguistic structure of speech.

PHONIC DECODING DEFICITS

The clinical importance of these findings is illuminated by the results of several studies we have conducted over the past three years. In one of these studies we compared a group of poor readers with a group of younger good readers who had been matched with the poor for basal vocabulary development.[13] We compared the decoding skill development of these two groups by using the Decoding Skills Test, or DST, a test which was developed for research on developmental dyslexia.[14] The DST provides criterion-referenced scores which reflect a child's basal vocabulary and phonic skills development, and it provides a variety of scores which characterize how decoding skills are expressed for individual children. Examples of these scores are response latency, transfer of phonic skills, contextual errors in oral reading, and the use of context clues. When we compared the good and poor reader groups on the variety of DST scores which characterize a child's decoding skills, we found that only those scores which involved the use of phonic skills consistently differentiated the two groups. The younger good readers had significantly better phonic decoding skills.

We have since replicated these results in a comparison of children who had been classified by their school district as "learning-disabled" with younger good readers.[15] The groups were matched for IQ and reading level. Results of this study showed that, while the two groups were equivalent on basal word recognition, the "learning disabled" (LD) children were particulary deficient in decoding phonetically regular words and nonsense (i.e., synthetic) words. In an extension of our study with the "learning disabled" sample, we found that the LD children made significantly more vowel errors which could be characterized as random guesses than did the younger normal readers.[16]

In summary, no validated diagnostic procedures for the positive identification of reading disabled children are yet available for general clinical use. However, several recent studies have identified related syndromes which may prove useful in the diagnosis of this disorder. The striking fact is that the majority of children identified in these studies fall into a category characterized by phonemic deficiencies. Moreover, a large number of recent studies have shown that performance on phonemic processing tasks relate to reading and reading disabilities. Finally, our own research has shown that reading-disabled children evidence a specific weakness in the use of phonic skills in decoding.

PHONEMIC PROCESSING MODEL

Taken together, the results of the studies reviewed above suggest a causal model of developmental dyslexia based on phonemic processing deficiences. According to this model, some children have difficulty apprehending the individual phonemes in spoken words. They are phoneme-deaf to language just as many of us are tone-deaf to music, although they may speak and understand normally. Logically, an understanding of phonemic sounds, their association with specific graphemes, and how they may vary in specific grapheme sequences (e.g., "at" versus "ate," "him" versus "whim") is important for normal reading development. Phonemic awareness should facilitate the acquisition of the First Grade reading vocabulary — the first few hundred words — and it may become essential for learning the several thousand additional words presented in the Second and Third Grade curriculum.

Normally, a beginning reader may use initial consonant sounds to help remember words such as "were," "does," and "says." Later, either through direct instruction or through inference, these children learn to respond to the spelling patterns of the language — to pronounce the sounds corresponding to specific spelling patterns such as *at*, *ate*, *ip*, *ipe*, *aw*, *ou*, and so forth. Thus, when the curriculum demands that they learn to read as many as 20 new words in a single day, they may already be able to decode many of these through their knowledge of phoneme-grapheme correspondence and spelling patterns.

Now let us consider what happens to the child who is less talented with regard to the phonemic structure of the language — the dysphonetic child. This child may even have learned the consonant sounds during First Grade, but does not understand how they apply to words like "were," "does", and "says." Deprived of this important clue, the phonemic dyslexic may struggle to learn the beginning reading vocabulary while his normal classmates learn these words with relative ease. Then, as the curriculum demands increase, the task of keeping up becomes more and more difficult. By Second or Third Grade, in a good school system, the dyslexic child may be identified as having a reading problem and be referred for special education or remedial reading.

Of course, we are not suggesting that phonemic processing deficits account for the whole of reading problems. Over the past three years I have taught and supervised the teaching of over 50 children with reading problems that were severe enough to prompt their parents to seek assistance from agencies outside the school system. Some have had difficulty memorizing words, some have had difficulty learning basic function words such as "were," "there," "when," and "which," some have had limited vocabulary development and some have even had pure comprehension problems — fluent decoding with little or no understanding. But, the striking fact is that most of these children evidenced difficulty with the use of the "letter-sound" system in reading.

A serious problem with research on developmental dyslexia has been that the clinical implications of the findings are not clear. Investigators are quick to suggest clinical implications of their results. For example, Mattis[17] cites several published programs which may be more or less appropriate for the three syndromes he has identified. However, the problem with clinical speculation based on research-generated hypotheses is that the link between the data and the clinical recommendation is theoretical rather than empirical and the research required to validate these speculations is expensive and administratively unwieldy. Thus, unfortunately, such applied research is rare.

METHOD

The Instructional Model

Over the past 15 years we have developed a model for reading instruction which can help bridge the gap between research and clinical practice. This model, called the Integrated Skills Method (ISM)[18] permits modality-independent control of the curriculum, (that is, independent emphasis on auditory versus visual teaching strategies may be exercised). Thus, a child's progress in these two aspects of reading instruction can be individually paced according to the child's behavior or according to a specified experimental protocol.

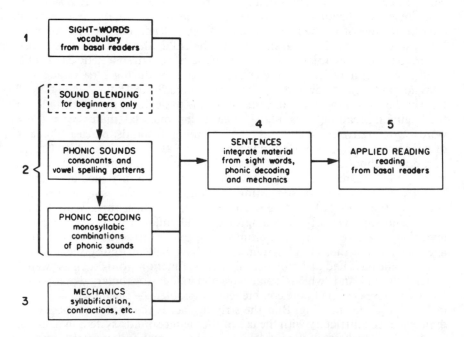

FIGURE 1. Diagram showing the five instructional components of the Integrated Skills Method Instructional Model.

FIGURE 1 provides a diagrammatic sketch of the ISM. The first component, Sight-Words, is designed to teach immediate recognition of words that are likely to be encountered at the child's reading level. The curriculum for this component is defined by the vocabulary sequence of any standard vocabulary-controlled basal reader program. We are currently using the Macmillan Series "r" readers in our clinics, but classroom applications of the ISM have used many different programs such as those of Houghton-Mifflin, Bank Street, and Allyn and Bacon. In our clinic, children are tested on the specific new words which will be introduced in the new stories to be read in the basal reader and those words which are not immediately recognized are written on index cards for rote drilling.

The second component of our model provides phonemic processing instruction for reading. It is designed to teach children to use the letter-sound system to decode unknown words. Much of the research on the development of the ISM has been devoted to the Phonic Decoding model we now use. We have published a review of the research[19] which demonstrates that it effectively produces transfer (that is, the ability to sound-out unknown words). The Phonic Decoding model includes three steps:

1. *Sound Blending*: The ability to synthesize whole word sounds from phoneme strings (for example, /m/,/an/ = man; /c/,/an/ = can).
2. *Phonic Sounds*: Production of phonemic sounds or blends in response to graphemes or grapheme strings (for example, m = /m/, c = /k/, st = /st/, an = /an/, ane = /ān/).
3. *Phonic Decoding*: The ability to decode unknown printed words (for example, man = "man," can = "can").

In the ISM, when a Phonic Sound is taught, it is fully exploited in terms of the accumulated Phonic Sounds. For example, if a child who knows the sounds for "m", "s," "c," "p," "at" and "an," is taught the sound for "f," the Phonic Decoding items "fat" and "fan," would be given in the same lesson. If that same child were later taught the Phonic Sound for "it," the words "sit," "pit," and "fit" would automatically be included in the Phonic Decoding step of the lesson. Finally, we have found it necessary to teach Sound Blending to children who are in the beginning stage of learning to read. Our review of the literature on Sound Blending[20] indicates that this skill is important in reading and we have demonstrated the face value of the decoding model in the research review cited above.[19] Although we suspect that most of the reading-disabled children we see in our clinics are deficient in Sound Blending, those who have mastered some of the First-Grade curriculum prior to treatment seem to get sufficient practice in Sound Blending by processing Phonic Decoding items, so that separate blending practice is not provided for them.

The third component of our model is called Mechanics for lack of a better word. It is used to teach a variety of material such as contractions and word endings, but it is used primarily to teach the application of phonic skills to polysyllabic forms. For example, a child who has mastered short *a* and *i* patterns in Phonic Decoding and can decode syllables such as "man," "ban," and "din," might be given items such as "manner," "banner," and "dinner" in the Mechanics step of the lesson.

The next component, called Sentences, is used to help the child transfer the skills taught in the earlier components to contextual reading. The teacher prepares sentences which integrate content from Sight-Words, Phonic Decoding and Mechanics into a single reading event. Consider, for example, the following sentence:

Tom put his dinner in the pot and went out to watch the parade.

In this sentence, which was prepared for an actual reading lesson, the words "Tom" and "pot" are Phonic Decoding items, "dinner" is a Mechanics item and "watch" and "parade" were selected from the basal vocabulary list (that is, are Sight-Word items). The other words ("put," "his," etc.) had been covered in previous lessons. The teachers prepare five or six such sentences for every lesson they design.

The final component of our model is called Applied Reading. This primarily involves reading stories in the basal readers which, by default, emphasize words from the Sight-Word component of the lesson. Although our model, as discussed to this point, emphasizes decoding skills, in Applied Reading the children are taught to use these decoding skills in reading for enjoyment and information. Thus, approximately one third to one half of every reading session is devoted to Applied Reading, and, although I have not emphasized this aspect of our model here, the data indicate that children who are taught by the ISM advance as rapidly in comprehension skills as they do in decoding.

Clinical Application of the Model

The ISM was reasonably well developed as long as ten years ago and there is a teacher's manual for its application in the classroom.[21] During the past several years our research has focused on how the ISM may be applied in various settings[22] and to improving the content sequence and specific instructional techniques. By far, our most successful effort to date has been a parent-involvement program which we have implemented at several major medical centers and in a few private learning centers.

In the parent-involvement program, a trained person, called the "reading therapist," designs weekly lessons for the child. During sessions the therapist checks the child on the previous lesson and demonstrates the new lesson, providing a role model for the parent who participates in the session. The parent and the child then practice at home with these materials each night for a week. During the week, the therapist designs the next lesson, making diagnostic decisions based on the child's performance in the previous session.

Each lesson includes five decks of index cards which correspond to the components of the model: (a) some 5 to 20 Sight-Word cards, (b) 4 to 8 Phonic Sound cards, (c) about 30 Phonic Decoding cards, (d) 10 to 20 Mechanics cards, and (e) 5 or 6 Sentence cards which have been prepared to integrate material from the entire lesson.

In a typical session, the child, parent and therapist gather around a small table. The therapist first checks the child with reference to the decks from the previous session, makes notes on the child's improvement, and decides what, if any, material should be carried over into the new lesson. At the beginning of the new lesson, the therapist has the child read the vocabulary list for the basal reader. Any words on which the child falters or which he misses are marked on the list and written on index cards. These constitute the Sight-Word deck for the week. Next, the therapist introduces the new Phonic Sounds and then has the child sound out the items in the Phonic Decoding deck. (The latter step will be preceded by a Sound Blending exercise if the child is a beginner.) As the lesson proceeds through Mechanics and Sentences, the therapist demonstrates specific teaching techniques to be used in daily home practice. Also, at each step of the session, the therapist may make diagnostic notes regarding any problems encountered. Finally, in the Applied Reading step of each session, the child reads a few pages from the sections of the basal reader that correspond to the words presented on the vocabulary list. The instructional emphasis of Applied Reading is, of course, oral fluency and comprehension.

Throughout each session, the teacher demonstrates and discusses specific teaching techniques for the parent and child — use of praise, prompting procedures for the Sight-Words, how to break words for Phonic Decoding, oral fluency and comprehension techniques for the sentences and basal readers, and so forth.

Measurement

Process Data

The structured clinic program offers a wealth of possible data for reading research. For example, a child's progress through the basal readers can be translated into grade equivalents (see Richardson and Freeman[23]) for the study of achievement rate. Responses to items on the basal vocabulary list are recorded each week and changes in a child's ability to decode these items can be studied. We are developing ways to measure a child's progress in the phonics curriculum and to measure the ease with which the child processes the material at each lesson step. The list could go on and we are just beginning to assemble data in order to explore the possibilities for a number of such measures. However, this presentation will be confined to data on basal reader program progress.

The Decoding Skills Test (DST)

The DST,[14] mentioned earlier in this presentation, is the most useful instrument we have at this point for studying changes in our children's decoding ability. It consists of three subtests: Subtest I, *Basal World Recognition*, Subtest II, *Phonic Decoding*, and Subtest III, *Oral Reading*.

The Basal Word Recognition Subtest includes 11 sets of 10 words each that were selected to be representative of the words taught at each of the 11 reader levels through Fifth Grade. TABLE 1 presents examples of items from each of these lists. The first list consists of Preprimer words, the second con-

TABLE 1. First Three Items in Reader Level Lists of DST Subtest I: Basal Word Recognition

Preprimer	Primer	First Reader	Two-One Reader	Two-Two Reader	Three-One Reader
to	so	sing	shop	strong	famous
yes	was	when	fine	able	daughter
the	went	next	end	almost	crowd

Three-Two Reader	Four-One Reader	Four-Two Reader	Five-One Reader	Five-Two Reader
natural	stalk	instruction	frequent	continent
mutter	project	contact	purchase	trudge
coin	stern	glare	advertise	desperate

sists of Primer words, and so on. This subtest provides criterion-referenced estimates of a child's instructional and frustration levels in word recognition. These estimates can be translated into grade equivalent scores for analysis. It also provides a variety of measures related to response latency and error types. (For a discussion of the variety of possible DST scores on each of the three subtests, see Richardson *et al.*[13])

DST Subtest II, Phonic Decoding, contains two sections: Real Words and Nonsense Words. (TABLE 2) Both sections consist of 12 lists, each containing five items. Half of the items are monosyllabic and half are polysyllabic, and each list represents a common spelling pattern. Each item in the Real Word section is a "regularly spelled" word. The items in the Nonsense Word section were constructed by changing consonants in the corresponding Real Words. This subtest also includes a variety of measures related to response latency and error types. Here I will present some individual response data, the total correct of the 60 items in each subtest section (Real and Nonsense Word) and the ratio of correct Nonsense Word responses to Real Word responses (the Phonic Transfer Index).

Subtest III, Oral Reading, consists of 11 passages which correspond to the 11 Subtest I word lists. The words from both Subtests I and II are systematically embedded in these passages as target items and a variety of types

TABLE 2. Examples of Items in Spelling Pattern Lists of DST Subtest II: Phonic Decoding

Spelling Pattern	Monosyllabic		Polysyllabic	
	Real	Nonsense	Real	Nonsense
CVC	nut	dut	mitten	pitten
CCVCC	stack	glick	publish	sublish
CVCe	doze	voze	confuse	monfuse
CCVCe	flake	grake	provide	drovide
CVVC	raw	taw	sausage	wausage
CCVVCC	choice	froice	creature	threature

of oral reading errors are recorded during administration. Owing to space constraints, no data from this subtest will be presented.

Norm-Referenced Measures

No evaluation of a child's reading development would be complete without the much-venerated standardized, norm-referenced, grade equivalent (GE) scores. In our evaluation we use the two reading subtests (Reading Recognition and Comprehension) of the Peabody Individual Achievement Test (PIAT) and the Gates-MacGinitie Reading Tests (Vocabulary and Comprehension). As we shall see in the data, the PIAT is perhaps an unfortunate choice of instruments since it provides GE scores which are often six months to a year higher than other estimates of a child's ability and since it seems at some times to overestimate and at other times to underestimate gains which are apparent from our other measures.

RESULTS

I am going to present case studies of two children treated in our clinics over the past two years and some preliminary results from 13 children who are participating in an experimental study being conducted in our laboratories. The case studies are presented in order to demonstrate how children respond to ISM treatment and to show some of the patterns one often observes in such children. The experimental data are presented to provide an example of how the ISM may be used to study developmental dyslexia. Although we feel that the progress made both by the individual cases and by the children in the experimental study is attributable to our treatment program, these data are not offered as validation evidence for the effectiveness of our program.

Clinical Case Studies

Since our clinic program has been a developmental effort with individual progress as the primary objective, it has been impossible for me to assemble data which could be summarized relating to the approximately 50 children we have treated. The two cases to be presented here were selected because they both received relatively consistent treatment on a long term basis, because we have a relatively complete set of data for them, and because they represent two very different types of cases. I present them here as two typical examples of how reading disabled children respond to our program.

Case 1: JC

The first case is that of a girl who came to our clinic in April, 1980 when she was in the eighth month of Fourth Grade (Grade Placement Grade Equivalent [GPGE] = 4.8). On most of our reading measures she scored in the low to middle Third Grade range, indicating a reading deficit of about 1½ years.

FIGURE 2 shows JC's progress over a year and a half in the basal reader program and on the DST's criterion-referenced estimate of her Instructional Level on Subtest I, Basal Word Recognition (the Instructional Level Grade Equivalent, ILGE). The solid curve in the upper part of the figure represents JC's school grade placement (GPGE) and, thus, the GE score which would be considered average for her at any given point in time.

Upon admission, JC scored 3-1 (first semester, Third Grade) on DST Subtest I which translates into a 3.3 ILGE score. On the basis of this and other data, she was placed at the beginning of the Third Grade Macmillan Series "r" readers. During the following five months (to September 1980) she attended eight clinic sessions. (The paucity of sessions was due, in large part, to the fact that clinic resources had to be redirected into other research efforts during that period.) Reference to FIGURE 2 indicates that JC gained five months in program placement and a full year on the DST ILGE during this period. By the end of the next three-month interval (December 1980), JC had received 12 more clinic sessions, had progressed eight months in Program Placement (that is, was reading Fourth Grade material), but her DST score remained constant at 4.3 (see FIGURE 2).

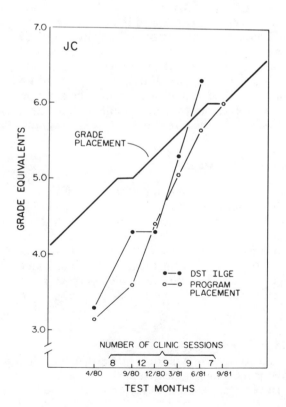

FIGURE 2. Reading achievement curves based on the criterion-referenced DST ILGE (closed circles) and Macmillan Series "r" Reading Program Placement (open circles) for subject JC.

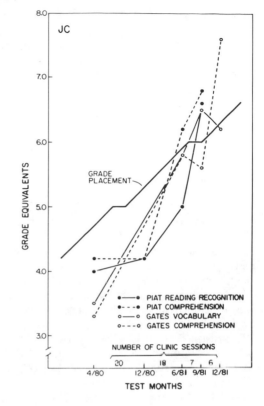

FIGURE 3. Reading achievement curves based on the standardized GE scores on the PIAT (closed circles) and Gates-MacGinitie (open circles) of subject JC. Word recognition curves (Reading Recognition and Vocabulary) are represented by broken lines, while comprehension curves are represented by solid lines.

Over the next three months (by March 1981), following nine additional sessions, JC completed the Fourth Grade readers and her DST score increased another full year (see FIGURE 2). Thus, in just under a year, she had progressed about two years in the instructional program (from beginning Third Grade readers to beginning Fifth Grade readers) and gained two years on the DST ILGE score (from 3.3 in April 1980 to 5.3 in March 1981). At that point her reading deficit was reduced to only about three to six months. By June 1981, she scored at the ceiling of the DST (ILGE = 6.3) and she was only about three months below the Grade Placement curve in Program Placement. By September, she had completed the Fifth Grade readers and was on grade level in Program Placement (at GE = 6.0).

FIGURE 3 shows JC's results on the norm-referenced PIAT and Gates-MacGinitie. Note that while the pretest results on the Gates confirm our original diagnosis (that JC was about 1½ years behind in reading), the PIAT results indicate only a six to eight month deficit (an obvious overestimate of JC's reading ability). After eight months of treatment, JC was retested with the PIAT (see the points at 12/80 in FIGURE 3). The results were most discouraging, indicating little or no gain for all of this effort. If we were to believe the PIAT, we might all have given up; however, we had the more reliable observations of the participants (child, parent, and teacher) that JC had made significant progress in reading, and we had the confirming evidence from the DST, so treatment was continued.

At the end of 14 months of treatment (see 6/81 in FIGURE 3), JC scored 5.8 on both Gates subtests, reflecting about 2½ years' gain over her pretest scores. A similar gain will be observed on the PIAT Comprehension subtest while the Reading Recognition score indicated a much more modest gain (from 4.0 at 4/80 to 4.9 at 6/81). Three months later (at 9/81), after JC had completed the Fifth-Grade readers and was on grade level in a criterion-referenced (and content-referenced) sense, she again was given both the PIAT and Gates. This time, the Gates Vocabulary and both PIAT scores were well above grade level. However, the Gates Comprehension score was about 4 months below grade level. Therefore, during the next three months, JC received 6 additional sessions aimed solely at improving her test taking strategy using the Scoring High in Reading Program.[24] Then, in December of 1981, she scored more than a year above grade level in comprehension and was discharged from the clinic.

To assess the role of phonemic processing in JC's reading problem and its correction, we will turn to the DST Subtest II, Phonic Decoding, scores. At pretest, she scored 35/60 on the Real Words and 19/60 on the Nonsense Words, resulting in a Phonic Transfer Index (PTI, which is equal to the Real Word score divided by the Nonsense Word score) of 0.57. Average readers we have tested generally score anywhere from 0.80 to 0.95 on the PTI (see Richardson et al.[14]). By the end of her treatment program JC had gotten a perfect score on the Real Words and 54/60 on the Nonsense Words for a PTI of 0.90, scores which are well within the normal range.

Some of her pretest responses provide a clue to her reading problem (see TABLE 3). The errors on Subtest II (with the exception of "shath" for sath) reflect weakness in the vowel component of the response and no difficulty with the consonant sounds. We may see how this deficiency in phonic decoding affected JC's basal vocabulary development when we review the Subtest I error responses (also in TABLE 3). For example, she decoded "desperate" as "dis/pā/rāt" and "distress" as "dis/trēz." Following five months of treatment, she was correct on most of the TABLE 3 items although they had not specifically been present in the instructional program. From this we conclude that

TABLE 3. Example of JC's Error Responses to DST Items

Subtest II Phonic Decoding, Nonsense Words		Subtest I Basal Word Recognition	
Test Item	Response	Test Item	Response
med	mid	continent	con/tent
pag	peg	desperate	dis/pā/rāt
thut	thôt	awkward	ak/ward
sath	shath	distress	dis/trēz
brop	broip	cautious	quan/tas
mide	mid	solemn	salm
voze	vēz	prairie	per/ry

the phonics instruction strengthened her use of vowels, thus improving her basal vocabulary or word recognition ability which, in turn, enabled her to progress rapidly through the program so that she was reading on grade level following a year and a half of treatment.

Case 2: JD

Now we will consider a very different case. JD was a hyperactive boy who was receiving Ritalin medication for his behavior problem when he began our clinic program. He was in the eighth month of his Sixth-Grade year in school but evidenced about a middle First-Grade reading level. Thus, JD had gained only about five months in reading from nearly 6 years of school instruction and he was about 5½ years behind in reading. The prognosis for such a child to catch up within two to three years of treatment is very poor. Not only must they gain about eight years in reading during that time, they must do this in spite of a most severe disability in the area. In fact, we have treated several such children and we are happy if we can simply keep the child's reading deficit from getting worse. (To avoid falling farther behind, the child must make "normal" progress.)

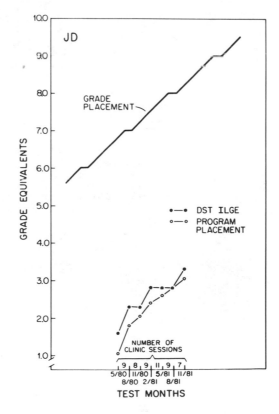

FIGURE 4. Reading achievement curves based on the criterion-referenced DST ILGE (closed circles) and Macmillan Series "r" Reading Program Placement (open circles) scores for JD.

FIGURE 4 shows that while JD was able to score a Primer level on the DST (ILGE = 1.6), he was actually started at the first Preprimer in the basal reader program. In such cases, we have found that although the child may know a sufficient number of words to score middle First-Grade on our tests, there are likely to be several Preprimer words which the child has not yet learned. Moreover, these children are able to complete the Preprimers with relative ease and this experience is an important motivating factor in the child's continued program progress. The steep slope of the Program Placement curve over the first three-month period in FIGURE 4 is simply a reflection of the initially low program placement. However, this does not necessarily account for the steep slope of the DST curve in this first period. This, we believe, is a function of the child finally making some sense out of the phonetic code as a result of our phonics program.

This progress, with the exception of the plateaus (which, as I have previously noted elsewhere, are best ignored by the participants), is confirmed by the DST results, which stay consistently two to three months above the child's Program Placement. By the end of 1½ years, JD was beginning the Third-Grade readers and his reading deficit had been slightly reduced to about five years (as opposed to 5½ years at the beginning of treatment).

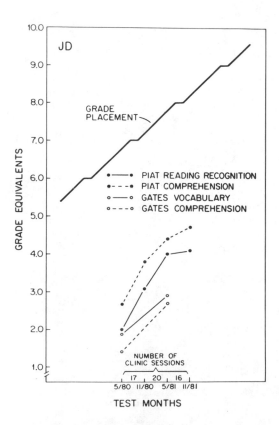

FIGURE 5. Reading achievement curves based on the standardized GE scores on the PIAT (closed circles) and Gates-MacGinitie (open circles) of subject JD. Word recognition curves (Reading Recognition and Vocabulary) are represented by broken lines, while comprehension curves are represented by solid lines.

TABLE 4. Example of JD's Error Responses to DST Items

Subtest II Phonic Decoding, Nonsense Words		Subtest I Basal Word Recognition	
Test Item	Response	Test Item	Response
jid	jīt	strong	strōn
med	mād	able	ab/bē
dut	brut	angry	an/jē
sath	sāth	else	el/lē
brop	broip	cautious	quan/tas
glick	glutch	short	strōt
blesh	brush	banana	ban/did

Now we will have a look at JD's results on our norm-referenced measures, the PIAT and Gates (see FIGURE 5). Note that, upon pretest, his Gates scores were 1.4 on Comprehension and about 1.9 (five months higher) on Vocabulary. The PIAT results, allowing for the 6-month to 1-year inflation on this measure, were just the opposite, with the comprehension score about 7 months above the Reading Recognition (i.e., Vocabulary) score. This teaches us to be very wary of drawing conclusions from standardized test results. After a year in our program, JD scored about 1 year higher on the two Gates subtests and nearly 2 years higher on the PIAT. Then, after an additional 6 months in the program, only the PIAT was given, but JD continued to display progress on this measure.

Now let us consider the impact of instruction in phonemic processing on JD's reading skills development. At pretest, JD responded correctly to 17 of the 60 Subtest II Real Word items but got only 7 of the 60 Nonsense Word items. This yielded a Phonic Transfer Index of 0.41, well below the 0.80 to 0.95 we have come to expect from average readers. By the end of his treatment program, a year and a half later, he scored 47 on the Real Word section and 43 of the Nonsense Word section of Subtest II for a Phonic Transfer Index of 0.92 — well within the average range. TABLE 4 shows how JD responded to several of the Nonsense Word items at pretest. Although there is a preponderance of vowel errors on these items, there are also a few instances of consonant errors. I have come to believe that the consonant errors in such cases are a result of the utter failure of the child's phonic knowledge to serve his decoding. This, I believe, results in a lack of detailed attention to the consonants. A similar phenomenon can, of course, be observed in JD's responses to the Subtest I, Basal Word Recognition items. To the stimulus items "able" and "else," JD responded "ab/bē" and "el/lē," ignoring the *l* in "able" and the *s* in "else" and pronouncing the silent *e* as a long *e* in both items. To "strong" he said "strug," giving the *o* a short *u* sound and ignoring the *n*.

Conclusions

Obviously, these two case studies do not conclusively demonstrate the impact of phonemic processing instruction on reading achievement in children with developmental dyslexia. However, I hasten to point out that these two children are typical of the many children we have seen in our clinics. I feel confident that further analysis of the response data of such children will considerably advance the case that carefully structured instruction in the phonetic code can provide tremendous assistance in helping children to overcome developmental dyslexia.

Ritalin and Reading Study

In developing and testing our treatment procedures, we have provided treatment for over 50 children. However, we have found it impossible to summarize our results in any meaningful way since our work was clinically oriented and evaluation was conducted as appropriate to each child's treatment rather than to suit research purposes. However, we have recently begun a study of the effects of Ritalin medication on the reading achievement of hyperactive children, using our reading clinic model to obtain rapid reading progress during the intervention period.

In this study, children are randomly assigned to one of four treatment groups (placebo, 0.3 mg/kg, 0.5 mg/kg and 0.7 mg/kg of Ritalin administered twice daily), and receive 6 months of treatment at our reading clinic. the DST,

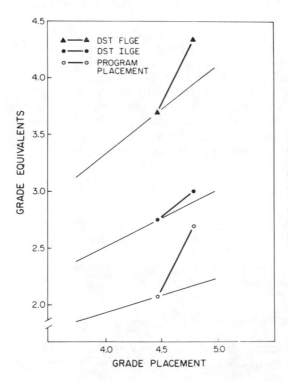

FIGURE 6. Reading achievement curves based on the mean criterion-referenced DST ILGE (closed circles), DST FLGE (closed triangles) and Macmillan Series "r" Reading Program Placement (open circles) scores of 13 hyperactive children participating in a study of the effects of Ritalin medication on reading achievement.

the PIAT, and the Gates-MacGinitie test are given as pretests, after 3 months, and after 6 months of treatment. Since we expect to take several years to gather sufficient data to evaluate our hypothesis regarding the effects of medication on reading achievement, we will not consider the various drug groups in this presentation. However, this study is currently providing us with systematic data with which to study the impact of instruction in phonemic processing on reading achievement. At present, we have data at the time of pretest and after 3 months of treatment for only 13 children. These data will be the focus of this present presentation.

The sample includes 12 boys and one girl. At the time of pretest, their mean age was 9 years, 6 months with a range from 8 years, 2 months to 11 years, 7 months. In grade placement, they ranged from 2.3 (the third month of Second Grade) to 6.3 (third month of Sixth Grade), with a mean grade placement of 4.48. Their averaged score on the Gates-MacGinitie test Total Reading at pretest time was 2.3. Thus, when they began treatment, these children were on the average, a little more than 2 years behind in reading.

Results

FIGURE 6 shows the averaged program placement and DST Instructional Level Grade Equivalent (ILGE) scores at pretest and after 3 months of intervention. According to these measures the children began our program at a beginning Second-Grade level. Following 3 months of treatment, they gained a little more than six months and were at a high Second-Grade level. Their averaged DST ILGE increased from about 2.7 to 3.0 — a gain of only 3 months for 3 months in the program. The real growth in these children's basal vocabulary development can be seen in the DST Frustration Level Grade Equivalent (FLGE) score. This measure reflects the number of "above-grade-level" words a child is able to decode. On this measure, the children gained approximately 7 months during the 3 months of the program. This means that the largest gains were evident for words which were not specifically covered in our instruction. I am willing to speculate that the large gains in the FLGE are due to the improvement in the children's ability to apply phonic decoding skills to basal vocabulary items. Although the actual research remains to be done, I submit that these data reflect the impact of phonemic processing instruction on the reading achievement of the participating children.

The light lines in FIGURE 6 represent the achievement curves for each of the scores extrapolated back in time from the pretest to the beginning of First Grade (1.0). Thus, these curves provide an estimate of the children's achievement rate prior to treatment. The resultant angles formed by these hypothetical curves with the actual achievement curves (that is, pretest to 3 months) provide an estimate of the impact of the treatment program on the children's achievement rate.

FIGURE 7 shows the results gotten from the standardized tests. The data reflect progress ranging from 3 to 5 months on all measures except the PIAT Reading Recognition. As in FIGURE 6, the light curves represent these children's averaged achievement curves extrapolated from their pretest scores.

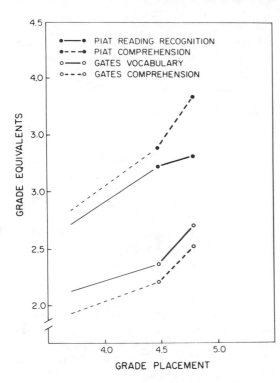

FIGURE 7. Reading achievement curves based on the mean standardized GE scores on the PIAT (closed circles) and Gates-MacGinitie (open circles) of 13 hyperactive children participating in a study of the effects of Ritalin medication on reading achievement. Word recognition curves (Reading Recognition and Vocabulary) are represented by broken lines, while comprehension curves are represented by solid lines.

In reviewing these data, it is important to bear in mind that 3 months is a very short period upon which to base an evaluation of a reading intervention program. Data from our clinic work would suggest that 6 months is a more reasonable period from which to expect measurable gains in phonic decoding skills. However, the children in our sample did, in fact, provide us with some evidence of gains in phonic decoding skills as measured by the DST Subtest II. At pretest time, the children scored an average of 29 correct of the 60 Real Word items and 19 on the Nonsense Word items. After 3 months they had gained 10 points on the Real Word section ($\overline{X} = 39$) and 11 points on the Nonsense Word section ($\overline{X} = 30$). The resultant Phonic Transfer Indices were 0.63 at pretest and 0.73 after 3 months of intervention.

An exploratory analysis was conducted in which the children were sorted into three groups on the basis of their pretest PTI and changes in this measure over three months. The three groups were defined as follows: (a) PTI greater than or equal to 0.80 at time of pretest (PTI Normal), (b) PTI less than 0.80 at pretest with a gain of more than 0.20 after 3 months (PTI Gain), and (c) PTI less than 0.80 at pretest with a gain of less than 0.20 after 3 months (No PTI Gain). The PTI Normal group includes children who evidenced relatively normal phonic decoding skill development and whose reading problems should be attributable to factors other than phonemic processing deficits. The PTI Gain group should include children with phonemic processing deficits (that is, who are phonemic dyslexic) who are responsive to phonics instruc-

TABLE 5. Averaged Pretest and Change Scores of Children in PTI Normal, PTI Gain, and No PTI Gain Categories

Measure	Normal PTI[a]	PTI Gain[b]	No PTI Gain[c]
n	4	5	4
Pretest scores			
Phonic transfer index	0.90	0.40	0.58
Expected grade placement	5.00	3.68	4.02
Gates total score	2.68	2.27	1.94
Gates discrepancy	− 2.32	− 1.41	− 2.06
Three-month change			
Phonic transfer index	− 0.10	0.44	0.11
Program placement	0.59	0.76	0.49
Gates vocabulary	0.13	0.54	0.28
Gates comprehension	0.13	0.42	0.33

[a] PTI > 0.80
[b] PTI < 0.80, Gain > 0.20
[c] PTI > 0.80, Gain < 0.20

tion. The last group, No PTI Gain, should include relatively non-responsive phonemic dyslexics.

Among the 13 subjects, four were in the PTI Normal group, five were in the PTI gain group and four were in the No PTI Gain group. TABLE 5 shows selected pretest scores and change scores of the children in each of the three groups. It will be noted from the table that the average PTI of the PTI Normal group was 0.90 while that for the PTI Gain and No PTI Gain groups was 0.40 and 0.58, respectively. The PTI Normal group was about 1 year older than the other two groups with an averaged Expected Grade Placement (that is, the grade placement expected if the child had not been held over) of 5.00. Thus, although the PTI Normal group earned higher Gates Total Scores than the other two groups, their Reading Discrepancy Score (Expected Grade Placement minus Gates Total Score) was greater than that of the other two groups.

An examination of the changes over 3 months in TABLE 5 reveals a negative change of −0.10 (down to 0.80 from 0.90) for the PTI Normal group and a small positive change of +0.11 (from 0.58 to 0.69) for the No PTI Gain group. In contrast, the PTI of the Gain group more than doubled from 0.40 at pretest to 0.84 after 3 months of treatment.

The importance of the relative changes in the PTIs of these children is revealed by referring to changes in their reading scores over the three month period (see TABLE 5). For example, the change in Program Placement (that is, progress in the Macmillan reading program) was 0.59 for the Normal PTI group (about six months of progress) and 0.49 (about five months) for the No PTI Gain group. However, the PTI Gain group progressed through about 7 and ½ months (0.76) in the Macmillan curriculum. On the two Gates measures, this effect was even more striking. While the PTI Normal group gained only 0.13 in Vocabulary and Comprehension and the No PTI Gain group improved only 0.28 in Vocabulary and 0.33 in Comprehension, the PTI Gain group improved by over five months (+0.54) in vocabulary and four months (+0.42) in Comprehension.

Discussion

Given the "after-the-fact" nature of this analysis and the small amount of data upon which it is based, no conclusions may be drawn. However, the results are suggestive of a promising avenue of investigation. It would seem that children can be sorted into three clinically relevant categories on the basis of their PTI scores: (a) children whose reading problem is *not* due to a phonemic processing deficit and who do not immediately benefit from intervention, (b) children whose reading problem is due, at least in part, to a phonemic processing deficit and who benefit immediately from remediation, and, (c) children whose reading problem is due, at least in part, to a phonemic processing deficit and who do not immediately benefit from remedial intervention.

It will be necessary to conduct further research to determine if, in fact, we are dealing here with actual, replicable results by which children may be classified in clinical programs, with consequent prognostic relevance. However, we will speculate at this time that we are dealing with the same syndromes described by Boder (1973). Our Normal PTI group may fit into Boder's dyseidetic category, the PTI Gain group may fit the dysphonetic category, and the No PTI Gain group may fit Boder's combined dyseidetic-dysphonetic category. If this is the case, we have a potentially powerful research tool in our intervention program for further describing these children in ways that are clinically relevant. We now have collected data from over 30 children in our Ritalin study and are beginning to explore in more detail the hypothesis that clinically relevant groups may be differentially diagnosed on the basis of PTI and achievement gains.

SUMMARY

It is hypothesized that a phonemic processing deficit is a primary causal factor in the reading problems of many children with developmental dyslexia. An instructional model which emphasizes phonics instruction as a key in the treatment of children with reading disorders is presented. Procedures for the application of this model in a parent-involvement clinic program are described.

Results from two typical children from the clinic sample who had received treatment for more than a year are presented. One Fourth-Grade child, who began the program with a 1½-year reading deficit, was reading grade-appropriate material and scoring about 1 year above grade-norms on a standardized test after 14 months of clinic treatment. The second child began the treatment program as a Sixth Grader who was virtually a non-reader. After 1½ years of intervention, this child had attained a Third-Grade reading level, but was still nearly 4 years behind in reading. The pretest error responses to individual words made by both children are reviewed to demonstrate the underlying phonetic deficiency—an apparent difficulty with vowel sound correspondence.

Averaged reading achievement results from 13 children who had received 3 months of instruction in an experimental study in which the instructional model is being used are presented. Results indicate a dramatic change in the children's rate of reading achievement during treatment. The children were divided into three groups on the basis of a measure of the transfer of phonic skills: (a) normal transfer, (b) poor transfer which improved dramatically in the first 3 months of treatment, and (c) poor transfer which failed to improve. Analysis of the achievement data of these three groups indicates that the second group improved more rapidly than did the other two groups. It is suggested that further analyses of phonic transfer data may prove to be very instructive concerning the causes and treatment of developmental dyslexia.

REFERENCES

1. SCHERE, R. A., E. RICHARDSON & I. BAILER. 1980. Toward operationalizing a psychoeducational definition of learning disabilities. J. Abnorm. Child Psychol. **8**: 5-20.
2. MATTIS, S., J. H. FRENCH & I. RAPIN. 1975. Dyslexia in children and young adults: Three independent neuropsychological syndromes. Dev. Med. Child Neurol. **17**: 150-163.
3. DECKER, S.N. & J. C. DEFRIES. 1986. Cognitive ability profiles in families of reading disabled children. Dev. Med. Child Neurol. **23**: 217-227.
4. BODER, E. 1973. Developmental dyslexia: A diagnostic approach based on three atypical reading-spelling patterns. Dev. Med. Child Neurol. **15**: 663-687.
5. BRADLEY, L. & P. E. BRYANT. 1978. Difficulties in auditory organization as a possible cause of reading backwardness. Nature **271**: 746-747.
6. FOX, B. & D. K. ROUTH. 1980. Phonemic analysis and severe reading disability in children. J. Psycholing. Res. **9**: 115-119.
7. FOX, B. & D. K. ROUTH. 1976. Phonemic analysis and synthesis as word-attack skills. J. Ed. Psychol. **68**: 70-74.
8. LIBERMAN, I. Y., D. SHANKWEILER, A. M. LIBERMAN, C. FOWLER & F. W. FISCHER. 1976. Phonetic segmentation and recoding in the beginning reader. *In* Toward a Psychology of Reading. A. S. Reber & D. Scarborough, Eds. Erlbaum. Hillsdale, NJ.
9. RICHARDSON, E., B. DIBENEDETTO, A. CHRIST & M. PRESS. 1980. Relationship of auditory and visual skills to reading retardation. J. Learn. Dis. **13**: 77-82.
10. SHANKWEILER, D., I. LIBERMAN, L. MARK, C. FOWLER & W. FISCHER. 1979. The speech code and learning to read. J. Exp. Psychol. Human Learn. Mem. **5**: 531-545.
11. ZIFCAK, M. 1981. Phonological awareness and reading acquisition. Contemp. Ed. Psychol. **6**: 117-126.
12. VELLUTINO, F. R. 1979. Dyslexia: Theory and Research. MIT Press. Cambridge, MA.
13. RICHARDSON, E., B. DIBENEDETTO & A. ADLER. 1982. Use of the Decoding Skills Test to study differences between good and poor readers. *In* Advances in Learning and Behavior Disabilities: An Annual Compilation of Theory and Research. K. Gadow & I. Bialer, Eds. JAI Press. Greenwich, CN.
14. RICHARDSON, E., B. DIBENEDETTO & A. ADLER. 1980. Interim Manual for the DST: Decoding Skills Test. Long Island Research Institute. Stony Brook, NY. (ERIC Document Reproduction Service No. ED 193 304.)
15. KOCHNOWER, J., E. RICHARDSON & B. DIBENEDETTO. 1983. A comparison of the phonic decoding ability of normal and learning disabled children. J. Learning Dis. **75**: 576-582.

16. DiBENDETTO, B., E. RICHARDSON & J. KOCHNOWER. 1983. Vowel generalizations in normal and learning disabled readers. J. Ed. Psychol. **75**: 576–582.
17. MATTIS, S. 1974. Childhood aphasia and dyslexia: Current issues and future research. Planning Conference on Essential Skills. National Institute of Education.
18. RICHRDSON, E. & C. M. BRADLEY, 1974. ISM: A teacher-oriented method of reading instruction for the child-oriented teacher. J. Learn. Dis. **7**: 344–352.
19. RICHARDSON, E. & B. DiBENEDETTO. 1977. Transfer effects of a phonic decoding model: A review. Reading Improvement **14**: 239–247.
20. RICHARDSON, E., B. DiBENEDETTO & C. M. BRADLEY. 1977. The relationship of sound blending to reading achievement. Rev. Ed. Res. **47**: 319–334.
21. RICHARDSON, E. 1974. The Integrated Skills Method Teacher's Manual. Interdependent Learning Model, Fordham University. New York, NY.
22. RICHARDSON, E., B DiBENEDETTO, A. CHRIST, M. PRESS & B. G. WINSBERG. 1978. An assessment of two methods for remediating reading deficiencies. Reading Improvement **15**: 82–95.
23. RICHARDSON, E. & H. FREEMAN. 1981. Reading Progress Feedback System. Interdependent Learning Model. Fordham University, New York, NY.
24. COHEN, S. A. & D. I. FOREMAN. 1978. Scoring High in Reading. Random House. New York, NY.

Introduction: Part II

VIRGINIA TELLER

Hunter College and the Graduate Center
The City University of New York
New York, New York 10021

The landscape of linguistic research in this country has changed remarkably over the last thirty years. The 1957 publication of *Syntactic Structures* created a revolution in the field and ushered in the modern era of linguistics. Chomsky's notion that grammatical transformations apply to abstract linguistic structures superseded Harris's view that transformations convert one surface sentence type into another. In the wake of the early successes of generative grammar, the concerns of many linguists turned to problems of syntax, often at the expense of other areas of research. Nearly a decade passed before the limits of this approach became apparent. With the realization that syntactic principles alone cannot account for language behavior, attention has increasingly focused on semantics, pragmatics, and discourse as well as syntax. These newer but now familiar terms all point to today's wider scope for linguistic studies. Language is more than a mathematical system for generating sentences; it is the primary means by which we communicate.

If a single theme links the six papers in this section, it is the importance of taking context into account. Originally presented as talks to the Academy's Linguistics Section between January, 1980, and May, 1982, they collectively attest to the diversity of stances possible with respect to what has recently been referred to as "situated" language. Each author takes a different vantage point on the issues involved. The contributions by McConnell-Ginet, Hoffman, and Verbrugge, all dealing with aspects of figurative language, cogently present the view that metaphoric structures themselves, both verbal and nonverbal, are relatively empty of content and are given significance only through their uses in a specific context such as discourse or problem solving. Bucci and Baxter's research describes how overt and subtle cross-cultural language differences can interfere with communication in a clinical setting. Baltin and Prince demonstrate that evidence from outside the domain of syntax can shed light on what have previously been considered purely syntactic problems.

McConnell-Ginet's inquiry into the influences of gender on discourse examines the social mechanisms that affect the meanings attached to linguistic forms. Drawing on evidence from recent research that indicates, among other things, that men tend to interrupt women, she builds a case for the quite different roles that men and women play in ordinary conversation: Women orient themselves toward it as a cooperative enterprise, while men view conversation as an arena for individual achievement. One consequence of this inequality is the greater likelihood that vocabulary will be marked by a predominantly male rather than a predominantly female viewpoint. As an illustration of the disparity, McConnell-Ginet traces an ingenious and convincing route by which *sissy* and *buddy*, diminutives of *sister* and *brother*, could have acquired their present meanings of "coward" or "effeminate" and "comrade" or "pal," respectively.

Although the first experiments on metaphor were conducted in the early 1900s, only in the last fifteen years have psychologists and psycholinguists begun to explore systematically the cognitive mechanisms that permit us to use figurative language so widely. Hoffman's purpose is twofold, first, to remind us how dominant metaphorical modes of expression are in our lives, and second, to review the extensive recent literature on the subject. His discussion reveals the pervasive use of nonliteral language at all levels — words, phrases, sentences, idioms, proverbs, and in problem solving, music, and computing. Although a variety of research methods and materials have been devised for investigating metaphor, it seems that we are still far from having a plausible model, much less a theory, of how figurative language is created, used, and interpreted.

Verbrugge's provocative paper goes a step further than either McConnell-Ginet or Hoffman in confronting and questioning the fundamental assumptions on which most linguistic research is based. He examines three metaphoric systems — microcosm, conduit, and representation — that have had a powerful influence on our understanding of cognition, meaning, and communication and argues that they may be our greatest impediment to progress in understanding linguistic processes. Verbrugge uses the chemist Kekulé's struggle to discover the structure of benzene as a pointed example of (i) how a notational system can be as prone to conceal the properties sought after as to reveal them and (ii) the danger of being trapped by a single metaphorical view. Instances of notations that have had constraining (and liberating) effects in linguistics abound, e.g. the phonetic transcriptions and visual acoustic displays so prevalent in speech research. Some of the potential pitfalls of metaphor can be avoided, Verbrugge claims, if we recognize that it is a mistake to regard metaphor and other symbolic phenomena as isolated properties of linguistic systems separate from the dynamic processes of human perception and action.

The sociolinguistic paper by Bucci and Baxter vividly depicts the ways in which communication between patients and therapists can break down on the psychiatric ward of an urban hospital where many patients speak nonstandard varieties of English in their interactions with therapists who speak Standard American English. Their study, which focuses on patients whose native dialects are Black English, Caribbean Creole, and Puerto Rican English, identifies three categories of cross-cultural communication problems: overt language differences, linguistic ambiguity, and linguistic insecurity. Linguistic insecurity is a subtle yet potentially severe problem characterized by a negative attitude toward one's speech. In an effort to assess this trait, Bucci and Baxter constructed a simple yet robust self-correction test in which the subject evaluates a recorded sample of his or her own speech. The measure has the advantage of being easily administered in almost any setting — psychiatric, medical, or educational — where there is a need to identify people at risk for this barrier to successful communication.

A theory of language that includes an account of language acquisition places stronger constraints on the notion "learnable" than a linguistic theory that views grammars as purely abstract mathematical objects. A learnable rule of grammar would be one for which evidence is available to a child. This point is not lost on Baltin as he considers the implications of the process of language acquisition for the structure of adult grammars. He proposes learnability as a criterion for positing syntactic rules and applies this criterion in an attempt to state the constraints governing two types of movement rules. The strategy Baltin adopts calls for more communication between child language researchers and linguistic theoreticians; data from each approach could affect the models constructed in both fields. His claim is that by analyzing particular features of grammar and exploring various accounts of their acquisition, we could gain further insight into both the universal aspects of grammar and the nature of the mental apparatus that can acquire language.

With Prince's paper we come, in a sense, nearly full circle. The linguistic tools — distributions, environments, and classification schemes — she uses to delve into the discourse functions of the constructions known as topicalization and left dislocation echo the approach of Harris. These two sentence types share an unusual feature of word order in that the object appears ahead of the subject. Since they are syntactically so similar, the question arises as to what, if anything, guides a speaker in choosing one over the other in discourse. Prince looks at the way people use the constructions in actual conversations, drawing on such sources as the monologues in Studs Terkel's *Working* for her data. She finds that they serve partially overlapping functions but each in addition has a unique role in focusing attention on a particular portion of an utterance. The rules she formulates to account for these differences distinguish a single function for topicalization and two for left dislocation based on the relationship between relevant elements of the sentence and entities in the preceding discourse.

The Origins of Sexist Language in Discourse

SALLY McCONNELL-GINET

Department of Modern Languages and Linguistics
Cornell University
Ithaca, New York 14853

"A rose by any other name would smell as sweet," says Juliet. "What's in a name?" For most of us, this familiar line serves to conjure up what I call the "code" view of language. On this view, the concepts of a language system function rather as name tags, like the little stakes in a garden that tell us that this flower is *rose*, that one *tulip*. It makes no real difference to their function as identifiers whether the tags are adhesive-backed or have pins in them, or whether the stakes are wooden or plastic. Similarly, it is argued, just what linguistic stuff we use to convey thoughts from one mind to another is inconsequential. The picture is something like this. Natural languages — English, Finnish, Japanese, Navajo — are codes that we use for public identification of concepts, for expressing our thoughts to ourselves and to one another. The basic concepts are words in some sort of universal "mentalese" or "language of thought." Just as the Morse code operator can turn an English expression into a sequence of dots and dashes that can enable an operator at the other end to retrieve the original English expression, so the English speaker can encode a mentally articulated thought into a structured string of English words that can subsequently be decoded by a hearer who also knows English in order to recover the transmitted thought. If this picture is right, then it is hard to see how the language-using process can be as fraught with social and psychological importance as is often suggested. What indeed could Juliet have in mind when she also says: "Romeo, doff thy name" and "'Tis but thy name that is my enemy."

These other lines of Juliet's suggest that there may indeed be much in a name. Unlike roses and other botanical specimens, social creatures derive their properties in large measure from systems of human thought and patterns of human action into which naming practices are integrated. These lines also serve to remind us of another, apparently very different, view of language as itself consequential in human life, an instrument of human thought and action, a tool serving some purposes perhaps better than others. It seems to be this instrumental view or something like it that lies behind feminist claims that men have "stolen the power of Naming," as Dale Spender[1] puts it. Spender is here protesting men's determining what is labeled and the content of the labels, protesting women's exclusion from the community of those whose concepts are linguistically articulated. Such a protest seems to presuppose, however, the view that access to linguistic articulation is a matter of importance. It also presupposes that such access may be problematic. The instrumental view even more obviously inspires feminist protests against sexist language.

But how can we understand such protests? For those of us trained in some version of the code view, it is difficult to know what is at stake here, difficult to understand what the issue is. Even if some speakers are less free than others to "name," how could it matter? After all, the person who decides whether garden labels should be plastic or paper hardly wields real power.

It is often alleged that what is conceptually problematic about feminist discussions of language is that they attribute potency to language itself, that they assume the rather shaky position that linguistic forms themselves have real import for society and culture. Does the mere existence of great numbers of derogatory or belittling words to refer to women make us think the less of women? No, goes the reply. The words themselves are harmless; it is only their use to insult which is harmful. It is because people have thought so little of women that an informal pronunciation of *housewife* descends to us as modern-day *hussy*, but the mere availability of the word *hussy* in its modern meaning has no particular social impact. Few analysts would argue that society and culture do not affect language. It is only the opposite direction of influence that is thought to be somehow suspect, something like magical belief in the efficacy of certain words to cure the sick or bring the rain. But how do social and cultural forms affect the development of language? In fact, we have no better understanding of influence in this direction than of influence exerted by language.

The central task as I see it is to develop an account of just how linguistic forms get attached to meanings and how the meanings they identify can change from generation to generation (indeed, far more rapidly). This way of putting it is still not quite right, for it seems to suggest that the meanings themselves are there, independently of their being labeled (just like the flowers in the garden). But is is precisely this picture that needs to be challenged. A rose is differentiated from a tulip through its structure: there is a systematic distinction in nature whether or not language happens to tag it. But Montague and Capulet are socially created categories not given in the scientist's inventory of natural kinds: the family names not only tag, but also point to a network of social relations and beliefs about them that have been produced by human minds and actions. The difference between *Montague/Capulet* and *rose/tulip* shows that we need to revise our first formulation and put the question somewhat differently: How is meaning created, transmitted, and transformed?

This paper makes two main points. First, sexist language is more than a matter of what Muriel Schulz[2] has called "the semantic derogation" of women or the "linguistic invisibility" of women created by so-called generic masculines. Sexism is involved to the extent that language reflects a male-centered view of the world and serves men's interests more readily than women's. Second, the key to understanding how language can serve one group's interests better than it does another's is understanding how it could come to reflect one group's views more fully and faithfully than another's. Or, to put it differently, to see how meanings are encoded is to see more clearly why it can matter which meanings are encoded. There is an "inequality among speakers," as Dell Hymes[3] has noted, and sexist language is the product of sexual inequality.

Specifically, I argue that linguistic structures themselves are relatively empty of content, but that they are given significance through their uses in actual discourse. This process of giving meaning is one in which social relationships and socially mediated beliefs and actions are crucially involved. Focusing on patterns of semantic shift and proposing a link between such shifts and the discourse settings in which they arise, I sketch a model of the mechanisms through which sexist attitudes and beliefs can contribute to lexical semantics. Using this model helps us give an account of how individual language users may stand in different positions with respect to their potential influence on the stock of conventional or preset meanings. It also suggests how that stock matters for what language users can mean and how they can mean it. In other words, it explains sexist language in terms of its origins in sexist discourse situations.

In fact, of course, we have no detailed knowledge of discourses in which, for example, the form *sissy* began to take on its present meanings of "coward," "effeminate," or "supra-feminine" and pretty much lost its use as a diminutive of *sister*, nor of those in which *buddy* began to lose its connection to *brother* while acquiring its meanings of "comrade," "pal," or (mainly male) "good friend." Similar extensions still occur — *a weak sister, the brotherhood of man*, and the like. There are, however, no tapes of the many conversations (and other linguistic transactions) during the course of which, presumably, *sissy* and *buddy* functioned in their evaluative uses less and less as figurative extensions of kin terminology and more and more as literal expressions of their current senses. My strategy therefore will be as follows: (1) I will examine some of the ways in which gender/sex systems enter into discourse processes; (2) I will sketch a view of the connection between linguistic meaning and language use that draws on recent work in theoretical semantics and pragmatics; and (3) I will suggest an explanation of the origins of sexist language by connecting investigations of sexual asymmetry in conversation with the theoretical analysis of how linguistic forms acquire meaning.

Gender is a complex system of cognitive, symbolic, behavioral, political, and social phenomena mediated by sorting of people according to their sex. The salience and content of "being a woman," for example, depend on many factors and vary significantly, not just cross-culturally, but also for different individuals in the same culture, as a self-identification and as an attribution made by others, for a given individual from situation to situation and at different stages in her life. Sociologists Helene Lopata and Barrie Thorne[4] have shown the problems with conceptualizing gender itself as a role; anthropologist Erving Goffman[5] has shown the ritual and symbolic distinctions between the "arrangement between the sexes" and cross-class relations. (This is not, however, his way of putting it; indeed, he speaks of sex-classes, but does not thereby invoke anything like a familiar theory of socioeconomically based classes.) Most studies of connections between gender/sex systems and discourse, however, ignore such complexities and begin by looking at effects of the sex of the speaker, the addressee, or interactions between the two. Yet investigations of this sort do provide somewhere to begin.

What I have to say about gender and discourse will inevitably oversimplify. For instance, I will say that men tend to interrupt women. This way of putting it ignores various complexities which are obviously important. It matters, for example, whether the woman is a professor and the man a student or vice versa, whether they are at a cocktail party or in a committee meeting, whether they are discussing a committee report about course requirements or the newspaper editorial about abortion, whether they are the same age or of different generations, whether she happens to be gregarious and he shy or vice versa, and so on. Gender modulates or works together with other features of power relationships, roles, situations, and personal attributes.

Nonetheless, to say that men interrupt women is to say that in certain familiar contexts — such as before-dinner conversations with one's living partner at home or over-coffee chats with one's friend in a restaurant or departmental meetings with one's colleagues — men are more likely to wrest the floor from women than vice versa. Much of the research addressing the question of interruptions has been done by Candace West and Don Zimmerman, both sociologists. West and Zimmerman have shown parallel asymmetries in interruption rates between men and women[6] and those between parents and children,[7] suggesting strongly that "control" or "dominance" in the situation is an important factor. One of West's studies[8] examined the hypothesis that men interrupted women because they were easy targets, that women's conversational demeanor was somehow such as to invite or at least not to discourage interruption. In fact, however, that research found women and men responding to attempts to interrupt them in much the same way and with much the same rates of success in warding off such attacks. The major difference seemed to lie in the proportion of attempts to interrupt. Women are more likely to be interrupt*ees* and men to be interrupt*ers*.

Related findings suggest that men tend to monopolize the conversational "floor" in other ways as well. Studies of professional conferences and of intimate conversations both show men tend to spend more time talking than do women when the two sexes are together. (Carole Edelsky in very interesting research[9] suggests that women thrive better in a special kind of discourse where there is suspension of the prevalent "one person at a time is in possession of the floor" norm.) This does not mean more time talking altogether — there are no real data on that score — but simply more time talking in certain common settings of cross-sex communication.

A third way in which men appear to dominate in cross-sex discourse is their disproportionate success in initiating conversations and in introducing new topics. Data are quite limited here, most coming from a single study by sociologist Pamela Fishman,[10] but they are certainly suggestive. The hypothesis one can draw from Fishman's study is, in a sense, the obverse of West's: men have more success with their topics, not because women fail to pursue their own suggestions with sufficient vigor, but because women reliably return the conversational ball served by men and not vice versa. Thus it isn't what *men* do that leads to their success in topic-initiation, but what *women* do (and men *fail* to do) in topic maintenance and development. The women in Fishman's study made plenty of conversational attempts — more, indeed, than their male companions — but did not get the sort of conversational cooperation that they themselves provided. In other words, what got talked about in any detail depended much more on the man's interests than the woman's.

Fishman's study dealt with intimates and with a setting where explicit norms of who should talk and when were not operative. Studies of talk in professional settings are not directly comparable. Nonetheless, a study by Swacker[11] found men's questions from the floor after a conference paper much more likely than women's to introduce new material ("you'll be interested in my study of Finnish relative clauses where I show that . . .") in addition to their being more frequent and lasting longer. Women who did comment were more likely to offer corroborating evidence or to ask a clarificatory question. When a woman, say Ms. A., does introduce a topic or make some suggestions in a faculty meeting, Eakins and Eakins[12] found that others tend to appropriate her idea: Mr. B., for example, may present it as if novel and then others identify it later as Mr. B.'s proposal. They may make this identification even if Mr. B. himself actually credits Ms. A. and just supports her. In sum, even where a woman does get her own point made, someone else may claim it as his own.

There are relatively few studies of the impact of gender in single-sex conversational groups. We might, however, hypothesize from Fishman's study that women would have more success getting their topics going in such groups than in those including men. Perhaps part of the stereotype of women as talkative comes from men who observe women speaking among themselves, the "off-stage" participants doing more in such groups to help along those "on-stage" than is typical in male-male conversation. This help includes not only responding fully and, in some cases, asking "leading" questions, but also contributing an accompanying "chorus" of interspersed or superimposed comments of understanding and/or approval.

Although I know of no studies of single-sex conversations using West's or Fishman's research methods, there are some investigations of single-sex groups. Anthropologist Susan Kalčik[13] looked at women's "rap" groups, a somewhat special context but nonetheless of a general type familiar to many women. She delineates the notion of a "kernel story," some particular anecdote or point first introduced by one member of the group, but returned to by others, often with further developments, and eventually coming to function as a mutually constructed conversational asset. The original contribution is appropriated by the group and becomes a shared resource, drawn on by various group members for different purposes. This is different from the kind of individualistic appropriation mentioned earlier, where the contribution is not so much seen as common to the group and available for mutual development, but as "owned" by its introducer (or by the person who later repeats it without attribution and as if novel). Also looking at women's rap groups, Mercilee Jenkins[14] found that women gave one another much the same kind of support that Fishman suggests they give men. In the women's group, in contrast to mixed groups and to men's groups, support is reciprocal and talk is collaboratively produced. Jenkins work supports and extends Kalčik's. Both suggest that women's conversations with one another benefit from the maintenance work that Fishman argues men exploit to their own advantage without reciprocating in cross-sex conversations.

Another single-sex study of children's play groups done by anthropologist Marjorie Goodwin[15] found boys tending to jockey for verbal "control." Ascendancy is achieved by one who refuses to respond to others who phrase directives towards him as straightforward imperatives rather than as requests but who himself issues imperatives and not requests. Examination of the boys' speech shows clearly this verbal negotiation of asymmetrical hierarchies. In contrast, the girls neither used the imperative forms among themselves nor struggled to get themselves deferentially addressed. The focus was on forms like *let's* and *shouldn't we*, suggesting a much more horizontally connected kind of talk and accompanying social organization. Goodwin's work with Black children's conversations is more subtle and complex than I can convey here. The girls she worked with certainly did not lack confrontational skills. In recent interesting work, Marsha Stanback[16] has proposed that Black middle-class women show somewhat more communicative flexibility than their white counterparts. Their conversations with one another are not precisely like those reported for white women, although they do appear to be supportive and collaborative.

Finally, several studies have shown women giving more "back-channel" signals that acknowledge verbal connection: for example, *mmhmm*. A related phenomenon is the somewhat greater proportion of rising intonational contours on women's declaratives. These contours frequently function as implicit requests for confirmation that understanding has been achieved, that the hearer has heard and properly noted what was said. If the declarative is a response to someone else's question — Robin Lakoff's[17] renowned dialogue

> "When will dinner be ready?"
> "Six o'clock?"

provides a good example — the intonational pattern may also signal some other covert question like "Why do you want to know?". Lakoff herself proposes a somewhat different view of why rising finals might be more common in women's speech. I have discussed the interaction of intonation with sex/gender systems in some detail elsewhere.[18] But in any case, like *mmhmm*, a rising final intonation pattern serves to mark and reinforce conversational connections, and helps to establish mutuality.

In short and oversimplifying considerably, the picture emerging from consideration of how gender interacts with discourse is that women in our society tend to orient themselves towards conversation as a cooperative enterprise, as a mutually constructed product for common interests. Men in turn tend to view conversation as an arena for individual achievement, a place to display individual prowess and control. Even in institutional settings like the classroom, studies find women teachers encourage discussion more than do men, who are more likely to lecture. Treichler and Kramarae[19] provide an excellent overview of women in higher education; the bibliography in Thorne *et al.*[20] discusses classroom interaction studies beginning with grade school. In addition, as the powerful tend to ignore the powerless in such aspects of conversation as allocation of speaking turns and time, so men tend to dominate women in these respects. We cannot, of course, assume that matters have always been so nor that this is precisely how conversational structure and gender interact in all cultural settings. And, as I have said, the picture presented is an abstraction from the particularities of specific contexts and is thus a somewhat distorted and inadequate picture, even for our own time and culture. The point, however, is that gender has consequences for how people think they ought to contribute to conversation (their notions of rights, responsibilities, effective strategies); how indeed they do contribute (which will depend not just on what they do but on what others do as well); and how they and others perceive that contribution.

The effect of gender on discourse depends on various ethnohistorical factors. Nonetheless, common features are found in different times and settings because they derive from features of gender-modulated roles, relationships, and behavioral norms that themselves cut across eras and cultural settings, even though other features of the gender/sex systems with which they are associated show striking variations. For example, assumptions of male privilege and of inter-male competitiveness are not limited to modern America. So we need not suppose that nineteenth-century American men interrupted women in the same way as West's subjects did in order to suppose that they nonetheless tended to dominate cross-sex discourse, especially in public settings. And we know that they had much greater access than did women to a variety of audiences and speakers, through their greater participation in education and travel. In addition, of course, insofar as what is said in certain institutional contexts carries extra weight, it is relevant to note that in nineteenth-century America, even more than now, men predominated in church, courtroom, stage, and the like.

But what do interruptions and the other forms of conversational control have to do with meaning and semantic shifts? To begin to answer this question, I want to draw on certain features of recent accounts of linguistic meaning and linguistic communication, namely, notions of mutual belief and of conventions of language use that rely on such mutual belief in a population. My informal account will only suggest the direction a fuller and more detailed exposition might take.

The basic idea is that to "mean" to express a certain thought x by utterance y is to try to get your hearers to recognize that your utterance of y is an attempt to get them to recognize x. The central notion of reflexive intentionality on which I am drawing here is based on ideas first presented by Paul Grice.[21] The standard or literal meaning can be thought of as what is recognizable solely on the basis of knowledge of standard practices in using and interpreting the language. As children acquire a vocabulary, they gain experience and form expectations as to how particular lexical items contribute to the thoughts expressed by utterances in which they are used. What precisely these meanings are that children attach to vocabulary forms is not my present concern. The point is rather that speakers do come to some kind of consensus as to what they and others are up to in using particular linguistic forms. There are also, however, mechanisms for doing nonstandard things in particular cases, and these mechanisms plant the seed for the standard practices of use and interpretation to shift, that is, for literal meanings to change.

Let us perform a thought experiment and transport ourselves back to the hypothetical era in which the form *buddy* was simply an alternative and familiar variant of *brother* and *sissy* an alternative and familiar variant of *sister*. What does this mean? It means that whatever one could literally communicate by uttering an expression of the form e1: . . . brother . . . , one could literally communicate by uttering an expression just like e1, save that occurrences of *brother* were replaced by *buddy*. Similarly, for e2: . . . sister . . . , there would be an equivalent expression with *sissy*. This is not to say that *brother* and *buddy* or *sister* and *sissy* need ever have been perfectly equivalent. The American Heritage Dictionary, for example, suggests that they originated as diminutive or familiar alternates of the standard kin terms, thus pointing to their use in somewhat different situations than those standard terms. Nonetheless, the assumption is that the propositional content speakers could intend to convey simply by virtue of having their hearers recognize that intent was essentially identical for utterance pairs differing only in the substitution of *buddy* for *brother*, or *sissy* for *sister*. What happened then? We will look first at *buddy*.

Presumably there were occasions, at first infrequent but later more common, where speakers managed to communicate by utterances in which *buddy* occurred something other than the literal "male sibling" meaning. More specifically, they intended to convey something about a positive comradely sort of relationship between male peers, and they succeeded in having that intention recognized. In other words, they did just what some present speakers might be able to do by saying *He was a brother to me*. For this to work, it has to rely on some kind of mutual belief of speaker and hearer, roughly that the most salient property of a brother is his affectionate support (or some such). For this new meaning to be conveyed in a wide variety of contexts and for speaker-hearer dyads without special knowledge of one another, there must be some kind of collective mutual belief about the salient properties of brotherhood. In other words, (1) the members of the speech community must generally recognize comradeliness as a salient property of brothers or of the relation between brothers; (2) they must also believe that the other members of the speech community generally have such a conception; and (3) they must believe that the others also generally hold that such a belief is prevalent in the speech community.

Why? For me to try to mean by an utterance of *He is my buddy* that he is a comrade and pal, I must be able to assume that hearers can recognize that I intend to express this thought, and this I can assume only if either (1) this is already established as the literal meaning of my utterance, knowledge of which I share with the other members of the speech community, or (2) it is clear that the context is one in which the literal meaning is not directly operative and in which I can take as a matter of mutual belief the distinctive salience of comradeship as a brotherly trait. That is, I need to be able to assume that my hearer will believe that I believe this and that my hearer will believe that I believe that she will believe this. None of us need really believe that brothers generally are (or should be) comrades; rather, what is needed is mutual belief that there is such a general association in people's minds. Suppose, in fact, that the hearer does not find comradeship the most salient feature of brotherhood. Perhaps for her, the notion of brother is most strongly linked with a conception of demanding selfishness, of a pest for whom she is forced to suffer various inconveniences and whose interests those in authority put before hers. Given such a down-on-brothers hearer, does communication come to a halt?

Not necessarily. Assume that our listener, despite her great distaste for brothers, is nonetheless very much interested in doing her share to make communication successful. She assumes that her conversational partner was trying to mean something, observes that he could not have intended to speak literally, and has reason to doubt that he shares her view of brothers. Although she herself does not believe that brotherliness and comradeliness are genuinely united, she does believe that many other members of the speech community so believe (and that the speaker may well be among them), and she also supposes that there is *not* mutual belief that any other trait is specially salient. In particular, she has no reason to think that the speaker realizes she does not share his outlook.

Thus she believes that conditions are such that her interlocutor may well have the false belief that there is general agreement about the special salience of comradeship on which he can rely to communicate, and thus may have the kind of intention he needs in order to mean by his utterance of *Joe was a brother to me* that Joe was a real pal. So she correctly understands what the speaker was up to and so indicates, probably without bothering to challenge the false presumption on which his attempt was predicated. Uptake is what is required here and what she provides, but it is unlikely that she will challenge the false assumption that he thinks secured the uptake because it is not the major issue in the present communication. He now has even more reason than before to think that there is a mutual belief in the speech community about the special salience of comradeship in brotherhood since his communication succeeded. In addition, a precedent is set; next time around, she knows immediately what he means by *buddy*. Eventually, she may even use the form as he did, depending on his example and not on his beliefs about brothers, at which point we are on the way to a new literal meaning—one that depends simply on previous usage and does not go through some way-station of a nonapplicable literal meaning.

Mutatis mutandis, we tell the same story for *sissy*. We do not have to suppose that misogyny is really the consensus of the community, just that some speakers think it is and are able, trading on that assumption, to mean something like "weak and cowardly" by using *sissy*. But the question is, why doesn't it go the other way? Why is my hypothetical brother-hater unlikely to make an utterance of *he was such a damn buddy to me* stick? Or, why didn't *sissy* come to mean a person of either sex from whom one expects and gets loving support?

There is the inverse case from the one we considered possibly applicable in the actual extension of *buddy* to its present "pal" applications. Namely, suppose a speaker (probably female) whose addressee (probably male) does not share the assumptions she must have in order to try to mean "pest" by using *buddy*, namely, (1) that "pestiness" is an especially salient trait of brothers; (2) that there is general recognition of this in the speech community; and (3) that it is also generally recognized that there is such a general recognition. In particular, suppose her addressee himself thinks comradeship is the most salient property of brothers, yet it is also clear to him that this is not what she intends to express in some context where her application is obviously not intended literally. The first difference that we can see between this hypothetical situation and the one we just discussed is that he is somewhat less likely to guess what alternative she might have in mind than she to infer his attitude, the reason being that he has in various ways monopolized their mutual conversations. Perhaps he has interrupted her, failed to return her openers, and talked a disproportionate share of the time. The second difference is that he is less likely to try to figure out her intent if it is not immediately apparent to him than she is to try to understand him. Their different stances towards conversation, associated with their different social networks and expectations, help to explain this: on his individualistic conception of talk, it is an "each man for himself" (my pronoun here is self-consciously masculine) competition. She has just lost, blown her chance, by having a false view of community opinion. In the parallel situation, where it was his false assumption at stake, her more social view of conversation led her to do whatever she could to make the collective enterprise work, to try to achieve the coordination of assumptions required for successful communication.

Is he cooperative in a similar fashion? I suspect not. Let us suppose that something does indeed tip him off to her perspective. He is probably more likely than she to point to the false assumption, to comment critically on her having incorrectly presumed operative a general belief in the pestiness of brothers. In part this may simply be due to there being rather little likelihood of his having been frequently exposed to expression of her sort of views and thus greater puzzlement that she is presenting them as common in the speech community. It may also reflect his general dominance in the particular conversation where she tried to mean "pest" by *buddy*—she might have failed to correct his false presumption not because of lack of effort, but because he afforded her no opportunity or ignored her comment. In any case, even should she succeed in having herself understood in this exchange, that success is more likely accompanied by a weakening than by a strengthening of her belief in the general recognition by the community of her outlook. She is thus not likely to build on the precedent, and this will affect future communication, not just with that particular partner but also with others.

Perhaps most important, however, the woman is less likely to try to use *buddy* to convey her "pestiness" conception in the first place than he is to use it to convey "pal." Why? Because she knows his expressed views better than he knows hers. She is unable to try to mean "pest" by *buddy* with him because she knows too much. His meaning what he did relied crucially on his ignorance of substantial contrary opinion. The more one talks and the less one listens, the more likely it is that one's viewpoint will function as if it were community consensus even if it is not, thus the more likely that one's viewpoint can be appealed to in novel expression of certain notions and thus ultimately set new precedents and leave some mark on community-wide meanings. The more attention one pays to perspectives different from one's own, the more likely one is to give tacit—indeed sometimes unwitting—support to these other views simply by being able to understand them. One's own distinctive perspective cannot function as a resource for going "beyond the letter" and is thus not likely to find as wide expression as the views of those less attuned to their co-conversationalists.

Positive *sissy* seems a more likely candidate for instantiation, given that we do find *she was like a sister to me* used positively by speakers of both sexes. Had *sissy* not developed pejorative associations, it might have been available for a more positive development. Indeed, the form is used by fashion writers simply to denote an especially decorative (though perhaps somewhat childish) form of dress. Thus the point is not that terms denoting female referents cannot have various positive associations affecting their subsequent semantic development nor that terms denoting male referents will always develop positively. We certainly know of many historical instances of negative development of terms for denoting males. (*Knave* is one instance, *churl* another. There appear, however, to be many more such cases of negative terms for women; for further discussion, see Schulz.[2]) Rather, what does seem to emerge is the greater likelihood that vocabulary will be marked by a viewpoint that is predominantly male than by viewpoints predominantly female.

I will close with a brief look at a much discussed contemporary case, that of the so-called generic masculines. Psychologist Wendy Martyna,[22] in very interesting and enlightening research, has shown that women are more likely than men to attach a non-sexual interpretation to *he* with a nonspecific or generic antecedent, but less likely to use it themselves in such a situation. This suggests a divided conception in the speech community of what the form really does. Indeed one could argue that it has become more and more difficult for people to try to express a generic meaning with this form (and even more so with the free form *man*), simply because it is less and less plausible to assume that others will share this view of its literal meaning or be willing to see the generic as a plausible "figurative" extension. Nonetheless, women seem willing to overlook such mistaken presumptions, but less inclined than men to continue to rely on them.

Matters are much more complex than I have been able to indicate, of course. The general claim is that the politics of discourse profoundly affects the course of semantic development. First, discourse circumstances limit what speakers can try to mean by affecting the perceptions they have of consensus in the speech community. Those with less advantageous positions as speakers will be less able to assume that their outlooks are shared and thus more restricted in what they can mean nonliterally. Second, the circumstances of discourse may offer greater assistance to some speakers than to others in their attempts to rely on perceived consensus: hearers differently situated are both differently inclined and differently able to understand. (As one reviewer of this paper reminded me, "inclined" understates the case. There is considerable evidence of active refusal to listen to women's meanings, of deliberate misunderstanding. I have not pursued here these and other ways in which men "control" meaning. For discussion, see Kramarae[23] and Blaubergs,[24] who have both discussed some of the other explanations for men's greater influence on the development of language.)

The meanings of individual forms are continually renegotiated in discourse. But not all members of the speech community are similarly equipped to participate in this renegotiation because their experience and expectations of discourse are different. When someone's views support a new application of a term, a precedent is established and others may well assume that the earlier successful use built on genuine rather than simply perceived consensus. So long as the old connection persists — so long as *sister* and *sissy* are thought to be related — not only linguists but also other speakers of the language will at times be misled by that link into believing a much stronger connection between the community's views of sisters and of sissies than may indeed exist. But to think that others think in a certain way affords some motivation for assuming the correctness of that way of thinking; this is especially likely for the child without wider experience. In other words, success as a discourse participant can lead in both direct and indirect ways to success in influence and perhaps to success in furthering one's line of thought. Spelling out that story I leave for further work. But I think that to begin to understand how our conventional modes of talk could come to be sexist in the sense of being shaped by a male-centered perspective is to begin to see how their being sexist might also matter.

REFERENCES

1. SPENDER, D. 1980. Man Made Language. Routledge & Kegan Paul. Boston, MA.
2. SCHULZ, M. R. 1975. The semantic derogation of woman. *In* Language and Sex: Difference and Dominance. B. Thorne & N. Henley, Eds.: 64–75. Newbury House. Rowley, MA.
3. HYMES, D. 1973. Speech and language: On the origins and foundations of inequality among speakers. *In* Language as a Human Problem. E. Haugen & M. Bloomfield, Eds.: 45–72. Norton. New York, NY.
4. LOPATA, H. Z. & B. THORNE. 1978. On the term "sex roles." Signs: Journal of Women in Culture and Society **3**: 718–721.
5. GOFFMAN, E. 1977. The arrangement between the sexes. Theory and Society **4**: 301–331.
6. ZIMMERMAN, D. H. & C. WEST. 1975. Sex roles, interruptions, and silences in conversation. *In* Language and Sex: Difference and Dominance. B. Thorne & N. Henley, Eds. Newbury House. Rowley, MA.
7. WEST, C. & D. H. ZIMMERMAN. 1977. Women's place in everyday talk: Reflections on parent-child interaction. Soc. Problems **24**: 521–529.
8. WEST, C. 1979. Against our will: Male interruptions of females in cross-sex conversation. *In* Language, Sex and Gender: Does "La Difference" Make a Difference? J. Orasanu, M. K. Slater & L. L. Adler, Eds. Ann. N. Y. Acad Sci. **327**: 81–97.
9. EDELSKY, C. 1981. Who's got the floor? Language in Society **10**: 383–422.
10. FISHMAN, P. 1978. What do couples talk about when they're alone? *In* Women's Language and Style. D. R. Butturff & E. L. Epstein, Eds. Language and Style Books **1**: 11–22. University of Akron Press. Akron, OH.
11. SWACKER, M. 1976. Women's verbal behavior at learned and professional conferences. *In* The Sociology of the Language of American Women. B. L. Dubois & I. Crouch, Eds. Papers in Southwest English **IV**: 155–160. Trinity University. San Antonio, TX.
12. EAKINS, B. & G. EAKINS. 1976. Verbal turn-taking and exchanges in faculty dialogue. *In* The Sociology of the Language of American Women. Papers in Southwest English **IV**: 53–62. Trinity University. San Antonio, TX.
13. KALCIK, S. 1975. ". . . like Ann's gynecologist or the time I was almost raped": Personal narratives in women's rap groups. J. Am. Folklore **88**: 3–11.

14. JENKINS, M. 1982. Stories women tell: An ethnographic study of personal experience narratives in a women's rap group. Paper given at the 10th World Congress of Society, Mexico City.

15. GOODWIN, M. H. 1980. Directive-response speech sequences in girls' and boys' task activities. *In* Women and Language in Literature and Society. S. McConnell-Ginet, R. Borker & N. Furman, Eds.: 157–173. Praeger. New York, NY.

16. STANBACK M. H. 1983. Code-Switching in Black Women's Speech. Unpublished Ph.D. dissertation, University of Massachusetts at Amherst.

17. LAKOFF, R. 1975. Language and Woman's Place. Harper. New York, NY.

18. McCONNELL-GINET, S. 1983. Intonation in a man's world. *In* Language, Gender and Society. B. Thorne, C. Kramarae & N. Henley, Eds.: 69–88. Newbury House. Rowley, MA.

19. TREICHLER, P. & C. KRAMARAE. 1983. Woman's talk in the ivory tower. Commun. Q. **31**: 118–132.

20. THORNE, B., C. KRAMARAE & N. HENLEY, Eds. 1983. Language, Gender and Society. Newbury House. Rowley, MA.

21. GRICE, H. P. 1957. Meaning. Philos. Rev. **66**: 377–388.

22. MARTYNA, W. 1980. The psychology of the generic masculine. *In* Women and Language in Literature and Society. S. McConnell-Ginet, R. Borker & N. Furman, Eds.: 69–78. Praeger. New York, NY.

23. KRAMARAE, C. 1980. Proprietors of language. *In* Women and Language in Literature and Society. S. McConnell-Ginet, R. Borker & N. Furman, Eds. : 58–68. Praeger. New York, NY.

24. BLAUBERGS, M. S. 1980. An analysis of classic arguments against changing sexist language. *In* The Voices and Words of Women and Men. Cheris Kramarae, Ed. Women's Studies Int. Q. **3**: 135–147.

Recent Psycholinguistic Research on Figurative Language[a]

ROBERT R. HOFFMAN

Department of Psychology
Adelphi University
Garden City, New York 11530

INTRODUCTION

The first actual experiments on metaphor were not conducted in 1975 or even 1970, but in the early 1900s in the psychological laboratories of Karl Buehler[1] and others of the "Wurzburg" school of thought. Psychology at that time was dominated by the influence of Wilhelm Wundt. Psychologists were trained as physical and medical scientists and focused primarily on the psychology of sensation and perception. Wundt was dubious as to whether psychology could be used to perform experiments on higher mental processes such as problem-solving and linguistic reasoning. The psychologists at Wurzburg disagreed and conducted research on exactly these topics.[2] For instance, in one experiment, subjects were presented with pairs of proverbs that had similar meanings and they then had to engage in various comprehension and paraphrase tasks. In the years after the Wurzburg studies, the topic of metaphor was not forgotten among psychologists (for more details, see Honeck[3]). In particular, Gestalt psychologists such as Heinz Werner and Solomon Asch discussed metaphor with regard to the development of languages and cognition. Asch[4] studied "double-function terms" in which aspects of one sensory modality are used to describe experiences in other modalities. For example, people are described as "hard," "bitter," "bright," and so on. In the 1950s the Neobehaviorists Roger Brown and Charles Osgood referred to metaphor and its importance in language. Osgood's semantic differential task has subjects rate various words and concepts on various affective and semantic dimensions to produce a scaling of word meanings. Both Brown and Osgood noticed the metaphors that the differential task would sometimes generate — for instance, "excitement" is regarded as "vertical," "colorful," and "crooked".[5]

Beginning in about 1970, interest in research on metaphor began to boom. We see in operation here a number of "Zeitgeist effects," such as dissatisfaction with the Chomsky-Katz-Folor approach to language and meaning. Andrew Ortony[6] organized a seminal conference at the University of Illinois in 1977 which brought linguists, philosophers, and psychologists together to discuss the theoretical issues. That same year, experimental psychologists began to organize symposia for the presentation of research.

---

[a] The paper is adapted from a lecture given at the New York Academy of Sciences, February 1, 1981.

It cannot be entirely coincidental that on the night I began to prepare this review, the news media were providing me with great examples of the use of metaphor. Budget Director David Stockman was being criticized for calling the Reagan budget a "Trojan horse." In response to the critics, the Director used other inappropriate metaphors, which seemed to get him into even deeper trouble. The economics news on a major television network included many metaphors:

"The President returned to Washington today, the place he'd been calling the *puzzle palace* of the U.S."

"The President seemed reluctant to *fight his economic battle*, but *stung by the cries* of his budget critics, he *stung* back."

"The President saw Washington's response as a *knee-jerk reaction*."

"He said that there was no *magic pencil* to yield a balanced budget on paper."

"The President *drew a line in the dirt* and said that those who were serious about a balanced budget would not cross it."

"The President's reply to his critics was a *strong offensive,* using *fighting words*. He is by no means *backed up against a wall*."

"One of the President's critics said that the sinking ship of Reaganomics cannot *bear the weight* of the new budget cuts, proposing instead a *freeze* on all spending levels."

As I listened to the news, I was struck that every sentence in the report used metaphor or idiom. Metaphor and discussions about metaphor are part of our current age. Figurative language is a hot topic in linguistics, philosophy, psychology, education, and other disciplines. There have been something on the order of 15 books, a few major conferences, scores of special meetings, and dozens of seminars on this subject. Since 1977, experimental psychologists alone have organized more than 15 symposia involving close to 100 researchers.

The fact that I can say that research on the development of figurative language comprehension is beyond the scope of this paper attests to the size of the field. The literature of experiments on development is about as large as the literature on adult comprehension (see for example recent papers by Bamberg[7], Loring and Kessel,[8] Marks,[9] Mendelsohn et al.,[10] Petrun,[11] Pickens and Pollio,[12] Reyna,[13] and Vosniadou and Ortony,[14]). The developmental research has been reviewed[15,16] but a thorough review of research methods is long overdue. The literature on philosophical and theoretical concerns is also voluminous and key theoretical issues and points of view have been amply summarized (see, for example, Johnson,[17] Ortony,[6] and Sachs[18]).

Figurative language, in general, involves a host of distinct forms and a host of important questions. With regard to its forms, one can distinguish idioms, proverbs, metaphors, similes, and various rhetorical forms such as metonymy, hyperbole, allegory, and so forth. I shall not define and refer to all of these in this paper, but will describe many of them. The approach I have taken is to demonstrate how varieties of figurative language occur at various levels of language (e.g., phonology, words, sentences), an approach that has the advantage of allowing me to show how pervasive figurative langauge is, and therefore how important it is to communication and cognition, even in scientific problem-solving itself.

Figurative language forces us to confront a number of important questions, such as "What is meaning?" and "Can computers be programmed to understand metaphors?" The approach I have taken here to explore these questions is to focus on recent psycholinguistic research, such as that on memory, mental imagery, and reaction time. While such questions have driven much of the research, the goal of this paper is not to explore them in depth, but rather to summarize and focus on recent research, in terms of methods and materials, and thereby point to significant issues and questions, which are "salted" throughout the paper.

PERSUASIVENESS OF NONLITERAL COMMUNICATION

Before getting into the research, let me begin by describing some recent demonstrations of how figurative language occurs in communication at different levels.

First, a recognition memory test. Below is a list of proverbs. The reader's task is to read each one and decide whether he or she has heard or seen it before:

"When the cat's away, the mice will play."
"Man does not live by bread alone."
"Life is just a bowl of cherries."
"A rolling stone gathers no moss."
"Don't look a gift horse in the mouth."
"Every dark cloud has a silver lining."
"Don't bite the hand that feeds you."
"Don't judge a book by its cover."
"A watched pot never boils."
"The early bird catches the worm."
"Let sleeping dogs lie."
"One picture is worth a thousand words."
"If the shoe fits, wear it."
"Too many cooks spoil the broth."
"You can't make a silk purse out of a sow's ear."
"A stitch in time saves nine."
"An ounce of prevention is worth a pound of cure."
"A bird in the hand is worth two in the bush."
"Roast geese do not come flying into the mouth."

If you are like most native English speakers, only the very last proverb is unfamiliar (it is from the Chinese). The proverbs that are shared by languages within a family far outnumber the proverbs that are unique to a language. Recognition and recall memory tests that I have conducted on populations in Minnesota (mostly of northern European descent) and on Long Island (mostly of southern European descent) have shown that most people have a good recognition memory of some three hundred or more proverbs! The interesting thing about our incredible memory storehouse of proverbs is that if you ask persons to simply recall the proverbs they know, they have a tough time of it; this is an extremely frustrating task. In about 30 minutes of quiet thought, most persons can only recall about 20–30 of the proverbs they know. Most individuals are also quite certain they must know many more proverbs than those they were able to recall. Why this difference between recall and recognition? The answer has to do with communication and event perception. Certain salient aspects of events are what triggers our memory of a proverb. So, in the free recall task, it is common for a person to say: "I imagined my grandmother in different situations and tried to think of what proverb she might say."

So, we all know some hundreds of proverbs. What about other forms of nonliteral language? Howard Pollio and his colleagues[19,20] have analyzed political debates, introductory psychology texts, novels, and psychotherapy sessions in an attempt to estimate overall use of nonliteral language. Most English speakers utter about 10 million novel metaphors per lifetime and 20 million idioms per lifetime. This works out to about 3,000 novel metaphors per week and 7,000 idioms per week. And there is more to nonliteral language than novel metaphors, idioms, and proverbs.

The Level of Words

Etymologically, many words in a given language have their meanings or origins in metaphor. My favorite example is how people (including psychologists) use the word "structure." In terms of its Latin origin as *struere*, it meant to arrange things into piles. We understand productive human activities in terms of structural parts and the operations that put the parts together. So, for example, a theory can be "unfounded" or can "rest on solid foundations." We use the structure metaphor to describe language and cognition: One can "construct" a sentence or "construe" a meaning. The mind is said to have a "structure"; a computer is said to have an "architecture." Many abstract words have their origins in metaphor. Over time, the metaphorical origins may be lost and may go unnoticed in day-to-day conversation. In other cases, it is hard not to notice metaphoricalness: People can be "shrimps," "fruitcakes," "chickens," "tomatoes," or "hot dogs."

Metaphor also plays a role at the level of phonology, via the semantics of monosyllables.[21] For example, words with the suffix *-oop* all refer to curved shapes or paths ("droop," "sloop," "swoop," "loop," "stoop," "scoop"). Words like "string," "strip," and "strap" all refer to flexibility. "Knoll," "nut," and "nugget" are all references to convex shapes whereas "niche," "notch," and "nick" all refer to concave shapes. These monosyllable clusters show how the language classifies objects and events. "Blank," "blanch," and "blush" all refer to color; "drop," "drink," "drain," and "drown" all refer to liquids. The metaphoricalness of the clusters shows best when one looks at other languages. For instance, among speakers of Ojibwe, words for travel all involve putting together a prefix for "*paddle*" plus a suffix indicating the type of path, as in "paddle + along," "paddle + around," and "paddle + away." Types of motion are described with reference to canoeing.

Thus, not only are words often of metaphorical origin, but the phonological chunks of which words are made can also be traced to metaphorical or sound-symbolic origins.

The Level of Phrases

At the level of phrases are idioms, tens of thousands of them in English[22]: "close shave," "wolf in sheep's clothing," "pulling a person's leg," "a sight for sore eyes," "lead a dog's life," "shadow of doubt," "a long shot," "start from scratch," "be in a rut," "keeping up with the Joneses," "have a chip on one's shoulder," "wild goose chase," "to give a person what for," "to sell someone short," "to have a lot of nerve," "to have no spine," "get the ball rolling," "far be it from me. . .," "pan out," "naked as a jay bird," "like peas from the same pod," "skinny as a bean pole," "red as a beet," "white as a sheet," "have a yellow streak," "plain as the nose on your face," "cute as a button," "flat as a pancake," "high as a kite."

The syntax of these phrases is fairly stuck (forms a continuum from the completely "frozen" to the almost fully productive). For example, the sentence "The bucket was kicked by Jim" might be taken to refer to literal kicking of a bucket rather than to Jim's death. Since their syntax is stuck, idioms behave more like lexical entries rather than phrases. However, they also rely on metaphor in a dynamic way. My favorite example is the idiom "red herring." Herring, a critic once pointed out to me, are not red. That is so, unless they are smoked and salted. And when so cured, a bunch of them can be tied together and dragged along the ground to leave a false-scent trail. This North American idiom originated as the phrase, "to drag the red herring," meaning to leave a false trail or to mislead. The experience has been lost over the years, but the origin of the idiom in experience and metaphor cannot be denied.

The Level of Sentences

At the level of sentences it is important to draw distinctions between a number of types of nonliteral forms, since different psychological processes are no doubt involved.[b] I have already mentioned proverbs, and we can certainly regard them as a separate class. We can also regard novel or poetic metaphors as a separate class. Much recent psychological research has been aimed at disclosing how we comprehend novel poetic metaphors. There are also what are called *metaphor formulas* or themes. These are sentence-level expressions, the syntax of which is generative rather than fixed, and which

---

[b] One helpful reviewer of this paper complained repeatedly that I only point to distinctions and only offer examples and no clear definitions. I do not think that I *could* offer air-tight definitions that would satisfy everyone. Besides, as I indicated earlier, my goal is not to discuss matters of theory or definition as much as it is to survey research areas. Hence, examples of materials and types of figurative language will have to suffice.

TABLE 1. Examples of the Spatial Orientation "Conduit" Theme in the Natural Language Metaphoric Understanding of the Relations of Consciousness to the World[23] and other Orientational Metaphors for Mind[25]

Metaphor Theme	Examples
WORDS OR IDEAS ARE OBJECTS	"The words carried great weight"
	"That thought has been around for centuries"
	"The concepts buried him"
WORDS CONTAIN INFORMATION AND MEANING	"The concepts got put into words"
	"The words held no meaning for me"
	"The ideas seemed air-tight"
THE MIND IS A CONTAINER	"I didn't get anything out of it"
	"Her mind was a sponge"
	"That thought really sank in"
	"I'm cramming for the test"
COMMUNICATION IS THE TRANSFER OF OBJECTS	"His meaning got across well"
	"The ideas poured out"
	"The words came across well"
HAPPY IS UP, SAD IS DOWN	"My spirits rose"
	"I felt low-down"
CONSCIOUSNESS IS UP, UNCONSCIOUS IS DOWN	"I fell asleep"
	"He sank into a coma"
	"It was a shallow trance"
CONTROL IS UP, CONTROLLED IS DOWN	"I'm on top of things"
	"He was under her thumb"

often relate to common experience and common concepts by means of metaphor. The previous examples of the way we use the word "structure" are examples of a theme in which sentence comprehension is described by means of a reference to buildings and construction.

The language we use to talk about language provides another example of a metaphor theme. This is a theme of language as a *conduit* for the communication of meanings from one mind to another.[23] One can say "The ideas came across well," "The poem was packed with meaning," and other expressions. In fact, most of the language that we use for talking about language is based on this metaphor theme. Its impact on theorizing about language in linguistics and psycholinguistics cannot be overemphasized.[24] TABLE 1 presents examples of the "conduit" metaphor theme for language.

Other examples of metaphor themes can be found in the language we use for talking about cognitive states, such as "love." One theme for love compares it to insanity: "He was crazy for her," "He was head over heels for her," "He was out of his mind with jealousy." Cognitive states involving the relation of consciousness to the unconscious are understood in terms of metaphor: "He sank into a coma," "His spirits rose." In a recent survey of the use of metaphor in natural language, Lakoff and Johnson[25] (see also Smith[26]) provide thousands of examples of concretizing metaphorical expressions used in daily communication to talk about abstract concepts such as time, love, debate, and others. They speculate that all abstract concepts are understood via metaphor themes. Consider the ways we talk about time: "I lost a lot of time," "I'm living on borrowed time," "I invested a lot of time in it," and others in which time is understood as a resource like money.

Returning to language about cognition, for examples of metaphor themes, we regard ideas as light sources: "It was a bright idea," "The theory was illuminating," "I couldn't see the theory at all." We also regard knowledge as a growth process and learning as a form of ingestion: "The idea grew on me," "The theory was a lot to sink your teeth into." "The paper was raw facts." "It had a germ of truth to it," "A new theory was born today."

The rule-based grammars of the sort envisioned by Chomsky[27] led psycholinguists to focus perhaps too much on linguistic creativity (i.e., recursiveness). Although metaphor would be a prime example of the creativity that commonly occurs in communication, much of language behavior is very repetitive, and is based on idioms and metaphor formulas. Do we ever say "spilled milk" without also saying "It's no use crying over spilled milk?" Do we ever say "ulterior" without saying "ulterior motives?" Becker[22] has estimated that most communication by English speakers is based in a shared memory for tens of thousands of idioms and metaphor formulas.

METAPHOR AND INFERENCE-MAKING

Metaphors seem to be special for a fundamental reason having to do with the structure of metaphor. First, metaphors have a *topic*, something that is being talked about. The topic is usually, though not always, in the subject phrase of the sentence. The topic can be explicit or implicit. An example is "Einstein was a good swimmer." When stated in this context-free way, it could be taken as a literal sentence. However, it can be taken as a metaphor with the actual topic implicit (i.e., the theory of relativity). In this and other such cases, an inference may be needed (based in part on contextual information) in order to determine what it is that the metaphor is about. Another structural component of a metaphor is called the *vehicle*. This is the part of the metaphor that makes a comment about the topic, the thing that is used to talk about the topic. In the above example "good swimmer" is the vehicle. The remaining aspect of a metaphor is always implicit — this is called the *ground* of the metaphor, that is, the underlying semantics of the meaning similarity of the topic and vehicle. The theory of relativity, like good swimmers, can "go a long way" in explaining data and can "swim a strong race" against competitors. In "He flung himself upon his horse and rode madly off in all directions," the topic is implicit — the event of riding and his manner of doing it. The vehicle involves a prepositional phrase. The ground might be stated as "an emotional and frantic behavior."

This topic-vehicle-ground structural scheme[28] along with the classification according to implicit or explicit topic[29] is the basic scheme used to talk about metaphors. It makes salient, how, in order to comprehend a metaphor, one may have to make a number of inferences and connections and comparisons. Inference-making can certainly be involved when one comprehends

TABLE 2. Representative Stimulus Materials Used in Recent Research on Figurative Language

Brewer and Bock[33]
  Proverb: Out of another's purse it is easy to be generous.
  Surface structure change: It is easy to be generous out of another's purse.
  Literal paraphrase: From someone else's pocketbook it is easy to be charitable.
  Synonymous proverb: Broad thongs are cut from other people's leather.
  Unrelated proverb: Even caviar tastes ill to him who is forced to eat it.

Brewer, Harris and Brewer[34]
  Proverb: Many little leaks sink a ship.
  Literal paraphrase: A lot of small holes cause a boat to go under.
  Figurative paraphrase: A lot of small problems can add up to serious trouble.

Dorfmueller and Honeck[35]
  Proverb: The best pears fall into the pig's mouth.
  Interpretation: The least deserving sometimes get the finest things.
  Scenario instantiation: The uncle chose the nephew who only wrote him once in the past
      ten years to go with him on a trip to Europe.

Hoffman[41]
  Anomaly: Colossal hoax of clocks and calendars.
  Good interpretation: Schedules are a joke the way they rule our lives.
  Mediocre interpretation: We make appointments for some unimportant things.
  Poor interpretation: Everything we do must take some amount of time.
  Unrelated interpretation: False beliefs can keep us from our goals.

Hoffman and Honeck[42]
  Proverb: Birth is much but breeding is more.
  Good interpretation: Inherited genius could not create without a good education.
  Mediocre interpretation: People of royal blood must still prove themselves worthy of
      respect.
  Poor interpretation: Those of esteemed parents must learn to behave properly.
  Unrelated interpretation: Nobility is sometimes gained through fateful circumstances.

Honeck[43,44]
  Proverb: Industry is fortune's right hand and stinginess her left.
  Surface structure change: Stinginess is fortune's left hand and industry her right.
  Paraphrase: You must work hard and spend money carefully to make a fortune.
  Unrelated interpretation: A fortune is made or lost nearly every day.

Honeck, Riechmann, and Hoffman[45]
  Experiment 1:
    Proverb: There is great force hidden in a sweet command.
    Good interpretation: A little kindness often persuades better than a rough order.
    Poor interpretation: A good leader can persuade without abusing power.
    Unrelated interpretation: Increasingly more people are being persuaded to live in the city.
  Experiment 2:
    Proverb: In due time, the fox is brought to the furrier.
    Story: A jewel thief was successful for a long time. However, a detective caught him after
        10 years. But the detective said that if he had not caught the thief someone else
        would have because . . .

Honeck, *et al.*[46]
  Proverb: Great weights hang on small wires.
  Target interpretation: The outcome of important events often depends on what would
      otherwise be minor details.
  Foil interpretation: Everything of importance is accomplished at the expense of something
      else.
  Target instantiation: The ball just squeezed by the outstretched glove of the shortstop
      and the winning run scored.

Foil instantiation: He practiced batting for long hours during training and developed a few blisters on his hand.

Kroll, *et al.*[47]
  Context: The totem pole was made out of wood.
  Target: The arrow was like a totem pole.
  Correct response: Bad simile
  Context: His personality was very pleasant.
  Target: His personality was like an anchor.
  Correct response: Good simile.

Malgady and Johnson[48]
  Literal: Robes are cloaks. Dew is water. Blossoms are roses.
  Figurative: Robes are shadows. Dew is tears. Blossoms are faces.
  Anomalous: Robes are kites. Dew is a radio. Blossoms are laws.

Malgady and Johnson[49]
  Metaphors and similes:
    White snow falls like confetti.
    Red blood pours like rain.
    Old memories fade like garments.
    An old schoolhouse is a ragged beggar.
    The round moon is a flying kite.
    Distant hair is fatal silk.

Pollio and Smith[50] and Pollio[19]
  Anomalies:
    The moon is a newspaper.
    The gymnasium is a cloud.
    The dust is a plant.
  Metaphors:
    The car is a lemon.
    The job is a snap.
    The mind is a mirror.

Riechmann, *et al.*[51]
  Low imagery, low comprehensibility:
    Proverb: Reputation is commonly measured by the acre.
    Interpretation: Someone's character may be judged more by his material goods than his moral fiber.
  Low imagery, high comprehensibility:
    Proverb: It takes many shovelfuls of earth to bury the truth.
    Interpretation: It is hard to conceal what is right.
  High imagery, low comprehensibility:
    Proverb: The best pears drop to the pig's mouth.
    Interpretation: The least deserving sometimes get the finer things in life.
  High imagery, high comprehensibility:
    Proverb: He who spits above himself will have it all in his face.
    Interpretation: It is not wise to insult someone who is more powerful than yourself.

Gildea and Glucksberg
  Some fish are trout.
  Some birds are eagles.
  Some jobs are jails.
  Some roads are snakes.
  Some words are daggers.
  Some schools are zoos.

Harris[37]
  Metaphor: He hates the slime that sticks on filthy deeds.
  Synonymous metaphor: He hates the venom that oozes from poison deeds.
  Synonymous nonmetaphor: He hates the rancour that stays on cruel deeds.

Synonymous nonmetaphor: He hates the malice that comes from dastardly deeds.

Harris and Hall,[38] Harris,[39] and Petrun and Belmore[40]
Metaphor: The gentle wind tickled the wheat.
"Dead" metaphor: The gentle wind rocked the wheat.
Nonmetaphor: The gentle wind blew through the wheat.

Kemper[52]
Proverb: Diamonds come in small packages.
  Paragraphs relevant to the literal meaning of the proverb:
    Short: Frank gave Beth a present in a tiny box for their wedding anniversary. Diamonds come in small packages.
    Long: Frank gave Beth a present in a tiny box for their wedding anniversary. The box was tiny but the present was expensive. Frank wanted Beth to have a new ring so he didn't need a very large box. Diamonds come in small packages.
  Paragraphs relevant to the figurative meaning of the proverb:
    Short: If you think that size is important, you have to be wrong a lot of the time. You shouldn't overlook something because it appears to be little. Diamonds come in small packages.
    Long: If you think that size is important, you have to be wrong a lot of the time. A short person may be a great thinker and a poem of only 5 lines can have great beauty. You shouldn't overlook something because it appears to be little. Diamonds come in small packages.

---

literal speech, such as in the use of requests like "Can you open the window?"[30] As another example, recall of a sentence like "The nurse washed the clothes" can be cued with inferentially related words, like "basket."[31] In our comprehension of sentences we construct images and "possible worlds" all the time.[32] Metaphor, however, seems to compound this inference-making process to the point of testing the adequacy of psychological and linguistic models of the comprehension process.

RESEARCH METHODS AND MATERIALS

Psycholinguistic research on figurative language (in all its diverse forms) has provided a considerable amount of basic information. TABLE 2 presents a representative sample of the sorts of materials that have been used. In the remainder of this paper I will have occasion to refer to many of the studies cited in this table. TABLE 3 presents a synopsis of the basic research methods that have been used.

Individuals can yield reliable and consistent judgments of the semantic similarity between two sentences, where either sentence can be anomalous, metaphorical, proverbial, or a paraphrase. Such judgments can show rates of 80% agreement or more, both in forced-choice categorization tasks and in scaling judgments tasks. Subjects can yield reliable judgments of the meanings of the terms in metaphors. They can yield reliable judgments of the similarity between metaphors, proverbs, and pictorial representatives of their meaning, and they can yield reliable judgments of the different categories of sentences (anomalous, redundant, metaphorical, and so forth). I may seem confident in discussing these experiments now, but back in 1970–1975, when this ground was being broken, nobody was exactly sure what to do or how to do it.

It makes most sense to discuss the research in terms of five general domains: metaphor versus anomaly, the role of mental imagery, memory for

---

TABLE 3. Research Methods

Semantic Judgments

How close in meaning are sentence$_1$ and sentence$_2$?

How close in meaning are word$_1$ and word$_2$ when given in or out of their metaphor context?

How "imageable" is this metaphor on a scale of 1 to 5?

How metaphoric is this sentence on a scale of 1 to 5?

How well does this proverb fit this instantiation or scenario?

Memory Tasks

Possible acquisition tasks	*Possible memory tasks*
Interpret or paraphrase these sentences.	*Free recall* of lists of sentences
Read these sentences in their prose contexts.	*Cued recall*
Semantic judgments.	

                              Types of cues:
                                    Topic, vehicle or ground
                                    Content words
                                    Interpretations
                          Recognition
                          Types of cues:
                                    The acquisition sentences plus a set of foils
                                    Paraphrases
                                    Scenarios to which the metaphors or proverbs might apply

Comprehension reaction time tasks

Comprehension teaction time:

    "Push this button as soon as you understand each of these sentences."

Classification decision task:

    "Read each sentence as it appears and decide as quickly as possible whether or not it is a ____" (metaphor or literal, literally true or literally false, anomalous or grammatical).

Paraphrase generation task:

    "For each sentence, generate a paraphrase of the meaning, putting it in your own words."

Semantic similarity decision task:

    "Decide as quickly as possible if sentence 1 and sentence 2 in each pair have the same (literal, metaphorical) meaning."

Rhyme monitoring task:

    "While listening to this sentence, try to detect any word that rhymes with *back*.
    'When Fred was working at the grain elevator, he wanted to hit the sack as soon as possible.' "

Cognitive capacity task:

    Task 1 — "Decide if sentence 1 and sentence 2 have the same meaning."
    Task 2 — "Listen for background click sounds."

Sentence priming decision task:

Context	Target	Decision
(time 1)	(time 2)	(time 2)
"COLD"	"His wife was a refrigerator"	"Is target literally acceptable or not?"
Rhyme cue: "falls"	"By his fourth day in the hospital he was climbing the	"Respond once you've detected a word in the target according to the
Category cue: "part of a building"	walls to go home"	cue type."

---

metaphors, reaction time studies, and studies of problem-solving. After discussing these areas of research I will be in a position to offer a few comments on the "granddaddy" issue that metaphor raises; What is meaning?, and I will be in a position to comment on the prospects for future research.

ANOMALY AND METAPHOR

Just about any sentence can be taken as metaphor given the right context. A classic example is "The old rock is becoming brittle with age." In the context of a geology class the sentence is perfectly logical and literal, it is non-redundant and grammatically acceptable. However, if uttered in reference to a professor emeritus, the sentence suddenly becomes a metaphor and violates semantic rules. Context-dependence is an aspect of figurative language that makes one hard-pressed to reliably distinguish the metaphorical from the literal.

Technically, metaphors are anomalies since they violate the rules for putting word meanings together. According to the transformational grammar approach, anomalous strings are devoid of meaning. They were therefore used in the 1960s as controls for meaning in experiments that attempted to demonstrate the "psychological reality" of syntactical and transformational rules. For example, research participants would have to repeat sentences out loud. The sentences were presented from audio tape against a background masking noise.[53,54] This is a much more difficult task to do for anomalous strings than for grammatically well-formed strings. Here are some examples of the "meaningless" sentences used in these early experiments on grammar:

> "The academic liquid attended a deep bar."
> "The ordorless child inspired a chocolate audience."
> "The witness appraised the shocking company dragon."
> "Gallant detergents fight accurate flames."
> "The dove will tell tires from sympathy to speak."
> "Mr. Hobbs is a remember in our community."
> "Extra rivers wished casually to cancel off."
> "Seventeen intuitions ate highly across the right."
> "Large factories utilize efficient hesitates."
> "Sensible ideas distrust politicians."

Most of these strings were rule-generated by shuffling the words between sentences. What resulted often were strings that were anything but meaningless (note the metaphor in the concept of meaninglessness, "Words are containers for meaning"). Pollio and Burns[55] found that if subjects are required to actively interpret such strings, then memory for them is not significantly worse than memory for grammatical strings.

Honeck and I did some experiments using anomalies that had been intentionally generated — these from the poetry of e.e. cummings. We selected lines that violated various types of linguistic rules and all possible combinations of types of rules. As with Honeck's earlier demonstrations, we found that persons can relate the meanings of any two strings (metaphors, anomalies, and proverbs all matched with sets of possible interpretations), even under the constraint that no two strings match on words, propositions, deep structures, or case-relation structures.[56,57]

What then distinguishes anomaly from metaphor? If one sets up a judgment task properly, one can get persons to reliably distinguish metaphors from anomalous strings. One idea is that these types of strings should fall on a continuum. For example, "Robes are trucks" should be regarded as anomalous since robes and trucks have little if anything in common. On the other hand, "Robes are wisdom" should be regarded as a metaphor since they do have some conceptual overlap. "Robes are garments" should be regarded as literal since they have many features in common. A number of experiments (reviewed in Malgady and Johnson[48] and Johnson and Malgady[58] have shown that subjects can yield reliable judgments of which type of sentence a given string is, and of the semantic relatedness of the two terms in each comparison. This result seems to confirm the continuum idea. Taking this a bit further, one can generate a more detailed classification system:

Redundancy: "A tulip is a flower."
Informative: "The thief is a banker."
Anomalous: "The mountain is a frog."
Contradictory: "The dog is a cat."

This classification scheme was used by Steinberg in experiments[59] to show that persons can reliably classify sentences according to these purely logical categories. Note, however, that if one is a bit flexible in interpreting these sentences, some can be reclassified. Over the long-term of geological history, some mountains are like frogs. Some thiefs are bankers. In other words, given the right event or situational context and the right "cognitive style" on the part of the interpreter, many of the logical types of sentences can be taken as metaphor. Pollio and his colleagues[55,60,61] replicated the classic Steinberg experiments, but allowed metaphor as one of the categories. Many of the sentences that Steinberg's participants took as Anomalous and as Informative now went into the Metaphor category. There were also considerable individual differences in cognitive style. Some persons perferred to think in terms of the logical categories, whereas others seemed to be in a poetic mode.

Thus, the realization or awareness of metaphoric meaning depends on context and on individual differences in cognitive style. Another important factor is mental imagery.

IMAGERY

Many of the first metaphor experiments were demonstrations about comprehension and the inadequacies of available theoretical concepts. When we look back on this work, we see that some problems with it. The metaphors used were often constructed *ad hoc* by the experimenter and took on forms ranging from verbal beasts ("I will take the sun in my mouth and leap into the ripe air") to mundane forms ("The moon is a round platter"). The sentences were often presented in the form of lists, with each sentence somewhat semantically isolated. The tasks do not seem to relate much to how people actually use nonliteral language (e.g., learning a set of proverbs versus recalling and using one in an actual conversation).

Another salient aspect of the early research is that almost all of the sentences (except for the proverb research) used highly concrete and "imageable" nouns and verbs. It is known that imagery is a potent variable in studies of comprehension and memory.[62] Imagery and metaphor are related in complex ways, but metaphors need not be concrete ("A theory is a wish") and the preponderance of event-specific imageable materials may have led researchers to overemphasize the role of imagery and perception in metaphor as opposed to the role of conceptual imageless thought.[63] In Riechmann's experiment,[51] subjects were given either highly imageable proverbs or highly abstract ones (examples of the materials are included in TABLE 2). Some subjects were told to concentrate on the image that the proverbs suggested, while others were told to concentrate on the abstract meaning. In the memory task that Riechmann devised, subjects were asked to recognize the interpretations of the original proverbs. The imagery instructions made it harder for subjects to recognize the meaning, especially for the more imageable proverbs.

As Riechmann prepared for the experiment on recognition of the interpretations of proverbs, he had to generate lists of proverbs that varied independently on imagery and comprehensibility. A group of subjects was asked to rate lists of proverbs in terms of their imagery and comprehensibility. It turned out that the order of the two ratings tasks made a difference in the judgments. If proverbs were first rated in terms of imagery value, subsequent comprehensibility ratings for other proverbs would be lowered somewhat. If comprehensibility was rated first, subsequent imagery ratings were somewhat inflated. Perhaps instructions to focus on the image that proverbs suggested kept subjects at a concrete level, lowering subsequent comprehensibility ratings. Conversely, initial focusing on underlying meaning subsequently made images more meaningful (see also Higbee and Millard[64]).

MEMORY FOR METAPHORS

Many persons believe that metaphors are special. Perhaps they yield especially vivid images or perhaps they are especially memorable, or perhaps they require special comprehension processing.[6,37] With a little help from Shakespeare, Harris[39,65] generated lists of poetic metaphors, and for each one, some paraphrases that expressed a highly similar meaning, but in a literal way. Some examples of the materials of Harris *et al.* are presented in TABLE 2. Next, they obtained ratings of imageability, comprehensibility, metaphoricalness, and other attributes. The metaphors and paraphrases were presented to subjects in the form of lists and the tasks were recall and recognition memory. These investigators did not find evidence that metaphors are especially memorable, especially evocative of vivid images, or especially difficult to understand. This pattern of results seemed to hold when the metaphors were presented in a dramatic context.

We now know that if metaphors are presented in the context of meaningful conversation or prose then they *can* be more memorable and their images more salient.[66,67] Furthermore, ratings of "aesthetic goodness" and "metaphori-calness" can be related to recall. What literary critics would call a "good" metaphor may be a more memorable thing.

A most elegant and influential series of experiments on metaphor and inference-making was carried out in the mid-1970s at the University of Minnesota by Verbrugge and McCarrell.[68] They presented to their participants metaphors such as "Billboards are warts on the landscape" and then later gave a recall test with either the topics, the vehicles, or statements of the implicit ground used as recall cues. For example, the ground cue for the billboards metaphor was "ugly protrusion on a surface." The experiments demonstrated that the meanings of topic and vehicle interact to specify their ground and that this ground is inferred during the initial comprehension of the metaphors.

Honeck, Riechmann, and I[45] made a similar demonstration for proverbs. Proverbs are like metaphors, except that they are general (nonpast tense) and they are topic-less. That is, the entire sentence is a vehicle term which makes reference to its current context of use (for example, many proverbs are admonitions). A paraphrase of a proverb, which says in a literal way what the vehicle (proverb) says figuratively, is also a potential statement for the implicit ground of the proverb. We presented subjects with novel proverbs like "Reputation is commonly measured by the acre" and found that recall could be prompted by the implicit ground ("Someone's character may be judged more on the basis of his material goods than his moral fiber").

Recently, Franklin and DeHart[69] modernized and refined the original Wurzburg experiment and successfully cued the recall of one set of proverbs with other proverbs of similar meaning or implicit ground.

The research on memory for metaphors shows that metaphors can be more memorable than literal statements under certain circumstances, such as on-going prose comprehension (see Arter[70] and Hofer[71], and that complex forms of inference-making are involved during comprehension and recall. Psychological theories of these processes will certainly have to accommodate these new findings.

METAPHOR AND REACTION TIME

Ideally, what we would like to have is a real-time model of all the processes that go on as a person comprehends, all the perceptual, memorial, and inference-making processes, all the images, concepts, and word meanings, and "world knowledge" to boot. One approch to this problem is to generate a computer model of the processes that are hypothetically required and then to test the model on a computer to see whether it behaves like a person does (e.g., can generate the types of paraphrases and translations that a person does). The earliest attempts at getting computers to translate languages had difficulty with metaphors. The apocryphal story is told of the language translation program that, when given the proverb "The spirit is willing but the flesh is weak," returned with a translation that said "The vodka is sweet but the meat is rotten." There can be little doubt that idioms, metaphor themes, and novel metaphors will all have to be dealt with before there can be any generally useful computer system for comprehending or translating languages.

In the case of figurative language, what one would like (aside from the translation problem) is a system that is capable of yielding paraphrases that say in a literal way what metaphors say in a nonliteral way. Thibadeau's READER program[72] was based on a general semantic feature transfer process, one not just tied to literal meaning. Russell[73] has described a system for interpreting the figurative meanings of verbs. In this system, word meanings are specified by levels as well as features. In the comprehension process, more than one type of transfer is possible, across the levels as well as across features. Both Thibadeau and Russell's systems rely on descriptions of "world knowledge" in one or another form (e.g., stored "scripts") in order to decide how to relax and alter the restrictions on word meaning.

Another approach to computer modeling has been taken by Carbonell.[74] He has programmed a computer to paraphrase metaphors which are based on common economics metaphor themes. For example, we understand time in terms of metaphorical comparisons to resources, such as money. So, the specific metaphor "I wasted a lot of time" is comprehended by reference to the general metaphor theme. Carbonnel has had considerable success in dealing with many common metaphor themes having to do with topics in politics and in economics (e.g., "Inflation is a disease"). This approach does not directly get at the problem of comprehending novel poetic metaphors, however.

Many researchers have used reaction-time methods to attempt to disclose the processes that occur during comprehension (TABLE 3 presents examples of the tasks). From the time of the Wurzburg experiments on proverbs and novel metaphors until only very recently, it has been notoriously difficult to use simple comprehension reaction-time measurements to disclose comprehension subprocesses and causal structures (in contrast with the ease of showing effects of syntactic structure, such as in the delay for understanding passive negative questions). The reason for the difficulty is variability. It might take from seconds to minutes to comprehend a novel proverb ("Silk and velvet can put out the kitchen fire") or a novel poetic metaphor such as those used by the researchers at Wurzburg ("The most glowing colors in which virtues shine are the inventions of those who lack them.")[2,33,37,52]

Brewer, Harris, and Brewer[34] used a semantic similarity decision task with pairs of sentences. Each sentence could be either a proverb, a paraphrase of its literal meaning, or a paraphrase of its figurative meaning. If the first sentence of each pair was a paraphrase of the figurative meaning, then it took extra-long to comprehend the proverb, implying that figurative meaning of proverbs is determined in stages. Overall reaction times were quite large (on the order of 3 to 10 seconds) with considerable variability. This result confirmed Buehler's contention[1] about the difficulty of comprehending novel figurative forms. Such forms seem to "stretch the comprehension process out" so that its subprocesses can perhaps be studied.

Researchers have recently been able to constrain tasks and materials to generate meaningful chronometric data on proverb comprehension,[52,69,75] simile comprehension,[47,76] and idiom comprehension.[77-80] Many experiments overcome the variability problem by presenting metaphors in the context of ongoing sentence comprehension without much in the way of cumbersome instructions or special tasks. Participants are given a single specific decision task, such as to decide whether each sentence is literally acceptable.

To successfully use reaction time measures, one must distinguish idioms and common metaphor themes from unconventional or novel poetic metaphors, and these from proverbs. In the case of idioms, there is no doubt that persons have a bias to perceive the nonliteral meaning.[77,81] Since idioms are fairly fixed in terms of syntax, they behave more like words or lexical entries than like phrases. So, reaction times to the comprehension of idioms are quite short, shorter than would be expected on the basis of the word length of the idiom phrases,[82,83] especially when idioms are presented in contexts. If the context is appropriately arranged, idioms can be comprehended literally (e.g., a sentence about a person giving someone else a pink slip), and since this is an unusual use of an idiom, memory for it can be better than memory for idioms when comprehended according to their intended nonliteral meaning.[78,79] Even so, comprehension of idioms is initially and primarily of the nonliteral meaning rather than the literal meaning.

Results confirm the notion that literal processing of figurative forms is a distinguishable mode. We have a bias to perceive figurative meaning and attempts to get people to take nonliteral utterances literally can impede the smooth flow of comprehension. For example, one can be presented with a paragraph about someone knocking over a jar of beans. If there is a statement about "spilling the beans," the context has biased the comprehender toward the literal meaning and the comprehender's cognition will be hung up on the unusual usage. A similar conclusion seems to hold for metaphor formulas, statements like "A road is a snake," "The surgeon is a butcher," and "His wife was a refrigerator." While more flexible and generative than idioms, these formulas are a standard part of the language community and, as is the case with idioms, reaction time to comprehension of them is generally quite short.[36]

In the case of novel poetic metaphors, on the other hand, the important effect of context lies at another level: The presence of clarifying context can significantly decrease the time it takes for a person to comprehend a novel metaphor.[80] The more context a person can rely on, the lower the reaction time, for novel metaphors and for novel proverbs.[52,75]

Petrum and Belmore[40] measured the time it takes a person to decide whether pairs of sentences (paraphrases and novel metaphors) are similar in meaning. Participants also had to listen for the occurrence of background "click" sounds as a secondary task which strained their concentration. If the sentence to be comprehended was a novel metaphor, it was harder for people to detect the clicks.

Because of the constraints imposed by our common cultural heritage of idioms and metaphor formulas, and because of constraints on contextual information, we are biased to perceive the figurative meaning of many nonliteral utterances. It takes special contextual manipulations to get persons to

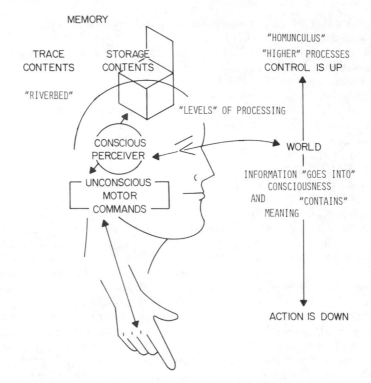

FIGURE 1. A general model for cognition which manifests some of the basic metaphor themes that are widely used to describe mental events.

take idioms and metaphor formulas in a literal way. In ordinary contexts, figurative language takes no longer to comprehend than ordinary communication, because figurative language *is* ordinary communication. It does not seem to require special comprehension processes, if to be "special" means "to take more time."

Recent chronometric research began as a reaction to the theoretical assumption that linguistic meanings are stored in the head as fundamentally literal things based on reference and perception of properties. Therefore, metaphor comprehension would require special inference-making processes. First, an input metaphor would be comprehended according to the usual rules and meanings. When this analysis fails, as it must in the case of metaphor, then some special process or processes get invoked to derive the intended figurative meaning on the basis of a rearrangement or transformation of the stored literal meanings of the words involved. This theoretical scheme is called the "two-stage" theory of metaphor comprehension.[37,84]

On a theoretical level, there are many classes of possible processing and representation models.[85-87] For instance, suppose that the semantic features of words are stored in the mind in the form of an ordered list or push-down stack. If the features that are needed for comprehension of the metaphor are stored low-down in the list, then it might take longer to comprehend the metaphor whether or not there is a special metaphor comprehension process. Conversely, if the semantic features can be scanned in parallel, then it might not take longer to comprehend metaphors even if there is a special process. No simple model, even a refined two-stage model, will suffice to explain the intricacies of figurative language comprehension. One is wise not to conclude that all metaphor comprehension is the process "x" for an given x.

METAPHOR IN SCIENTIFIC PROBLEM-SOLVING

Metaphor plays a necessary and critical role in cognitive science and artificial intelligence.[20,88-90] Metaphors are used to generate ideas for experiments (e.g., the notion that short-term memory is like a computer memory "pushdown stack") as well as ideas for theories. Cognitive science relies quite heavily on metaphors that are part of our Cartesian heritage: Perception is the input of sensory data which need to be processed in order to be presented to the mind in the form of percepts. The modern computer metaphors for mind have altered this Cartesian theme, to the effect that perceptual and linguistic processes are logical or computational processes. FIGURE 1 represents some of the basic metaphor themes that modern psychology and computer science use to describe the activities of the intellect.

TABLE 4 presents some exemplary mentalistic metaphor themes that are used in the area of artificial intelligence.

TABLE 4. Some Examples of the Metaphors of Cognitive Science and Their Themes as found in Brachman and Smith[91]

Buildings and Structures	Entities
Programs can "build" schemas, representations, or prototypes. Programs have a "logical architecture," thought can be modelled with "embedded structures," there are "fixed skeletons," "data structures," and "relaxation nets."	Ideas can be "embodied as formal objects," Procedures can be "anchored or unanchored," There are "mental dictionaries," "servants and demons," and "indivisible entities."
Paths	**Languages**
"Links" and "nodes" can represent propositions and relations, one can "fetch" information and have "search" problems, there are "cognitive maps," "associative pathways," "inheritance networks," and "conceptual hierarchies."	Computers use "computational languages," languages can be "universal" and they can be "equivalent," information gets "translated" into representations, there are "tree-like abstract syntax," "layers of language," and a "primitive vocabulary."
Machines	**Causality and Intention**
Tasks can be "hard" or "easy" for a machine, there are "inference machinery," "focus mechanisms," "pattern-matching engines," "mental apparatus," and "mechanical procedures."	Computers "manipulate" information, programs "activate" entities and they "behave" like experts, interpreters "look" for symbols, and programs "guide" inferences.

From Freud's theory of consciousness as the "tip of the iceberg," to conversational ways for talking about time ("We must face the future together"), figurative language is pervasive in all forms of discourse, so pervasive that one is often hard-pressed to distinguish metaphor from literal truth, from symbols, from archetypes, from myths. Indeed, it is a mistake to regard metaphor as either (1) a property of isolated sentences, or (2) a property of isolated linguistic systems separate from perception and action.[92] My favorite example is an advertisement by the SONY Corporation for their audio cassette tapes. In the ad, musical staffs are depicted with pastel blotches of color in among the musical notations. Visually the ad is quite striking. Music is color.

In linguistics, philosophy, and rhetoric, even theories of the meaning of metaphor are themselves based on metaphorical notions of what meaning is: A metaphor is regarded as an "ornament" of language, a "puzzle" to figure out, a "mask" of the truth, a "filter" of meanings, a "tension" in the fabric of discourse, a "mapping" of meanings, and interactions of "semantic atoms." Attendant to each of these metaphors is a full, formal theory of the semantics of metaphor. Theorists of metaphor are not always explicit in their reliance on metaphor. How ironic this must seem to positivists, who believe that all true scientific theories must be literal, logical things!

It should come as little surprise that metaphor is an important tool in problem-solving (see for example, Gordon[93] and the "synectics" technique). The use of metaphors and mental images in the physical sciences has been amply documented.[90,94-97] Much of the available research on scientific problem-solving assumes that most problem-solving boils down to the use of analogy. This is an oversimplification made on the basis of an old abstract metaphor, "Thought is logic." Since scientists' actual analogies usually come long after the metaphors and images (and mathematics) have been played with, one is not compelled to assume that all metaphor comprehension is the comprehension of analogy or should be reduced to this one logical form.

Howard Pollio and his colleagues[61,98] have conducted a number of experiments in which subjects' ability to interpret metaphors is compared to their ability to solve analogies and other types of thinking and problem-solving tasks. These experiments have shown that, while metaphor comprehension and analogistic reasoning are related to overall reasoning ability, the two are not the same, and that they tap different cognitive operations and styles, and show differing developmental patterns.[16]

Modern researchers are now using metaphor itself as a tool in the teaching of science and of the problem-solving process.[88,99] Analyses of the steps involved as scientists use images and metaphors have revealed complexities and phenomena that beg for further study. I find fascinating the ways in which scientists go from metaphors to mathematical equations. A favorite example of a scientific metaphor is the physics metaphor, "An atom is a solar system." This metaphor was used by Ernest Rutherford and Niels Bohr to generate the mathematical equations which formed the beginnings of quantum mechanics. Bohr took certain equations from astronomy and translated them rather directly into equations which led to predictions of atomic spectra and explanations of the properties of elements as indicated in the periodic table (itself a metaphor based on suits of cards). It is striking how Bohr and other physicists were explicit in the use of metaphor. James Clerk Maxwell, in particular, advocated the use of poetry, metaphor, and mental image models in the generation of mathematical equations (see Hoffman[90]).

Gentner[99,100] has pioneered in the generation of ideas for research based on the analysis of the use of metaphor in problem-solving. She has distinguished ways in which scientific metaphors can differ: In terms of their scope or richness, in terms of their precision or detail, in terms of their abstractness (i.e., the mapping of properties versus higher-order relations), and the specificity or clarity of the mapping (i.e., one-to-one mapping or many-to-many mapping). Good scientific metaphors are judged to be richer, more precise, abstract, and yet clear. In another set of her experiments, she charts (in verbal problem-solving protocols) the progress and errors that students make in learning to apply one system (e.g., plumbing) to comprehend another system (e.g., electronics) by fleshing out an analogy into mathematical equations (e.g., a resistor is like a block in the fluid flow).

Carroll and Thomas[101] have begun to analyze the use of metaphor in the design of computer languages. If we assume that learning is the metaphoric extension of known ideas, then the metaphors a computer language has should be used in a consistent way (often they are not). The various metaphors in a computer language should be coherent rather than mixed (e.g., not using language about "trees" and "nets" in the same system). Carroll and other computer scientists (e.g., Chandrasekarian[88]) advocate the use of metaphor as a tool in designing languages and computer systems because of the role of metaphor in comprehension and learning. A number of researchers now advocate explicit use of metaphor as a tool in the teaching of science and the writing of science texts.[20]

METAPHOR AND MEANING

Honeck had done studies[43,44] showing that individuals could reliably rate the semantic relatedness of proverbs and their interpretations. This was no small demonstration, for the materials were rigged—no proverb/interpretation pair had overlap in terms of words, propositions, or deep structure. In short, subjects could see semantic relations that available theories could not readily describe.

The big question that figurative language confronts us with is: What is meaning? It would be impossible to provide philosophers, logicians, and psycholinguists with an answer that would satisfy all. Most treatments of what meaning "is" themselves rely on metaphorical conceptions.[86,87,102] It is commonly assumed in linguistics and philosophy that word meaning is a matter of reference or "pointing," that word meaning is a matter of "primitive semantic atoms," that sentence comprehension consists of "looking up" the meanings of the component words and then combining them according to "computational rules" to arrive at the intended sentence meaning. These assumptions, and some others, characterize the "literalist" approach to semantics, which dominated until very recently.[63] The Achilles heel of the literalist view is that "semantic primitives" are too "timeless" and detached from the dynamic cognitions of actual people. In its concern for logical structure, it freezes out creative possibilities. For instance, a linguistic theory (of the type advocated by Chomsky[27] and Katz and Fodor[103] might claim that the meaning of the word "bachelor" would involve general features such as ANIMATE and HUMAN along with subsidiary features like MALE and UNMARRIED. The metaphors, "She looked right through the bachelor" and "She welded her eyes on the bachelor" would require bachelors to be not only METALLIC but TRANSPARENT. Sentence comprehension is so dynamic that it makes more sense to talk about it "from the world up" by looking experimentally at the dynamics of comprehension. It is edifying to take a metaphor and attempt to render the "deep structure" along with some semantic features for each content word (salient features when the word is comprehended *outside* the metaphor context). It is difficult to capture a metaphor's possible meanings in such a static way.

For the topic and for the vehicle, one can arrange a set or list of relevant distinctions or properties. The ground of the metaphor would involve the properties the topic and vehicle share. In a good metaphor, the amount of overlap would be "just right," that is, they would share a moderate amount of features, features that are highly salient for the vehicle and of low salience for the topic. The features that are not shared can also be important in specifying the ground.[104-107]

One might admit temporal change into the semantics scheme, such as Gentner[99] has done for analogy-mapping in problem-solving. I have tried to show how this might be done in FIGURE 2.

The representation of the creation and use of a metaphor usually begins with "semantic features" or similar distinctions, along with set theory, but can be broadened to describe properties, relations, dispositions, events, and other types of "meaning elements" besides linguistic features. In FIGURE 2, topic, vehicle and ground concepts are represented as sets by uppercase letters. Properties, relations, and so forth, are represented by lowercase letters. The place of the topic and vehicle concepts in their respective domains must also be represented, as in panel A. The ground is shown in panel B as a form of set overlap which effectively distinguishes the elements in the vehicle into two subsets: Those which may be literally true of the vehicle (1) and those which may be figuratively applied to the topic (f).

One might realize a particular property of the vehicle (say, that solar systems are very large) and then try to apply that to the topic. One would not want to say that atoms have diameters of billions of miles. But the relative expanses between atomic particles may be comparable to solar systems and a relational aspect of meaning would "map" between topic and vehicle. In the creative use of metaphor shown in panel C, properties of the vehicle that were initially ignored or thought to be literal or irrelevant (1) are reconceptualized, leading to the creative discovery of relations, dispositions, actions, events, or similar properties (f) that may be regarded as figuratively applicable to the topic. This creative act may alter the theory or domain of

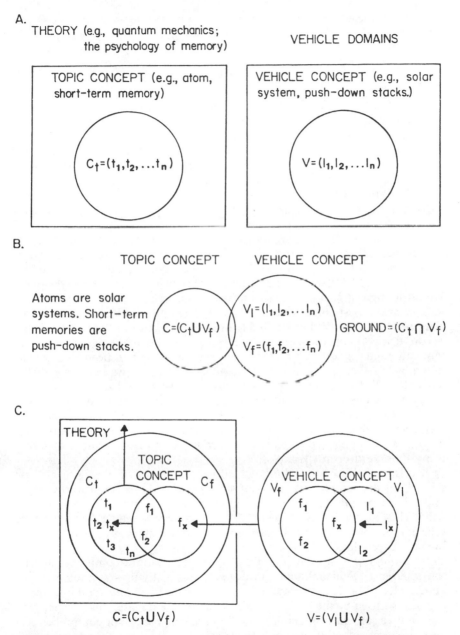

FIGURE 2. A dynamic approach to the meaning of metaphor with examples taken from the sciences. In panel **A**, topic and vehicle are juxtaposed. Panel **B** is a set-theoretic representation of the metaphor ground in terms of set overlap. Panel **C** shows one possible dynamic of comprehension and inference.

which the topic concept is one part, just as Bohr's solar-system-based equations had implications for all of particle physics.

PROSPECTS

The belief that the field of figurative language is an exciting one has persisted since the first meetings and symposia on it were held in 1977.

Today, the research seems to be dovetailng with another modern trend, the trend toward ecological, contextualistic, and functionalistic views which seem to be prominent in life-span developmental psychology,[108] the psychology of learning,[109] and the psychology of perception.[110] A description of the philosophy that underlies these modern trends would take me too far afield. An indication of trends in terms of research directions is entirely appropriate.

Researchers seem to be turning toward examinations of the uses of metaphors in real-world contexts, such as art criticism and art interpretation,[111] music theory,[112] political rhetoric and communication,[113] communication about sports and sports headlines,[26] college texts,[20] prose comprehension,[70,71] and street slang.[114] Many practical questions are being asked about metaphor. Would foreign language instruction best proceed by explicit instruction in idioms, or is it best done as we now do it by beginning with drills on pronunciation?[115] Harwood[116] has studied the use of metaphor in the sign language of the deaf. Comprehension was tested by asking for judgments of the semantic similarity of topic and vehicle terms, showing that hearing-impaired individuals are as adept at metaphor interpretation as we hearing individuals. McNeill[117,118] has analyzed the relations between hand gestures and communication content and has found that metaphoric understanding and mental imagery seem to express the observed relations. For example, the mathematician who is talking about the "dual" of a function makes a gesture of turning his hands from palm up to palm down, mimicking the movement of something flipping over in space.

Dorfmueller and Honeck[35] cued subjects' memory of novel proverbs by using brief descriptions of events or scenarios to which the proverbs might apply. For example, "The best pears fall into the pig's mouth" could be cued with "The co-ed who never lifted a finger in college landed a nice job." This type of experiment successfully brings the ecology and pragmatics of proverbs into the psychological laboratory.

Billow et al.[119] have instituted a project on metaphor comprehension by schizophrenics. Schizophrenics have characteristically bizarre nonliteral language. Metaphor can be a way of expressing conflicts and symbols, and it can also be used by the patient to hide things. The research involves varying the emotive content of metaphors and comparing metaphor comprehension with a battery of other psychological tests.

I look forward to considerable progress in computer understanding of metaphor, including a more careful use of metaphor in computer programming languages and in instruction in computer programming. Figurative language promises to be an invaluable tool in the interface between human and computer.

Figurative language occupies a wide domain, and it cuts across all disciplines and contexts. There are scores of research projects out there waiting to be done, exciting projects with the potential for theoretical and practical payoffs.

SUMMARY

Modern experiments on memory and comprehension of poetic metaphor, proverbs, and idioms have significantly advanced our knowledge about the flexibility of cognition and learning. Research using new recall, recognition, and reaction-time methods has led to interesting discoveries about the relations of conceptual knowledge, mental imagery, word meaning, and event perception. The work has also led to practical research on the psychology of communication involving figurative language in various contexts: The teaching of a foreign language, programming in computer languages, the teaching of music theory, and the use of metaphor in creative scientific problem-solving.

ACKNOWLEDGMENT

I would like to thank Dr. Sheila J. White for her support and perseverance.

REFERENCES

1. BUEHLER, K. 1908/1951. On thought connections. *In* Organization and Pathology of Thought. D. Rapaport, Ed. Columbia University Press. New York, NY.
2. STAEHLIN, W. 1914. Zur Psychologie und Statistik der Metephern. Arch. Gesamte Psychologie **31**: 299–425.
3. HONECK R. P. 1980. Historical notes on figurative language. *In* Cognition and Figurative Language. R. P. Honeck & R. R. Hoffman, Eds. Erlbaum. Hillsdale, NJ.
4. ASCH, S. 1955. On the use of metaphor in the description of persons. *In* On Expressive Language. H. Werner, Ed. Clark University Press. Worcester, MA.
5. OSGOOD, C. 1980. The cognitive dynamics of synesthesia and metaphor. *In* Cognition and Figurative Language. R. P. Honeck & R. R. Hoffman, Eds. Erlbaum. Hillsdale, NJ.
6. ORTONY, A., Ed. 1975. Metaphor and Thought. Cambridge University Press. Cambridge, England.
7. BAMBERG M. 1982. Metaphor and play-interaction. *In* The World of Play. F. Manning, Ed. Leisure Press. New York, NY.
8. LORING, D. & F. KESSEL. 1982. Playing with meanings: Figurative language in the elementary school years. Department of Psychology, University of Houston, Houston, TX. Manuscript in preparation.
9. MARKS, L. 1982. Synesthetic perception and poetic metaphor. J. Exp. Psychol. Hum. Percept. Perform. **8**: 15–23.
10. MENDELSOHN, E., S. ROBINSON, H. GARDNER & E. WINNER. 1982. Preschooler's renamings are genuine metaphors. Paper presented at the convention of the American Psychological Association.
11. PETRUN, C. 1980. Metaphor comprehension and cognitive development in col-

lege students. Paper presented at the annual convention of the Midwest Psychological Association.

12. PICKENS, J. & H. POLLIO. Metaphoric competency and reading skills. Department of Psychology, University of Tennessee, Knoxville, TN. Manuscript in preparation.

13. REYNA, V. 1982. Children's metaphor in the resolution of semantic inconsistency. Department of Psychology, University of Texas, Dallas, TX. Manuscript in preparation.

14. VOSNIADOU, S. & A. ORTONY. 1982. Effects of linguistic and cognitive variables on children's ability to comprehend figurative language. Center for Reading Research, University of Illinois, Urbana, IL. Manuscript in preparation.

15. BILLOW, R. 1977. Metaphor: A review of the psychological literature. Psychol. Bull. **84**: 81–92.

16. GARDNER, H., E. WINNER, R. BECHOFER & D. WOLF. 1978. The development of figurative language. *In* Children's Language. K. Nelson, Ed. Garner Press. New York, NY.

17. JOHNSON, M., Ed. 1982. Philosophical Perspectives on Metaphor. University of Minnesota Press. Minneapolis, MN.

18. SACHS, S., Ed. 1980. On Metaphor. University of Chicago Press. Chicago, IL.

19. POLLIO, R., J. BARLOW, H. FINE & M. POLLIO. 1977. The poetics of growth: Figurative language in psychology, psychotherapy, and education. Erlbaum. Hillsdale, NJ.

20. SMITH, M., B. COHEN & H. POLLIO. 1981. Metaphorical models of thinking in introductory psychology textbooks. Paper presented at the annual convention of the American Psychological Association.

21. RHODES, R. & J. LAWLER. 1981. Athematic metaphors. Proceedings of the Chicago Linguistics Society.

22. BECKER, J. 1975. The Phrasal Lexicon. Report No. 3081. Bolt, Beranek and Newman. Cambridge, MA.

23. REDDY, M. 1979. The conduit metaphor: A case of frame conflict in our language about language. *In* Metaphor and Thought. A. Ortony, Ed. Cambridge University Press. Cambridge, England.

24. LAWLER, J. 1979. Mimicry in natural language. Proceedings of the Chicago Linguistics Society.

25. LAKOFF, G. & M. JOHNSON. 1980. Metaphors We Live By. University of Chicago Press. Chicago, IL.

26. SMITH, M. 1982. Review of *Metaphors We Live By* (Lakoff and Johnson). Am. Speech **57**: 128–134.

27. CHOMSKY, N. 1965. Aspects of the Theory of Syntax. MIT Press. Cambridge, MA.

28. RICHARDS, I. A. 1936. The Philosophy of Rhetoric. Oxford University Press. Oxford, England.

29. PERRINE, L. 1971. Four Forms of Metaphor. College English **33**: 125–138.

30. CLARK, H. & P. LUCY. 1975. Understanding what is said from what is meant: A study in conversationally conveyed requests. J. Verb. Learn. Verb. Behav. **14**: 56–72.

31. ANDERSON, R. & A. ORTONY. 1975. On putting apples into bottles: Problem of polysemy. Cognit. Psychol. **7**: 167–180.

32. MILLER, G. 1979. Images and models, similes, and metaphors. *In* Metaphor and Thought. A. Ortony, Ed. Cambridge University Press. Cambridge, England.

33. BREWER, W. & J. BOCK. 1975. Comprehension and memory of the literal and

figurative meaning of proverbs. Unpublished manuscript. Department of Psychology, University of Illinois, Urbana, IL.

34. BREWER, W., R. HARRIS & E. BREWER. 1976. Comprehension of literal and figurative meaning. Unpublished manuscript. University of Illinois, Urbana, IL.

35. DORFMUELLER, M. & R. HONECK. 1981. Centrality and generativity within a linguistic family: Toward a conceptual base theory of groups. Psychol. Rec. **30:** 95–109.

36. GILDEA, P. & S. GLUCKSBERG. 1983. On understanding metaphor: The role of context. J. Verb. Learn. Verb. Behav. **22:** 577–590.

37. HARRIS, R. 1976. Comprehension of metaphors: A test of the two-stage processing model. Bull. Psychonom. Soc. **8:** 312–314.

38. HARRIS, R. & F. HALL. 1971. The Use of Imagery in Remembering Metaphors. Human Information Processing Institute Report 77-2, Kansas State University Psychological Series, Manhattan, KS.

39. HARRIS, R. 1979. Memory for metaphors. J. Psycholinguist. Res. **8:** 61–71.

40. PETRUN, C. & S. BELMORE. 1981. Metaphor comprehension and cognitive effort. Paper presented at the convention of the Eastern Psychological Association.

41. HOFFMAN, R. R. 1976. Conceptual Similarity among the Interpretations of Anomalous Sentences. Ph.D. thesis, Department of Psychology, University of Cincinnati, Cincinnati, OH.

42. HOFFMAN, R. & R. HONECK. 1976. The bidirectionality of judgments of synonymy. J. Psycholinguist. Res. **5:** 173–183.

43. HONECK, R. P. 1973. Semantic similarity between sentences. J. Psycholinguist. Res. **2:** 137–151.

44. HONECK, R. P. 1973. Interpretive vs. structural effects on semantic memory. J. Verb. Learn. Verb. Behav. **12:** 448–455.

45. HONECK, R. P., P. RIECHMANN & R. HOFFMAN. 1975. Semantic memory for metaphor: The conceptual base hypothesis. Mem. Cognit. **3:** 309–415.

46. HONECK, R., B. SOWRY & K. VOEGTLE. 1978. Proverbial understanding in a pictorial context. Child Dev. **49:** 327–331.

47. KROLL, N., A. KREISLER & R. BERRIAN. 1981. A metaphor is like a foggy day: Developing an empirical basis for the understanding of metaphors. *In* Conditioning, cognition, and methodology: Contemporary Issues in Experimental Psychology. J. Sidowski, Ed. Erlbaum. Hillsdale, NJ.

48. MALGADY, R. & M. G. JOHNSON. 1980. Measurement of figurative language: Semantic feature models of comprehension and appreciation. *In* Cognition and Figurative Language. R. P. Honeck & R. R. Hoffman, Eds. Erlbaum. Hillsdale, NJ.

49. Malgady, R. & M. Johnson. 1976. Modifiers in metaphors: Effects of constituent phrase similarity on the interpretation of figurative sentences. J. Psycholinguist. Res. **5:** 43–52.

50. POLLIO, H. & M. SMITH. 1979. Sense and nonsense in thinking about anomaly and metaphor. Bull. Psychon. Soc. **13:** 323–326.

51. RIECHMANN, P. & E. COSTE. 1980. Mental imagery and the comprehension of figurative language. *In* Cognition and Figurative Language. R. P. Honeck & R. R Hoffman, Eds. Erlbaum. Hillsdale, NJ.

52. KEMPER, S. 1981. Comprehension and the interpretation of proverbs. J. Psycholinguist. Res. **10:** 179–198.

53. MARKS, L. & G. MILLER. 1964. The role of semantic and syntactic constraints in the memorization of English sentences. J. Verb. Learn. Verb. Behav. **3:** 1–5.

54. MILLER, G. & S. ISARD. 1963. Some perceptual consequences of violating linguistics rules. J. Verb. Learn. Verb. Behav. **2**: 217–228.
55. POLLIO, H. & B. BURNS. 1977. The anomaly of anomaly. J. Psycholinguist. Res. **6**: 247–260.
56. HOFFMAN, R. & R. HONECK. 1979. "She laughed his joy and she cried his grief": Psycholinguistic theory and anomaly. Psychol. Rec. **29**: 321–328.
57. HONECK, R. P. & R. R. HOFFMAN. 1979. Synonymy and anomaly. Bull. Psychon. Soc. **14**: 37–40.
58. JOHNSON, M. G. & R. MALGADY. 1980. Toward a perceptual theory of metaphoric comprehension. *In* Cognition and Figurative Language. R. P. Honeck & R. R. Hoffman, Eds. Erlbaum. Hillsdale, NJ.
59. STEINBERG, D. 1975. Semantic universals in sentence processing and interpretation. J. Psycholinguist. Res. **4**: 169–193.
60. POLLIO, H., M. FABRIZI, A. SILLS & M. SMITH. 1981. Is metaphor comprehension a period derived process? Department of Psychology, University of Tennessee, Knoxville, TN. Unpublished manuscript.
61. POLLIO, H. & M. SMITH. 1980. Metaphoric competence and complex human problem solving. *In* Cognition and Figurative Language. R. P. Honeck & R. R. Hoffman, Eds. Erlbaum. Hillsdale, NJ.
62. PAIVIO, A. 1979. Imagery and Verbal Processes. Erlbaum. Hillsdale, NJ.
63. HONECK, R. P., K. VOEGTLE, M. DORFMUELLER, & R. R. HOFFMAN. 1980. Proverbs, meaning, and group structure. *In* Cognition and Figurative Language. R. P. Honeck & R. R. Hoffman, Eds. Erlbaum. Hillsdale, NJ.
64. HIGBEE, K. & R. MILLARD. 1981. Effects of imagery value and an imagery mnemonic on memory for savings. Bull. Psychon. Soc. **17**: 215–216.
65. HARRIS, R. M. LAHEY & F. MARSALEK. 1980. Metaphors and images: Rating, reporting, and remembering. *In* Cognition and Figurative Language. R. P. Honeck & R. R. Hoffman, Eds. Erlbaum. Hillsdale, NJ.
66. McCABE, A. 1980. Memory for metaphor. Paper presented at the annual convention of the Eastern Psychological Association.
67. McCABE, A. 1981. Memory for metaphor in the context of spontaneous speech. Paper presented at the annual convention of the American Psychological Association.
68. VERBRUGGE, R. & N. McCARRELL. 1977. Metaphoric comprehension: Studies in reminding and resembling. Cognit. Psychol. **9**: 494–533.
69. FRANKLIN, L. & G. DEHART. 1981. The cued recall of proverbs as a function of comprehension. Paper presented at the annual convention of the Midwest Psychological Association.
70. ARTER, J. L. 1976. Affects of Metaphor on Reading Comprehension. Doctoral dissertation, Department of Psychology, University of Illinois, Urbana, IL.
71. HOFER, E. F. An Exploratory Study to Investigate the Effects of Figurative Language on the Comprehension of Expository Text. Master's thesis, Department of Psychology, University of Illinois, Urbana, IL.
72. THIBADEAU, R. 1980. The metaphor metaphor: A clue to language understanding. paper presented at the annual convention of the American Psychological Association.
73. RUSSELL, S. W. 1976. Computer understanding of metaphorically used verbs. Am. J. Comput. Linguistics. **44**: 1–73.
74. CARBONELL, J. 1981. Metaphor — a key to extensible semantic analysis. Proceedings of the Annual Convention of the American Computational Linguistics Society: 17–21.
75. KEMPER, S. 1978. The role of conversational implication in proverb compre-

hension. Paper presented at the Fourth Annual Interdisciplinary Conference on Linguistics, University of Kentucky, Louisville, KY.

76. KROLL, N., R. BERRIAN & A. KREISLER. 1978. The comprehension and memory of similes as a function of context. *In* Practical Aspects of Memory. H. Gruneberg, P. Morris & R. Sykes, Eds. Academic Press. New York, NY.

77. KEMPER, S. & R. ESTILL. 1981. Interpreting idioms. Paper presented at the annual convention of the American Psychological Association.

78. GIBBS, R. 1980. Spilling the beans on understanding and meaning for idioms in conversation. Mem. Cognit. **8**: 149–156.

79. GIBBS, R. 1981. Understanding metaphoric utterances in discourse. Paper presented at the annual convention of the American Psychological Association.

80. ORTONY, A., D. SCHALLERT, R. REYNOLDS & S. ANTOS. 1978. Interpreting metaphors and idioms: Some effects of context on comprehension. J. Verb. Learn. Verb. Behav. **17**: 465–477.

81. BOBROW, S. & S. BELL. 1973. On catching on to idiomatic expressions. Mem. Cognit. **1**: 343, 346.

82. SWINNEY, D. & A. CUTLER. 1979. The access and processing of idiomatic expressions. J. Verb. Learn. Verb. Behav. **18**: 523–534.

83. SWINNEY, D. 1980. On the time course of processing idioms. Paper presented at the annual convention of the American Psychological Association.

84. CLARK, H. & E. CLARK. 1978. The Psychology of Language. Harcourt Brace Jovanovich. New York, NY.

85. HANSON, R. 1982. A systematic investigation of the similarity and contrast models in categorical and metaphorical processing. Paper presented at the annual convention of the American Psychological Association.

86. HOFFMAN, R. & J. NEAD. 1981. Contextualist ontology: A new metaphor for cognitive science. Paper presented at the annual meeting of the American Psychological Association.

87. HOFFMAN, R. & J. NEAD. 1983. General contextualism, ecological science and cognitive research. J. Mind Behav. **4**: 507–560.

88. CHANDRASEKARAN, B. 1981. Natural and social system metaphors for distributed problem solving. IEEE Trans. Systems, Man Cybern. **11**: 1–5.

89. CRITELLI, J. 1981. The metaphor of mind as behavior. Paper presented at the convention of the American Psychological Association.

90. HOFFMAN, R. R. 1980. Metaphor in science. *In* Cognition and Figurative Language. R. Honeck & R. Hoffman, Eds. Erlbaum. Hillsdale, NJ.

91. BRACHMAN, R. J. & B. C. SMITH. 1980. Special issue on knowledge representation. SIGART Newsletter, No. 70, February.

92. VERBRUGGE, R. 1980. Transformations in knowing. *In* Cognition and Figurative Language. R. P. Honeck & R. R. Hoffman, Eds. Erlbaum. Hillsdale, NJ.

93. GORDON, R. 1961. Synectics. Harper & Row. New York, NY.

94. BLACK, M. 1962. Models and Metaphors. Cornell University Press. Ithaca, NY.

95. BOYD, R. 1979. Metaphor and theory change: What is "metaphor?" *In* Metaphor and Thought. A. Ortony, Ed. Cambridge University Press. Cambridge, England.

96. HESSE, M. 1966. Models and Analogies in Science. University of Notre Dame Press. Notre Dame, IN.

97. JONES, R. 1980. Physics as Metaphor. University of Minnesota Press. Minneapolis, MN.

98. PITTS, M., H. POLLIO & M. K. SMITH. 1982. An evaluation of three different series of metaphor production through the use of an intentional category

mistake procedure. J. Psycholinguist. Res. **11**: 347–368.

99.   GENTNER, D. 1980. The role of analogical models in learning scientific topics. Paper presented at the annual convention of the American Psychological Association.

100. GENTNER, D. 1979. The Structure of Analogical Models in Science. Technical Report No. NR 157–482. Office of Naval Research.

101. CARROLL, J. & J. THOMAS. 1980. Metaphor and the Cognitive Representation of Computing Systems. Report RC 8302. IBM Research Division. Yorktown Heights, NY.

102. ROEDIGER, H. 1980. Memory metaphors in cognitive psychology. Mem. Cognit. **8**: 231–246.

103. KATZ, J. & J. FODOR. 1963. The structure of a semantic theory. Language **39**: 170–210.

104. VONDRUSKA, R. & A. ORTONY. 1980. Metaphor and Similarity. Paper presented at the annual convention of The American Psychological Association.

105. VONDRUSKA, R. 1982. The role of similarity and prediction in the comprehension of metaphor. Paper presented at the annual convention of the American Psychological Association.

106. DENT, C. & C. W. DENT. 1982. Cognitive dimensions of the metaphor. Paper presented at the Annual Meeting of the American Psychological Association.

107. JOHNSON, J. & J. PASCUAL-LEONE. 1981. Metaphoric processing in children and adults. Paper presented at the annual convention of the American Psychological Association.

108. BALTES, P. 1980. On the potential and limits of child development. Newsl. Soc. Res. Child. Dev. (Summer): 1.

109. JENKINS, J. J. 1980. Can we have a fruitful cognitive psychology? *In* Nebraska Symposium on Motivation. H. Howe, Ed. University of Nebraska Press. Lincoln, NE.

110. TURVEY, M., R. SHAW, E. REED & W. MACE. 1981. Ecological laws of perceiving and acting. Cognition **9**: 237–304.

111. FEINSTEIN, H. 1982. The effects of relaxed attention exercises on the metaphoric interpretation of paintings. Department of Art Education, University of Cincinnati, Cincinnati, OH. Manuscript in preparation.

112. GUCK, M. 1982. Metaphoric responses to music. Department of Music, University of Michigan, Ann Arbor, MI. Manuscript in preparation.

113. NYBERG, A., ED. 1983. Secretariat News **37** (1): 3.

114. TAYLOR, M. & A. ORTONY. 1981. Figurative Devices in Black Language. Report No. 20, Center for the Study of Reading, University of Illinois, Urbana, IL.

115. KOCH, T. 1982. Idioms in Foreign Language Instruction. Gesamthochschule Kassel, West Germany. Manuscript in preparation.

116. HARWOOD, D. 1981. Comprehension of metaphor by the hearing-impaired. Paper presented at the annual convention of the American Psychological Association.

117. MCNEILL, D. 1981. Action, thought, and language. Cognition **10**: 201–208.

118. MCNEIL, D. & E. LEVY. 1982. Conceptual representations in language activity and gesture. *In* Speech Place, and Action. R. Jarvella & W. Klein, Eds. Wiley. New York, NY.

119. BILLOW, R., D. PALERMO, J. ROSSMAN & N. WOLOVSKY. 1981. The metaphoric process in schizophrenia. Paper presented at the annual convention of the American Psychological Association.

The Role of Metaphor in Our Perception of Language[a]

ROBERT R. VERBRUGGE[b]

Department of Psychology
University of Connecticut
Storrs, Connecticut 06268

> A *picture* held us captive. And we could not get outside it, for it lay in our language and language seemed to repeat it to us inexorably.[1]
> — LUDWIG WITTGENSTEIN

Our metaphors for language and cognition have constrained our perception of linguistic events in many ways. While these constraints have been fruitful for our perception of some properties, they have impeded our understanding of other important properties. The irony of this is that our metaphors for language have limited our perception of metaphor itself. As we become more sensitive to the metaphoric processes involved in our own efforts to understand metaphors, we should find it easier to avoid being trapped by the limitations of a single metaphoric view.

Before I discuss this problem directly, I would like to summarize my general approach to metaphoric phenomena. First, metaphor is not uniquely a *literary* phenomenon, limited to poetic discourse or poetic people. It is pervasive in ordinary language. Second, metaphor is not strictly a *linguistic* phenomenon. It is possible for perception, thought, and action to be metaphoric in the absence of language. Language can induce or express metaphoric perception or action, but the linguistic forms are not themselves metaphoric. Metaphor is better conceived to be a type of dynamic process in living systems — a process that can alter perception, thought, or action in particular ways, but does not necessarily have language as a catalyst or consequence. In short, metaphoric processes are a class of biological events, a class not limited to literary contexts, not limited to linguistic behavior, and perhaps not limited to humans.

A wide variety of phenomena have been called metaphoric or analogic, and it is not clear whether a singular definition can be given for this class of processes. Metaphoric language can provoke processes that are brief or long-term, private or social, that do or do not alter our understanding of a topic, that lead us to attend to a preexisting similarity or to create a new one, and that are fanciful or realistic in experienced quality. There is one type

[a] This paper is based on a talk entitled "The Groundwork of Metaphor," presented to the Linguistics Section of the New York Academy of Sciences on January 14, 1980, and on a talk entitled "The Role of Metaphor in Our Perception of Language," presented during a symposium entitled "Metaphor as Knowledge" at the meeting of the American Psychological Association, Montreal, September 1980.

[b] Address for correspondence: Robert R. Verbrugge, AT&T Bell Laboratories, Room 2B-638A, Crawfords Corner Road, Holmdel, New Jersey 07733.

of process that I find especially intriguing and most prototypic of the family of metaphoric processes. It is a process I call *transformational*, because it involves transforming one event into another event that was previously experienced as very different in kind.[2] The process is related to one that has been called "seeing as,"[1] which means roughly that a person experiences one thing as if it were another. For example, you might see a cloud as a lion, imagine a highway as a writhing snake, or perceive your own movements as catlike or bearlike.

The transformational process is typically *fanciful* in quality, since it alters conventional identities. It is *directional*, in that one event (the topic) is transformed by a second (the vehicle). It is *partial*, in that the topic is not completely reidentified as the vehicle (as seems to happen in some schizophrenic processes). And finally, it is *fusional*, because there is a plastic remodeling of the topic by the vehicle, rather than a preservation of separate identities. In all cases, perception of the topic is warped by constraints that typify the vehicle. This warping can be weird and useless, or it can be the starting point for a productive change in our sensitivity to structure in some event. In the latter case, metaphoric processes produce changes in *knowing*.

My focus in this paper is the role of metaphor in our efforts to understand linguistic events, including metaphor itself. For this purpose, I will need to construe "metaphor" broadly enough to include a variety of symbolization systems beyond spoken language, such as writing systems and diagrams. Similarly, the phrase "metaphoric processes" must be broad enough to include all of the transformational, cognitive processes that are supported by this full range of symbol systems.

I will focus on the potential *pitfalls* of metaphor as a path to knowledge about language, as exemplified in our own work as psychologists and linguists. While metaphor can initiate our perception of some aspects of structure, it can also *limit* our perception of the events of interest. As a result, it can be an impediment to explaining the full range of properties exhibited by those events. While this general principle may be obvious, its operation in practice is insidious and its effects are very difficult to unravel.

CONVENTIONAL WISDOM

Aided by the work of Reddy,[3] Lakoff and Johnson,[4] and others, I would like to sketch three of the metaphoric systems that have had a powerful influence on our understanding of cognition, meaning, and communication. These systems are found both in ordinary language and in theoretical language, they have historical roots as ancient as you please, and they may be our greatest impediment to progress in understanding linguistic processes.

Microcosm Metaphor

The first metaphoric system views mind as a miniature inner world, a replica or model of the outer world. The microcosm has *contents*, such as ideas and concepts, that correspond to objects in the world. One of these contents is an active agent, called the homunculus, spirit, or mind. Like people in the outer world, this agent is capable of many *actions:* viewing, manipulating, comparing, constructing, and so on. This pervasive metaphor has its roots at least as early as pre-Socratic speculations on perception and cognition, and has found its most recent expression in research on mental imagery.[5-7]

Contemporary models of language processes include numerous microcosmic metaphors. The notion of a "mental lexicon" implies, in part, that a mind comprehends a word by a process analogous to that employed in looking up the meaning of a word in a dictionary. Similarly, in many models of speech, it is assumed that a mind can listen or prepare to speak only by making reference to an internal model of the speaker's mouth (its anatomy, physiology, physical acoustics, and so forth). Not surprisingly, the internal models proposed for use by the mind are patterned closely on the models used by speech scientists for representing articulation in other people. It is convenient to assume that the representation systems we find useful in our own scientific activities are useful (even necessary) within the speech process itself.

There are several intuitive bases for this kind of metaphoric self-description. Perhaps the most powerful source is our range of imaginal experiences, those that occur in the absence of corresponding events in our immediate environment. These virtual experiences of objects and actions tend to shape the *explanations* we give for them — namely, we tend to attribute those experiences to the presence of internal objects (representations) in a mental microcosm. This is a seductive approach to "explaining" imaginal processes, but it is little more than description masquerading as explanation.

The microcosmic style of explanation has often been extended to a much wider range of psychological processes (perception, recollection, action, and so on). These processes are often attributed, in whole or in part, to mediation by microcosmic processes (internal representations and operations on them). This broadening of the microcosm assumes that imaginal events mediate everything we do, even when we are not conscious of them. The fruitfulness of this extended metaphor is open to question, and there are efforts underway to find alternative styles of explanation.[8-10] Several motivations for theoretical uses of the microcosm have been identified, and all are problematic. In visual perception, for example, it is often assumed that the light at an eye is largely uninformative about the world, and one is left with the puzzle of how we perceive a world in such rich detail. A common solution is to attribute this experience to a richly structured internal microcosm. However this still leaves unexplained how such a richly structured experience originates; the problem has simply been transplanted inward. Similarly, complex patterning in action (e.g., linguistic behavior) is often attributed to an internal patterning of a similar kind (e.g., knowledge of grammatical rules) on the assumption that the physical body itself is not inherently capable of complex action and exhibits it only when manipulated by an intricately structured mind. Again, this simply transplants the problem of how such regularities arise in a biological system, without explaining them.

Conduit Metaphor

The second metaphoric system, the *conduit metaphor*, is a metaphor for communication.[3] It views communication as a conduit, a channel through which mental contents (ideas, thoughts, and feelings) are carried from one person to another. Basic to this metaphor is the notion that meaning is somehow embodied in the carrier, that it is transported bodily from sender to receiver. Our expressions in English are "loaded" with this kind of meaning. The speaker puts meaning *into* words, and the listener *unpacks* the meaning from the words. In the meantime, the words are said to *contain* the meaning, they *carry* it, *convey* it. This metaphoric system extends the microcosm, by enabling homunculi in neighboring inner worlds to send each other ideas and thus to exchange knowledge.

Although this metaphoric system is patently absurd when made fully explicit, it nonetheless has a powerful influence on how we talk about symbols, texts, comprehension, and other aspects of communication. Perhaps the most problematic part of this metaphoric system is its reification of meaning. It treats meaning as an object. Meaning must therefore be *located* somewhere, in the mind (as an idea), the body (as a predisposition to act), or in the world (as something "contained" in printed or spoken words). At one extreme, this encourages the view that understanding can be exhaustively rendered in symbols themselves (in books, lectures, notations, diagrams, computers, and so forth), in isolation from *users* of those symbols. I would argue, on the contrary, that these symbol systems are only meaningful in relation to "educated" readers and listeners.

At the other extreme, the reification of meaning encourages the view that understanding is a set of subjective contents that cannot be externalized at all, but can be imposed freely on any symbols the person encounters. This radical subjectivism has no means of motivating regularities in symbol use or explaining occasions of effective communication.

In the middle ground is the view that words are a partial conduit, carrying only part of a communicator's subjective intent. This uneasy hybrid is the most common form of the conduit both in ordinary language and in theories of communication. Its problems as an explanatory tool arise from having to locate meaning both in people and in words, with varying degrees of match between the two. It might be more fruitful to talk of meaning not as an object to be located and moved, but as a property of an interaction among users and symbols. It may be possible to talk about the successful or meaningful use of symbols without referring to localized meanings at all.

Representation Metaphor

The third metaphoric system, fundamental to both the microcosm and the conduit, runs even deeper in our language and thought: the *representation* or *picture metaphor*. This metaphor views the components of language and mind as representations of the physical world; words and ideas are treated as substitutes or surrogates for that world. To *know* something is to possess a surrogate for it (an idea). To *communicate* is to send words that serve as surrogates for objects referred to; for example, we speak of *describing* something in words, or *painting a picture* with words.

There is an enormous literature discussing the types and qualities of representational relations, including the issue of whether they are best conceived as iconic (more picture-like) or arbitrary. The *underlying* metaphor treats these relations as basically iconic: the symbols "re-present" or "depict" aspects of the world (or body or mind). More precisely, elements or relations-over-elements in the symbol sytem are similar to elements or relations-over-elements in what is represented. In its weaker forms, the representation metaphor suggests only a *correspondence* between components of the symbols and what they represent. In this case, the symbols simply are "associated with" or "carry" a meaning, and the meaning is only "arbitrarily" related to the structure of the symbols.

The representation metaphor carries assumptions about the function of symbols as well as their structure. In particular, it promotes a preoccupation with the descriptive or depictive functions of symbols. In many accounts of knowledge, the prototypic representation is one that records "facts" about states-of-affairs in the world; the knowledge embodied in skill or action is not held to be prototypic. Tests for the *validity* of knowledge focus on the iconicity or correspondence between the representations and the states-of-affairs represented. In analyses of communication, there has been a corresponding preoccupation with the descriptive functions of written or spoken speech. To speak is to make statements about the world around us. To read a book is to view a series of events depicted by the author. The validity of a statement, book, diagram, and so forth is a function of how structure in the representation preserves that of actual events (either physical events or mental intentions).

When we stop to reflect on the problem, we discover that the descriptive functions of symbols probably have a more pervasive effect on our thinking than we would wish. We know that there are many other functions served by communication, and that considerable efforts have been devoted to their analysis in such fields as sociolinguistics, animal communication, speech act theory, and rhetoric. We know that there are serious limitations to the view that the meaning of a word is what it refers to, or that the validity of a theory, statement, or text depends on its isomorphism to observables. And yet when we talk about knowledge or symbolization, the metaphor of *representation* seems unavoidable (perhaps because it is so pervasive in colloquial language and thought). The consequences of this pervasive metaphor include the following: it leads to an overemphasis on correspondences between symbols and things even when this is not intended, and it tends to imply that symbols *embody* structure as isolated objects.

Alternatives are difficult to describe in detail, but at least the outlines of an alternative can be sketched if we adopt two changes in perspective. First, we can view knowledge and symbolization not as things, but as activities or processes. We can focus on the dynamics of cognitive activity or symbol use, rather than the properties of ideas or words. Second, we can view symbols as fundamentally *indexical*, in roughly the sense proposed by Peirce[11] (compare Alston,[12] and Verbrugge[13]). Indexes are integral components of events. They may be natural precursors of an event (such as thunderclouds on the horizon) or products of an event (such as footprints). More particularly, they are components of an event that can "signify" that event to a perceiver (i.e., they can catalyze appropriate activities, cognitive and otherwise). Indexes are neither iconic nor arbitrary with respect to the full event (though they may be structurally similar to *part* of the event). A hammer is not a "model" of a nail, a carpenter, or the act of hammering, nor is it arbitrarily related to them; there is a "natural fit" between them. The hammer can therefore be an index for any of them.

By extension, we can view *cognitive activity* as an index of the event someone is participating in. Thought is a natural component of that participation, and it need not bear any similarity to the event itself. Thus, the knowledge that permits us to act need not be viewed as a model of the world in which we act.

By a similar extension, we can view all forms of *external symbolization* as indexes of the activities of the people who shape them. Symbols are both products of those activities and catalysts for such activities. When considering the function of a symbol, it is irrelevant (or at best secondary) whether the symbol resembles any other component of the event it is a part of. The critical question to ask of a word, a novel, a diagram, a stop sign, a curve sign, and so forth, is how it selectively catalyzes human activities (smiling, imagining an event, understanding a proof, hitting the brakes, preparing for a curve in the road, and so on). Resemblance can *support* such functions (as in the case of a diagram, a landscape painting, the curved arrow on a curve sign, etc.), but it is not the essential ingredient.

What *is* essential? It seems to have more to do with a systematic "fit" between the symbol and the rest of the event it is a part of. A rough analogy is the fit between a catalyst and the chemical reaction it catalyzes.[13] As catalysts, both chemicals and symbols can facilitate and direct a process, without necessarily resembling other components of the process or embodying its outcome. Local isomorphisms (e.g., between two chemicals, or between symbols and actions) are only one of many factors that shape the resulting dynamics, and thus are only one contributor to defining an effective fit between the catalyst and the process as a whole. (There is an important difference between chemical catalysts and symbols, however. The fit of chemical "indexes" does not, outside of living systems, develop through a history of interaction. The fit of human symbols is far more labile.)

From this alternative perspective (viewing symbols as indexical components of processes), two limitations of the representation metaphor are especially clear: it tends to overemphasize a property (iconicity) that is irrelevant or secondary to symbol use, and it tends to focus on symbols as isolated meaning-bearing objects, rather than components of interactions among people, symbols, events, and other people.

One consequence of treating symbols too iconically can be to permit irrelevant properties of the symbol to intrude on our perception of events. This is a metaphorically induced paralysis: a particular representation serves as the only vehicle by which we come to understand the topic at hand. Representations do not *necessarily* serve metaphoric functions for their users (indeed, metaphoric processes are only one of many kinds of processes that symbolic indexes can catalyze). When they do act metaphorically, however, they are as prone to conceal as reveal. This problem is the focus of the next section.

EXTERNAL REPRESENTATION AS METAPHOR

The mischief created by representation systems can be broken down into two types: the mischief created by *external representations* (such as speech, written orthographies, formulas, and notation systems of all kinds), and the mischief created by *internal representations* (the hypothetical residents of mind). Unraveling the "internal representation" metaphor would be a long and arduous task; I will restrict myself here to some of the consequences of *external* representations.

Perhaps the most important danger of external representation is that the structure of the notation system can affect our perception of the event being notated, whether the notation is intended to be iconic or not. The notation will, in any case, be only partially structure-preserving and it will also have structural properties not shared by the event. Treating the notation as a *metaphor* for the event can therefore have two effects: first, it can limit perception of the event to those properties preserved iconically in the current notation system; and second, it can lead to ascribing extraneous properties of the notation system to the event itself. Clearly, these effects are not unavoidable — otherwise understanding would stagnate. It is interesting to note that as understanding changes, notation systems themselves evolve to record the altered perception.

A few examples of this kind of effect will probably be helpful, before I look at the metaphoric influence our notation systems have had on our studies of meaning and of metaphor itself. My first (and most detailed) example will seem rather distant at first, for it concerns the history of chemistry in the 1800s.[c]

The events of interest to nineteenth-century chemists were reactions involving chemical compounds. These compounds were represented by a variety of notations. In the early and mid 1800s, most chemists were content to manipulate formulas that summarized the *total* number of atoms of each type (carbon, hydrogen, and so on); an example would be C_6H_6. Subgroupings of atoms were also indicated to represent families of compounds with similar reactive properties. Four types of groupings were recognized: H_2O, H_2, HCl, and NH_3; all other groupings (no matter how large the compound) fell into one of these four types. In effect, these formulas provided a simple syntax of compounds, capable of generating novel combinations which could then be sought in the laboratory. The system was adequate for denoting *some* regularities in composition and reactive properties, but there were annoying

[c] Background information for this example derives from the following sources: Japp,[14] Anschütz,[15,16] Winderlich,[17] Ihde,[18] Findlay,[19] and Gillis.[20]

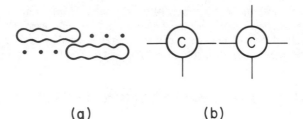

(a)   (b)

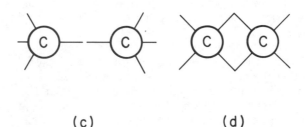

(c)   (d)

FIGURE 1. Kekulé's early formulas: **(a)** sausage model of carbon atom (illustrated here in formula for ethane, C_2H_6); **(b)** circle-and-line model of carbon atom (two-dimensional projection of a "flat" ball-and-stick model); **(c)** tetrahedral model of carbon atom (two-dimensional projection of a "three-dimensional" ball-and-stick model); **(d)** model of double bond (illustrated here in formula for ethylene, C_2H_4, using the circle-and-line notation).

exceptions. For example, there were many pairs of compounds with the same structural formula, but different functional properties (a kind of formal ambiguity). The complementary problem was also noted: a single compound with a single set of functional properties could have multiple structural formulas; for example, ethane could be $(C_2H_5)(H)$ or $(CH_3)(CH_3)$. Defenders of the formulas would argue that they were intended for notational convenience in classifying compounds; they were not intended to represent the internal structure of the substances themselves, and they were open to only limited proof or disproof by tests of a compound's functional properties in reactions. In spite of these denials, it was clear that much of the motivation for the formulas came from functional considerations. Moreover, since the formulas were, in practice, guiding chemists' perception of chemical events, they had become a barrier to understanding the kinds of anomalies noted above.

The German chemist Kekulé was one of the first to begin thinking of the architecture of compounds in terms distinct from the structure of these conventional written formulas. He visualized compounds in two and three dimensions, as chains of atoms of various sizes, and sought to work out the internal architecture of the groupings in the old formulas. He worked out the theory of valences (roughly, the idea that each type of atom forms a constant number of linkages to neighboring atoms — for example, carbon has four bonds, while hydrogen has only one). He tried out new notations to represent these valences: one depicted carbon atoms as "sausages" with four positions for linkages (FIGURE 1a); another depicted carbon as a circle with four lines at 90° angles (FIGURE 1b). Using wooden balls and brass rods, he built corresponding "ball-and-stick" models for use in teaching. By casting their shadows on a blackboard, he could produce a structural formula and illustrate the relation between the formula and the structure of the object itself. While this relation was relatively trivial when the models were "flat" (as in FIGURE 1b), the projection technique became a more powerful tool when three-dimensional models of atoms were introduced. For example, Kekulé later introduced a tetrahedral model of carbon, yielding formulas like that in FIGURE 1c.

Kekulé's architectural approach to compounds was able to break the constraints of the old formulas on imagined chemical structures. Kekulé's vision of carbon compounds as *chains* of carbon atoms opened new possibilities for explanation and prediction, and permitted resolution of many of the earlier ambiguities. For example, many of the pairs of compounds that appeared to have the same composition and formula, but different properties, could be shown to have *different* structures, with component groupings in mirror-image positions. In the complementary case, where the old system provided multiple formulas for a single compound, Kekulé's could provide a single, unambiguous structural description.

However, there were several families of compounds that could not be explained in terms of his chain-like structures. One family was the "unsaturated" compounds. Kekulé's solution here was to permit "double bonds" between adjacent carbon atoms (as illustrated in FIGURE 1d). A more difficult family was the "aromatic" compounds, including benzene, whose reactive properties could not be rationalized by any of the possible chain structures generated by Kekulé's theory. Benzene, for example, had only six carbon atoms and six hydrogen atoms. These could be arranged in a chain of six carbon atoms with four double bonds and one single bond in various positions, but none of these arrangements could explain the energy associated with benzene's reactions or the kinds of compounds that could be formed with it.

In retrospect, we can see that the problem was the assumption that the *chain* structure would serve to represent all carbon compounds. The new notation had itself become a barrier to understanding. Recognition of this struck Kekulé suddenly one night while he was dozing off before the fire. He was dreaming, as he often did, about atoms and chains. On this occasion, the chains were "twining and twisting in snake-like motion." Suddenly "one of the snakes . . . seized hold of its own tail, and the form whirled mockingly before [his] eyes."[14] In this metaphoric transformation, the familiar image of a snake swallowing its tail prompted Kekulé to imagine a similar structure on one of the carbon chains. This was the origin of Kekulé's insight that the carbons in the benzene nucleus of aromatic compounds are arranged in a *ring* (closed chain) structure rather than an open chain.

The ring structure, like the chain, permitted explanation of a wide range of properties that had earlier seemed anomalous, and corresponding ring *no-*

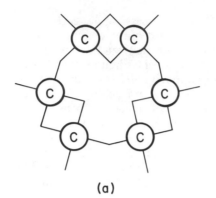

(a)

FIGURE 2. (a) Kekulé's early ring formula for benzene. (b) Modernized schematic diagram of Kekulé's oscillation formula for benzene.

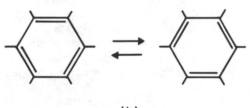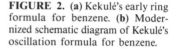

(b)

tations were developed as an aid to thought and communication. One of Kekulé's early formulas is illustrated in FIGURE 2a. More than a matter of convenience, these formulas became integral to the experimental analysis of benzene's properties and were a subject of much contention among different researchers. For example, some researchers noted that Kekulé's formula (FIGURE 2a) did not correctly predict the variety of "substitution" compounds benzene could form. Kekulé proposed a solution to this problem that again broke with notational conventions: he proposed that benzene oscillates in form between one ring structure and another. In effect, he was arguing that change is inherent to the "structure" of benzene; benzene is as much an event as a structure.

This insight demanded a new notation that would represent *change* over time, since all earlier notations had treated chemicals as static forms, abstracted out of time. Here the limitations of written notations as *iconic* indexes become especially salient: written marks can depict traces of events, or cross-sections of events in progress, but not the change itself. Kekulé's solution (one that has been carried down into more recent texts) was to represent benzene by the endpoints of the oscillation between two structures (FIGURE 2b). This represented a tremendous advance from the old formulas with which he began his career. It reflected his concern that chemical notations must not simply denote a compound, but must depict critical aspects of its spatial and temporal structure. Accuracy of *iconic* properties was important, in this case, if the notations were to be useful indexes for chemical researchers. In short, Kekulé wanted the best visual metaphors for chemical events that he could find.

This story from a distant land and time has several potential morals for students of language. First, it illustrates how a representation system can both liberate and constrain the imaginal activities of a user. On the constraining side, it is clear that a representation system can confine one's perception of an event to the properties currently represented, thereby limiting the types of properties that can be explained and that one even seeks to explain. In particular, a notation system can support the perception that the "event" being notated is, like the notation itself, essentially static in form, abstracted out of time. At its worst, this can lead to viewing dynamic or functional properties of the event as being irrelevant to its underlying form. Linguistic theories that seek sharp distinctions between competence and performance, language and paralanguage, semantics and pragmatics, phonology and phonetics, and so on, all risk this error.

Second, this story suggests that a *new perception of structure* is a major impetus for the development of notation systems, and that notations, at their best, are *derivative* from the dynamic event as newly perceived. Giving primacy to a notation system is a treacherous inversion of this relationship. It implies that the notation is the primary guide to perception, that perception must be derivative from some currently favored notation. Allegiance to particular representation systems is common in linguistics and psycholinguistics, sometimes motivated explicitly (e.g., by reference to deep-rooted mental structures), and sometimes more a product of convenience or tradition (e.g., the use of particular physical descriptors for speech acoustics). As Kekulé's example makes clear, scientific understanding develops only when we are prepared to reshape our representation systems in fundamental ways.

Finally, the story suggests that it is dangerous to impose any single formalism onto all of the events one is investigating. While it is natural and desirable to look for generality of this kind, premature selection of a "universal form" renders the notation incapable of handling important qualitative differences. As Kekulé and other chemists discovered, no single structure or set of types was adequate to represent the qualitative differences among the various families of chemical compounds. Linguistics and psychology face similar problems of explaining a wide variety of utterances, languages, conversational styles, and literary genres. We would need a crystal ball to identify with certainty the alluring generalities that now stand in the way of understanding this diversity. However, we need to consider the possibility that they include such formal conventions as binary oppositions, the universal phonetic alphabet, feature sets, associative networks, predicate calculi, story grammars, and other notations in common currency.

Examples of the constraining (and liberating) effects of notations can be found throughout the history of linguistics and in every subdivision of the field (including phonetics, syntax, and semantics). Developing this history in detail is clearly beyond my scope in this paper. Instead, I would like to present a few examples drawn from recent linguistic history that are particularly salient for me. I will begin with some brief examples from phonetics and syntax, and then turn to related problems in the semantics of metaphor.

External representations of many kinds have had a strong impact on the development of theories of phonetics and speech perception. In particular, alphabetic orthographies and other phonetic transcription systems have influenced how we conceptualize speech events, and they have arguably impeded progress in speech research. Alphabetic writing is a frozen metaphor for speech. It depicts some important properties of speech events as we perceive them; in particular, we can perceive speech as an ordering of discrete components of relatively stable identity. In alphabetic writing, these components are represented by sequences of nonoverlapping letters. This graphic representation has no doubt promoted the common-sense view that, in speech itself, phonemes are arrayed like "beads on a string." This simple structural view has proved to be a very poor guide to understanding the dynamic events of articulation and acoustics, in which phonemes appear to merge continuously and to be highly variable in expression.[21,22] Some researchers have suggested that phonemes can be characterized as "overlapping" gestures whose onsets are ordered.[23] This approach preserves a kind of discreteness for phonemes in production, but it rejects the idea that phonemes are *successive* elements (like letters on a page) at any stage in production; in particular, there is no planning stage at which utterances are represented in strings analogous to linguists' phonetic representations. Instead, phonemes are viewed essentially as interdependent actions of a complex biomechanical system, and therefore need to be defined in terms of the substantive structures and dynamics of that system. As in the case of chemical formulas, it follows that notation systems for speech must model as much of the internal architecture and dynamics of the speech event as is possible. If this approach is fruitful, future advances in understanding speech may gain more from biophysical notations or notations for movement (e.g., for locomotion or dance), than from the structure of alphabetic or phonetic notation systems.

The study of speech has also been strongly influenced by the physical descriptors and graphic displays used to characterize its acoustic structure. Spectrograms, oscillograms, and other displays have proven very useful in research on speech, and have given rise to a corresponding vocabulary of acoustic components and measures (transitions, steady states, silences, center formant frequencies, durations, and so forth). It is a common mistake to treat these displays as if they *define* the event (exhaustively or objectively). Speech is not simply the collage of acoustic segments visible on a spectrogram. It is easy to forget that acoustic displays are no more than visual metaphors for acoustic events. They index these events, but only partially embody their structure. Like any representation viewed metaphorically, these displays are necessarily partial in iconic function, and can as easily obscure structure as reveal it. No one has yet developed a generally successful system for speech recognition based on the kinds of properties represented in these displays. One of the major barriers to progress in this area may be the kinds of graphic representations that currently govern our conceptions of speech.

A final example, also from recent linguistic history, concerns syntax. The structure of our writing system promotes the perception of language as a chain of words, or as a series of nested phrases. Thus, the notation system provides intuitive support for any grammar that identifies words, word classes, or phrase structures as the principal components of language structure. Transformational syntax, whatever its faults, sought to break the perceptual grip of these surface structure properties, and it identified properties that could only be accounted for by structures of a different order. Written sentences, like spectrograms, are visual metaphors that only partially index the structure of speech events at the sentence level. Transformational grammar sought to identify organizational principles that were not manifest in the surface regularities of written sentences and that were not captured in the many kinds of phrase structure notations in general use. Its success may have been limited most by its efforts to distance these principles from the dynamics of performance. If the history of chemistry is a good analogical guide, the most useful linguistic "formulas" (syntaxes) of the future will be motivated by viewing language as a dynamic event (including its full temporal, biomechanical, and interpersonal structure), not as a set of rules for arranging elements.

METAPHORS AND MEANING

Let me return now to the problems of linguistic meaning and metaphor, and to the irony with which I began: our conventional metaphors for communication and mind may be hindering our understanding of metaphor itself. The problematic metaphors include not only the three metaphoric systems outlined earlier, but also a variety of notation systems used to represent meaning. These conventional metaphors pose several problems for developing an adequate theory of metaphoric meaning.

One problem is that, in some respects, we have viewed our formalisms for language as self-contained systems that exhaustively represent the phenomena of interest. In particular, they are treated as if they contain or even *embody* meaning. But the formalisms are not really the appropriate medium in which to define such properties as meaning or significance, since these are properties of *relations* holding over language users and the signs they use. Meaning is not contained in words or sentences, as the conduit metaphor suggests. To say that words *have* meaning or *contain* meaning is to indulge in synecdoche, to attribute a property of the whole to a part — in this case, a property of a linguistic event to the component sign. It is useful shorthand to speak of word meaning or sentence meaning, but it seems to me to be fallacious to suggest that "a sentence has a meaning" in isolation from a user and a context of use. One implication of this is that efforts to define metaphoric sentences or metaphoric quality cannot gain closure in a self-contained logic that makes no reference to processes in a language user. Thus, it is not strictly appropriate to ask whether a particular sentence is a metaphor, or whether it is a metaphor of high quality.

A second problem also derives from the study of symbols in isolation from their full dynamic context, and that is an overemphasis on the arbitrariness of the relation between symbol and referent. To focus on arbitrariness requires at least two treacherous steps of analysis: first, *isolate* symbol and referent from their natural context (including their relation to human users), and second, *compare* them (on the assumption that their relationship to each other is essentially representational). It is generally agreed that, in natural languages at least, the *representational* relation between symbols and things is largely arbitrary (noniconic). Other investigators, looking at the broader range of human symbol systems, may argue that representational relations are better viewed as fundamentally iconic, with departures from this norm coming only by degrees.[24] My own preference is to view the relation between symbols and *users* as fundamental, and to see this relation as *indexical*, rather than to view the fundamental relation as that between symbols and things.[13] We should be in the business of investigating indexical relationships between symbols and people, not the rules relating signs and meanings. In particular, as students of metaphor, we should seek to define and explain the array of symbol-user interactions that are *metaphoric* in nature, considering this as just one of many types of indexical relations.[d]

The representational view of symbols is one type of metaphoric interaction between people and symbols; specifically, it is an interaction in which we treat a symbol as a substitute or likeness for some other aspect of our world. While this metaphoric approach to symbols is of limited value as a *general* theory of how symbols function, it is *one* way in which we use symbols and thus deserves attention as a special case. As noted throughout this paper, iconic and metaphoric uses of symbols are common, if not always desirable or productive. On these occasions (when a symbol is treated *as representation*), the iconicity of the symbol becomes a relevant issue and the literature focusing on iconicity and arbitrariness can serve as a useful guide. However, the iconicity of a symbol *in use* is not simply a function of the similarity of symbol and referent, judged in some observer-neutral fashion. It depends also on the situation, the task, and the person involved. Iconicity is not a property inhering in the symbol itself, but is a way of describing the influence of that symbol on someone who reads or hears it. The important question to ask is whether the form of a symbol is active metaphorically in shaping someone's perception or action. This strikes me as a more productive way to phrase the traditional issue of iconicity versus arbitrariness.

A third problem with most logics and notations for language is that they are atemporal, abstracted from time. While they may partially represent temporal order in terms of spatial order, they fail in general to represent any of the dynamic relations that characterize comprehension and production of speech. The consequence of this for metaphor is that these static notations provide a poor starting point for explaining many of the dynamic properties

---

[d] It should be noted that there is no inherent contradiction in saying that symbol-user interactions can be both *indexical* and partially *iconic*. There are many cases where some aspect of the form of an index is preserved in the process it catalyzes, or where its form mimics some aspect of the event that it indexes. In natural languages, the classic example of this is onomatopoeia, but there are also more subtle iconicities involving temporal patterning and proximity relations (e.g., see Lakoff and Johnson,[4] Chapt. 20). The presence of an iconic component in such cases does *not* refute the general principle that all symbols operate indexically. It simply demonstrates that some indexes achieve their effects, in part, through similarity of structure.

of metaphoric processes—for example, the time course of a metaphoric process, the degree of permanence of the changes in perceptual sensitivity that result, and the shifts in direction of transformation over time. As in the case of benzene, we need to recognize that sentences and meanings are not *structures*, but *events* (or properties of events), and we need to develop notations to index that perception.

A fourth problem has to do with the types of structures we use for representing events in symbols (such as feature lists, predicate calculi, networks, and the like). The symbols in these notation systems fail to denote many other aspects of the process besides its temporal organization. Even so, we often proceed as if those unexplicated properties *are* embodied in our notations, not our interactions with them. For example, if we say that the metaphor *Juliet is the sun* means that *Juliet is like the sun* because both *Juliet* and *the sun* have the feature "radiant," we are playing a slippery game.[25] Certainly the *label* "radiant" (associated with Juliet) is identical to the *label* "radiant" (associated with the sun), but radiance in a person is not identical to radiance of the sun. Our ability to detect a similarity even so, and to choose a common label to denote it, depends itself on a metaphoric process. If we use common features (labels) to *represent* metaphoric meanings, those features cannot themselves depend on metaphoric interpretation, if we wish to avoid infinite regress. Semantic representations for metaphor do not (and cannot) exhaust the experiences we have on reading them. They are indexes, capable of catalyzing far more than they can embody. Our ability to read these *representations* with understanding is as mysterious as our ability to read the metaphors on which they are based.

The semantic representations proposed for metaphoric meanings are disturbingly *post hoc* and incomplete.[26,27] They only partially label the results of a process, and they do not begin to explain the process itself. However agreeable they may seem in what they *do* represent, they are seriously incomplete in representing the full impact of a metaphor on a comprehender. As a result, they provide little basis for predicting the kinds of processes or commonalities that will underlie the comprehension of novel cases. I suspect one reason for this is the tendency of these representation systems to assimilate all objects and events into a single structural grid, and to simply label a feature or predicate, instead of noting the finer grain of physical relationships that underlie our perception of that property. If a semantics of language is to be useful to us, it must be cast in terms of the full range of physical invariants that underlie our perception and action. The events in which we participate (and which provide the fuel for our metaphoric activity) are highly diverse. No single type of representation can handle this range of events, without severely distorting or occluding what we wish to explain. A single representation system serves our needs no better than the early formulas would serve modern chemistry.

A final problem with our notation systems is that their graphic structure, acting metaphorically, encourages inappropriate views of the comprehension process. For example, the separation of lexical items in speech, writing, and other representation systems has encouraged the view that the topic and vehicle of a metaphor are functionally separate, not fused, in the process of comprehension. There are strong reasons to believe that a fusional process mediates both comprehension and production of metaphor,[2,28,29] but this kind of process is difficult to represent in current notation systems. Another example relates more specifically to metaphor: the structure of many formalisms for metaphors and analogies has suggested that a topic and vehicle should be functionally symmetric. A formal notation for "X and Y share A" would be equivalent to one for "Y and X share A." The four-term analogy A:B::C:D is formally equivalent to C:D::A:B. However, the psychological functions of topic and vehicle are not equivalent,[2,30,31] and this suggests the need for a better notation system. Similarly, many structural descriptions have suggested that similes and metaphors are functionally identical (e.g., some investigators represented both sentence types using the common underlying form of a comparison). Again, there is intuitive and empirical support for a psychological difference that is not indexed by these notations.[2,32] In each of these cases, one can argue that our notation systems, acting metaphorically, have had misleading effects on our perception of metaphoric processes.

All of these problems illustrate the irony we face: the process we are eager to explain may be our worst enemy. We need to become more aware of the metaphoric self-descriptions that underlie our discussions of language and cognition. As Churchill put it in another context, we must beware lest our civil servants become our uncivil masters.

ACKNOWLEDGMENTS

I would like to thank Sheila White, Virginia Teller, and Robert Hoffman for their encouragement and for their roles in organizing the events at which I presented the two lectures that form the basis for this paper. I am also indebted to numerous colleagues, reviewers, and audience members for their insightful comments and suggestions.

REFERENCES

1. WITTGENSTEIN, L. 1935. Philosophical Investigations, 3rd ed. (1958). Macmillan. New York, NY.
2. VERBRUGGE, R. R. 1980. Transformations in knowing: A realist view of metaphor. In Cognition and Figurative Language. R. P. Honeck & R. R. Hoffman, Eds. Erlbaum. Hillsdale, NJ.
3. REDDY, M. J. 1979. The conduit metaphor—A case of frame conflict in our language about language. In Metaphor and Thought. A. Ortony, Ed. Cambridge University Press. Cambridge, England.
4. LAKOFF, G., & M. JOHNSON. 1980. Metaphors We Live By. University of Chicago Press. Chicago, IL.
5. PYLYSHYN, Z. W. 1973. What the mind's eye tells the mind's brain. Psychol. Bull. 80: 1–24.
6. SHEPARD, R. N. 1975. Form, formation and transformation of mental representations. In Information Processing and Cognition. R. Solso, Ed. Erlbaum. Hillsdale, NJ.
7. KOSSLYN, S. M., S. PINKER, G. E. SMITH, & S. P. SHWARTZ. 1979. On the demystification of mental imagery. Behav. Brain Sci. 2: 535–581.

8. SHAW, R. E. & M. T. TURVEY. 1981. Coalitions as models for ecosystems: A realist perspective on perceptual organization. *In* Perceptual Organization. M. Kubovy & J. Pomerantz, Eds. Erlbaum. Hillsdale, NJ.

9. TURVEY, M. T. & C. CARELLO. 1981. Cognition: The view from ecological realism. Cogition **10**: 313–321.

10. KUGLER, P. N., J. A. S. KELSO & M. T. TURVEY. 1980. On the concept of coordinative structures as dissipative structures. I. Theoretical lines of convergence. *In* Tutorials in Motor Behavior. G. E. Stelmach & J. Requin, Eds. North-Holland. Amsterdam.

11. PEIRCE, C. S. 1931. Collected papers (Vol. 2). Harvard University Press. Cambridge, MA.

12. ALSTON, W. P. 1964. Philosophy of Language. Prentice-Hall. Englewood Cliffs, NJ.

13. VERBRUGGE, R. R. Language and perception: Steps toward a synthesis. *In* Persistence and Change: Proceedings of the First International Conference on Event Perception. W. H. Warren & R. Shaw, Eds. Erlbaum. Hillsdale, NJ. In press.

14. JAPP, F. R. 1898. Kekulé memorial lecture. J. Chem. Soc. **73**: 97–138.

15. ANSCHÜTZ, R. 1929. August Kekulé (2 vols.). Verlag Chemie. Berlin.

16. ANSCHÜTZ, R. 1961. August Kekulé *In* Great Chemists. E. Farber, Ed. Interscience. New York, NY.

17. WINDERLICH, R. 1930. Kekulé. *In* Das Buch der grossen Chemiker, Vol. 2. G. Bugge, Ed. Verlag Chemie. Berlin.

18. IHDE, A. J. 1964. The Development of Modern Chemistry. Harper & Row. New York, NY. 1964.

19. FINDLAY, A. 1965. A Hundred Years of Chemistry, 3rd ed. Duckworth. London.

20. GILLIS, J. 1973. August Kekulé von Stradonitz. *In* Dictionary of Scientific Biography, Vol. 7. C. C. Gillispie, Ed. Scribner's. New York, NY.

21. LIBERMAN, A. M., F. S. COOPER, D. P. SHANKWEILER & M. STUDDERT-KENNEDY. 1967. Perception of the speech code. Psychol. Rev. **74**: 431–461.

22. LIBERMAN, A. M. & M. STUDDERT-KENNEDY. 1978. Phonetic perception. *In* R. Held, H. W. Leibowitz & H.-L. Teuber, Eds. Handbook of Sensory Physiology (Vol. 8: Perception). Springer-Verlag. Berlin.

23. FOWLER, C. A., P. RUBIN, R. E. REMEZ & M. T. TURVEY. 1980. Implications for speech production of a general theory of action. *In* Language Production. B. Butterworth, Ed. Academic Press. New York, NY.

24. HANSON, N. R. 1970. A picture theory of theory meaning. *In* The Nature and Function of Scientific Theories. R. G. Colodny, Ed. University of Pittsburgh Press. Pittsburgh, PA.

25. BERNSTEIN, L. 1976. The Unanswered Question. Harvard University Press. Cambridge, MA.

26. KINTSCH, W. 1974. The Representation of Meaning in Memory. Erlbaum. Hillsdale, NJ.

27. MILLER, G. A. Images and models, similes and metaphors. *In* Metaphor and Thought. A. Ortony, Ed. Cambridge University Press. Cambridge, England.

28. WERNER, H. & B. KAPLAN. 1963. Symbol Formation. Wiley. New York, NY.

29. VERBRUGGE, R. R. & N. S. MCCARRELL. 1977. Metaphoric comprehension: Studies in reminding and resembling. Cognit. Psychol. **9**: 494–533.

30. ORTONY, A. 1979. Beyond literal similarity. Psychol. Rev. **86**: 161–180.

31. CONNOR, K. & N. KOGAN. 1980. Topic-vehicle relations in metaphor: The issue of asymmetry. *In* Cognition and Figurative Language. R. P. Honeck & R. R. Hoffman, Eds. Erlbaum. Hillsdale, NJ.

32. BLACK, M. 1955. Metaphor. Proc. Aristotelian Soc. **55**: 273–294.

Problems of Linguistic Insecurity in Multicultural Speech Contexts

WILMA BUCCI

Institute of Advanced Psychological Studies
Adelphi University
Garden City, New York 11530

MILTON BAXTER

Department of English
Borough of Manhattan Community College
New York, New York 10007

A wide range of sociolinguistic problems may arise wherever speakers of non-standard varieties of English must communicate with speakers of the standard forms. In most of the important institutions in our multiethnic urban centers — in schools, businesses, government offices, and medical and psychiatric clinics — standard English is the dominant mode of discourse, spoken by the persons in authority; speakers of nonstandard forms of English enter these settings in search of services that are of crucial importance in their lives. The problems that arise range from total communication breakdowns involving foreign language speakers to subtle difficulties involving bilingual and bidialectal speakers of nonstandard English dialects.

In this paper we first discuss several major types of communication problems that were observed in a study of a psychiatric ward and examine the impact of these problems on the patient's treatment and adjustment to the therapeutic milieu. We then introduce a procedure that we have developed for detecting one such problem, *linguistic insecurity*, and present a pilot experimental study testing this approach. The pilot procedure was carried out with a group of dialect speakers in a remedial English class at a community college in New York.

CROSS-CULTURAL COMMUNICATION PROBLEMS IN AN INPATIENT PSYCHIATRIC SERVICE

The observations to be reported here were made during the years 1979–1980 in an inpatient psychiatric unit, operated as a open ward community, serving a multicultural, multiethnic urban area in Brooklyn, New York. The setting and its sociolinguistic characteristics have been described in Baxter and Bucci[1]; some of the relevant features will be summarized briefly here. Most of the therapists on the unit were whites from middle-class and upper working-class backgrounds. The nurses were from similar backgrounds, with more working-class concentration, and were evenly divided between whites and blacks, including native Americans, and non-native Americans from the West Indies.

The patients were primarily from working-class backgrounds and included blacks, Hispanics, and whites. Most of the Hispanics were Puerto Rican; among the blacks were native Americans and non-natives (e.g., Panamanians, Jamaicans, and Trinidadians).

A number of contrasting dyadic relationships were noted, reflecting the many socioeconomic and demographic differences among patients and staff. From a sociolinguistic perspective we decided to focus on the following contrastive therapist/patient pairs:

(a) white therapist / black native American patient;
(b) white therapist / black non-native American patient;
(c) non-Hispanic therapist / Hispanic patient.

The linguistic significance of these contrastive pairings becomes clearer on investigating the differences in language usage among members of the psychiatric unit. All of the therapists speak the standard varieties of English. Among the patients, however, there is much more diversity in language styles, including the black English vernacular (BEV), spoken by some of the native American black patients; a variety of Creole dialects spoken by the non-native American blacks, e.g., the Jamaican and Trinidadian forms; and the Spanish-English dialect as spoken by Puerto Ricans in New York.

The analysis of the nonstandard varieties of English spoken by the black and Hispanic patients, vis-à-vis the standard varieties of English used by the staff, permit us to define the contrastive pairings in the psychiatric unit along linguistic rather than sociological dimensions, as follows:

(a) therapist: SAE / patient: BEV
(b) therapist: SAE / patient: Creole
(c) therapist: SAE / patient: non-native accented English.

Each of these contrastive linguistic pairings, which are related to the social, ethnic and cultural differences of English speakers, are dyadic relationships in which effective communication between therapist and patient is impaired.

The linguistic situation is complicated by the fact that the different varieties of English spoken by the patient are not always apparent. Frequently, cross-cultural communication conflicts are ameliorated by linguistic code-switching abilities of the patients. Many of the bidialectal black patients, for example, are able to use both the standard and nonstandard codes, moving effectively from one to another in the appropriate social settings. Since they are aware that SAE is the norm for communication on the ward, they carry on their interactions there in that code, completely masking their dialectal versatility.

However, not all code-switchers use both the standard and nonstandard forms with equal facility. There are some individuals who appear to use both BEV and SAE codes well, but lack confidence in their use of the standard forms; their insecurity can be heightened in a social context in which standard English is the norm. There are also BEV speakers who are unable to switch codes. These are classified as monodialectal. Since they are locked into their nonstandard dialect, it may be extremely difficult and stressful for them to engage in a conversation in a social setting that calls for SAE.

Thus, speakers of the same dialect do not form a homogeneous group in terms of their facility with SAE. Speakers of BEV can be divided into several categories: (a) bidialectal speakers fluent in BEV and SAE; (b) bidialectal speakers fluent in BEV and insecure with SAE; and (c) monodialectal speakers fluent in BEV only.

OBSERVATIONS IN THE
THERAPEUTIC CONTEXT

Several examples may be given to illustrate the impact of the different possible pairings on patient diagnosis and treatment. (In all examples, names have been changed to ensure confidentiality.)

Rosa H.: "I can do all right at home." The first example concerns the experience of a bilingual Spanish-dominant patient with limited command of English. Rosa H. was born in Puerto Rico and lived there until she was 15; she has been in the United States for the past 30 years. She was admitted to the ward with symptoms of serious depression, and was characterized after her intake examination as "an alert, sensible woman, who spoke in a goal-directed, logical manner, but with a heavy Spanish accent. She was using a limited vocabulary, both because of her language problem and lack of education". After 2 weeks on the ward, Rosa handed in a "3-day letter," the official channel by which a patient may request to leave the hospital. At the ward community meeting, she explained her request only by repeating the same curt response, "I can do all right at home." Her refusal to say more than this prompted Maria, a Spanish-speaking bilingual patient, to explain to the community that Rosa was unhappy on the ward. She wasn't eating well. She had been on the ward for 2 weeks and had been eating hamburgers for lunch and dinner. Maria explained that Rosa could not understand the hospital menu, which was written in English, and thus continued to order hamburgers, even though she "doesn't like them." (Such lack of facility in English is common among Hispanic women in New York, even those who, like Rosa, have been here for many years; they spend their lives in their own speech communities and have little contact with other groups.) We interviewed Rosa's therapist, who said that the communication between the two of them was "beautiful." Rosa also stated that she had no problem communicating with her therapist.

Here is a case where the patient's mastery of English was insufficient to meet even her basic physical needs, and certainly to permit her meaningful participation in the shared community life. The community interaction is, of course, a central aspect of the socialization and treatment process, as well as an important source of emotional support for the patient. Neither the patient nor, surprisingly, the therapist recognized (or admitted to) problems in the treatment. However, this deeply depressed woman, whose basic personality structure indicated a good prognosis for treatment, left the hospital after a brief stay, at her own request and against medical advice.

Maria V.: Emotion and the "mother tongue." The next example concerns the contrastive pairing of an SAE-speaking therapist and a bilingual Hispanic patient who is fluent in both English and Spanish. Maria was born and raised in a Puerto Rican family in New York City, and was one of the patients who assisted us in communicating with Rosa H. We asked her if there was any type of experience that she felt she could not express adequately in English. Maria's response was that she had difficulty expressing intense anger in English because she curses only in Spanish. She could not give vent to these emotions with her therapist, who "wouldn't understand." Afterwards, we interviewed Maria's therapist, who spontaneously noted that she was having trouble getting Maria to express emotion in her treatment.

We suggest that this is a pervasive problem, not limited to the expression of anger, but affecting the articulation of emotion in a general sense. Even fully bilingual individuals, who can express all manner of complex ideas in their second language, may find it difficult to express emotional experience in a code other than the "mother tongue." Verbalization of emotional experience may be at least partially dependent on the use of language forms associated with the intimate experiences of one's family and one's early years.[2,3]

Brenda L.: "I see peeny wally." The next example concerns a contrastive pairing of an SAE-speaking therapist and a Creole-speaking patient with code-switching abilities. Brenda L., a 75-year-old black woman who was born in Jamaica, West Indies, was admitted to the ward with symptoms of auditory, visual, and tactile hallucinations and persecutory ideation. One of her chief complaints, as reported in her chart, was that she was seeing and feeling "stars," which ran through her body, skin, and vagina.

We interviewed the admitting nurse, who said that when she first met Brenda, they discussed her complaint about seeing twinkling stars and flashing lights that were on her body, head and "all over." During the discussion, the nurse mentioned to Brenda that she was also Jamaican. When Brenda then attempted again to describe her hallucination for the therapist present, she turned to the nurse and said, "You're from Jamaica, so you know what I'm saying. I see *peeny wally.*" The nurse explained that this expression is commonly used in Jamaica to refer to fireflies.

"Stars" have different connotations from "fireflies"; the distinction was important to Brenda. The presence of the nurse enabled her to use a term that more accurately described her complaint. One can imagine the frustration of a patient who has a word to describe a phenomenon that has specific significance to her as a source of mental distress, but is unable to use that word because it is not the SAE code. This type of correction, in itself, does not directly affect diagnosis or treatment. However, repeated over and over again, failure to communicate meaning in this way and the expectation of such failure can be a serious obstacle in the therapeutic process.

Jimmy R.: The problem of "muteness." Next we consider the effect of the ward on a patient who is a BEV speaker. According to medical records, Jimmy R., a young black man of 19, was admitted to the psychiatric unit because of "an altered state of consciousness, stupor and muteness, resulting from a series of epileptic seizures." Jimmy appeared to be extremely reluctant to talk during the ward community meetings; however, he made a few utterances which indicated to us that he was a BEV speaker. His charts noted that: (1) the patient has a "speech defect"; (2) the patient "speaks slowly and only with monosyllables"; (3) the patient has a "problem of muteness"; thus the nursing plan is to "speak to patient in such a way that he must answer verbally and not gesture," and "to attempt to engage in conversation"; (4) the patient is "withdrawn."

A therapist said "Jimmy would not speak. He had a lot of difficulty with words and refused to respond to words." Another therapist told us that Jimmy had a "sociopathic personality." As evidence for this, she pointed out that Jimmy's conversation was normal when he talked about nonconflictual topics, but when the topic was conflictual he stammered and there was a definite breakdown in communication. Also, when she spoke with Jimmy casually in the halls, communication was good, but in the office there was some difficulty. In giving her impression of Jimmy's family interaction, a therapist writes: "It seems that because of the son's quasi-muteness—the mother claims he always spoke like this—he doesn't assert himself too much, but allows his mother to run the show, including his life." According to the records, Jimmy's mother, with whom he lives, "describes the family relationship as good." Jimmy "sees himself as active socially . . . " and he "denies any problems with ears, nose, throat or voice."

These apparently divergent perceptions prompted us to arrange an interview with Jimmy. He was somewhat hesitant at the beginning of the interview, but after warming up, he began to talk quite extensively about his experiences in high school and about being a member of a Brooklyn street gang called the Tomahawks.

Jimmy's background provided some basis for the therapist's belief that his "muteness" resulted from emotional or neurophysiological factors. However, there was also evidence indicating that Jimmy is a monodialectal BEV speaker who is reluctant to speak in a social setting for which SAE is the norm, but is capable of fluent and expressive language in his own speech community. These sociolinguistic data need to be considered in forming a balanced picture of the case.

Arlene H.: "What do you mean by that?". Our final example concerns the contrastive pairing of an SAE-speaking therapist and a bidialectal patient fluent in BEV, and competent, but insecure, in SAE. Arlene H., a 35-year-old black woman, was born in the southern United States and then moved to New York City at the age of 12. She did not complete high school, but later received a high school equivalency diploma, and was employed in a steady and responsible job. She seemed fully competent in the SAE code; in listening to her talk, it was also evident that she was a BEV speaker. During our interview with her, she told us that her speech was "bad," and that she did not use the more acceptable speech patterns of the doctors. She said that she had not had speech problems in the South and had done well in school. Her speech deficiencies had first been recognized by her teachers when she moved to the North. She felt that her manner of speech was an obstacle to communication and caused difficulties for her therapist. When we asked how she knew this, she said that her therapist often responded to her statements by telling her that he did not know what she meant.

Arlene's therapist indicated that there were no language problems. He felt that Arlene's difficulty in expressing herself was directly related to her psychopathology, and reflected her difficulty in getting in touch with her feelings. Part of the therapist's treatment plan, in dealing with this, was to facilitate communication by frequent use of such promptings as "What do you mean by that?"; "I don't understand"; and "I'm a little bit confused." These are, of course, widely used therapeutic interventions whose purpose is to elicit a more elaborated utterance by the patient.

However, such standard therapeutic techniques may have a converse and negative effect for the patient who is linguistically insecure. The intervention which was intended to encourage Arlene to speak more freely actually caused her to feel defensive and withdrawn. She felt that attention was being focused on the inadequacy of her language style rather than on the content of her speech; and she responded by saying less rather than more.

THREE CATEGORIES OF COMMUNICATION PROBLEMS

On the basis of our observational study of the inpatient service, three major categories of cross-cultural communication problems were identified: overt language differences, linguistic ambiguity, and linguistic insecurity. These will be described briefly here.

Overt Language Differences

These problems, involving speakers of English as a second language, constitute the most acute, but in some sense the simplest case. Here the obstacles to communication are generally obvious, although their implications may be unrecognized, as in the case of Rosa H. In extreme cases, i.e., where the patient has essentially no English, interpreters may be used. In many instances, however, the assumption is made that if patients are able to communicate at all in English, they are able to *say what they mean.* Thus the customary interview procedures are carried out as if there were no language barriers at all, with significant negative consequences for both diagnosis and treatment.

In a study by Marcos *et al.*[4], the same standardized interview was administered to bilingual Spanish-dominant psychiatric patients in Spanish and in English. Psychiatric ratings indicated greater psychopathology when the English interview was used than when the same interview was carried out in Spanish. As Marcos *et al.* point out, the patients' behavior actually changes when they are required to communicate in English, in ways that affect both differential diagnosis and ratings of pathology. The patient may appear more tense, speak slowly and haltingly in a flat tone, be unable to express emotion, or appear withdrawn, uncooperative, or hostile. Increased pause time and slower articulation rate may contribute to a diagnosis of depression; certain speech disturbances may cause a patient to be suspected of organic brain damage; flatness of expression may be associated with thought disorder.

It is surprising that such basic language difficulties are often overlooked in evaluating a patient and prescribing a treatment course. The same lack of recognition may occur in evaluating students, and in many other contexts where similar issues are at stake. We have all had experiences of helplessness and isolation while attempting to communicate in an unfamiliar language in a foreign country—have spoken slowly and haltingly in a market in Mexico, have appeared withdrawn and dull in a dinner party in Paris. The English-speaking staffs of our institutions would do well to keep those experiences in mind when dealing with bilingual individuals who are dominant in their native tongues.

Problems of Linguistic Ambiguity

For speakers of a foreign language, the language differences are obvious, even though the problems that arise are sometimes not adequately understood, as discussed above. In contrast, nonstandard dialects of English use much of the same vocabulary as SAE, but in some cases with different meaning, and use similar syntactic forms with certain rule-governed variation. Thus, a more complex set of cross-cultural communication problems may arise. Differences in meaning of lexical items are likely to be unrecognized by persons unfamiliar with the dialect and with the cultural forms, and may lead to real misunderstandings. The black patient who tells his therapist that he is a "bad" doctor is expressing a type of positive feeling that the white therapist is likely to miss. The Creole-speaking patients, who use "he" and "she" interchangeably, are operating within the rules of their own dialect, while the SAE-speaking therapist may interpret this as reflecting a confused sexual identification. Other unfamiliar grammatical constructions, e.g., reversals of accepted SAE word order, which follow the rules of the patient's dialect, may be interpreted as evidence of language or thought disorders, even schizophrenic "word salad." Such unrecognized misunderstandings are likely to arise when white therapists, teachers, and others are locked within their standard code without awareness of the possibility of dialectal shifts. The nonstandard-English-speaker, who is bidialectal, is more likely than the SAE speaker to recognize the possibility of linguistic ambiguity, and to seek to avoid it by shifting codes.

Problems of Linguistic Insecurity

The third type of problem concerns the individual's *attitudes* towards his or her language rather than linguistic functioning per se. The bidialectal code-switching speaker, who is aware of contextual linguistic norms and attempts to adapt his speech to them, is most vulnerable to this problem. Linguistically insecure speakers usually appear to be fully competent in SAE, but suffer from a negative attitude to their own speech forms and to the speech of their dialect group; the problem is illustrated most poignantly in the case of Arlene H. above.

Linguistic insecurity may be characterized as a negative or poor "speech image," comparable to a poor "body image," that is, a bad feeling about the way one talks like a bad feeling about the way one looks. It is defined in terms of the following major characteristics:

(*a*) It is situationally induced, a matter of performance in certain contexts rather than a fixed attribute of an individual. A person may be fluent and expressive in informal settings in his own speech community, but his language behavior and attitudes change in contexts in which SAE is the expected norm.

(*b*) It leads to a focus on the form rather than the content of speech. The individual is concentrating on how he talks rather than on what he says; thus, language becomes overintellectualized, stilted, and hypercorrect.

(*c*) It is not necessarily related to level of competence in standard English. Some individuals with full linguistic competence may have low linguistic self-esteem. Others with less competence may have more confidence and show linguistic patterns associated with a positive speech image.[a]

(*d*) It may be but is not necessarily consciously recognized by the speaker; it is almost certain not to be recognized by the listener. The speaker who is uncomfortable about the way he talks may attribute this to dislike on the part of the listener or other aspects of the discourse context; the listener may attribute the speaker's behavior to cognitive or emotional deficits, as discussed above.

(*e*) It is a function of upward social mobility rather than of social class per se. For example, Labov found that upwardly mobile individuals tended to use phonological variants associated with more prestigious styles and to reject the forms associated with their own social class in interview contexts characterized as calling for "careful speech."[5]

DETECTION OF LINGUISTIC INSECURITY

The problem of linguistic insecurity is more subtle than overt language differences. We suggest that its impact is potentially more severe. Overt language differences are relatively easy to recognize; the resulting communication breakdowns may be dealt with directly. In contrast, linguistic insecurity may affect feelings and be manifest in behavior in a variety of disguised ways which color both the individual's entire experience of a situation and others' perceptions of him. The speaker who is uncomfortable about the way he talks may believe that it is caused by the listener's negative judgments or he may attribute his own discomfort to the situation in general; the listener may attribute the speaker's behavior to cognitive or emotional deficits. The individual who doubts his ability to express his meaning adequately in words in certain contexts may give up in this attempt; this can be a central problem in a wide

---

[a] Some aspects of linguistic insecurity may, in fact, be an indicator of linguistic competence rather than the converse. The constraints placed on oneself by the code-switching speaker may be interpreted as reflecting an awareness of cross-cultural differences—a sense of what is appropriate in a given context—that is more sophisticated than that held by the monolingual SAE speaker. William Stewart (personal communication) has noted that the linguistically insecure bidialectal speaker may in fact be basing his expectations and his behavior on a *realistic* view of the negative response to be expected from SAE speakers to dialect speech forms.

range of situations, from psychotherapy to the classroom. It is important to try to detect communication problems that are a function of the context, and to distinguish these from cases where actual cognitive, emotional, or linguistic impairment is involved.

As we have suggested, linguistic insecurity may be disguised in a variety of forms, and is by its very nature particularly difficult to detect. It is not a matter of competence, so that tests of linguistic ability do not apply. Furthermore, since the linguistically unsure individual is often unaware of his negative attitude, measures based on direct questioning or self-report are likely to be ineffective.

Several methods of measuring linguistic attitudes have been developed elsewhere. These include general linguistic attitude questionnaires; phonemic matched-pairs tests, which involve selection of one of a pair of words with competing pronunciations in the subject's dialect; and ratings of character traits based on speech samples recorded in varying dialect forms. The latter taps aspects of linguistic insecurity when the subject is asked to rate speakers whose dialect or accent resembles his own.

None of these approaches are adequate for assessing linguistic insecurity as conceptualized here. The use of general linguistic attitude questionnaires relies entirely on self-report and thus misses those negative linguistic attitudes that exist outside of awareness. These may, in fact, be the most serious instances of linguistic insecurity. The more negative an individual's "speech image," the more those unpleasant feelings are likely to be kept out of consciousness, and thus to affect speech behavior in unrecognized ways.

The matched-pairs test is presented as an objective measure of behavior; however there is, in fact, a self-report element in this test as well. The individual must be able and willing to report that his own usage deviates from the "correct" form. In this respect, the matched-pairs test is subject to the same objection as the linguistic attitudes questionnaire discussed above.

Another problem with this measure is that it requires selection of phonemic pairs which are in free variation in the subject's speech community; thus, they must be chosen individually for each specific dialect. Both the selection of the items and their accurate pronunciation require the services of a trained linguist. Therefore the measure cannot be used routinely as a standard assessment procedure in the kind of multilingual community setting in which the problem of linguistic insecurity is most likely to arise.

In contrast to the former two measures, the rating of character traits on the basis of prepared speech samples does not require consciousness of negative linguistic attitudes or willingness to report them. The listener is asked to evaluate the speaker's personality rather than his language. The assumption is made that judgments of personality in this context are necessarily determined by language style, whether or not the person making the judgment is aware of this connection. Linguistic samples constitute the entire data base for the judgment; factors other than linguistic style can presumably be ruled out in the experimental design.

This approach might be used as a measure of linguistic insecurity if speech samples matching the subject's own dialect were included. However, this raises a practical problem which is similar to that found in application of the matched-pairs test. We can approximate this matching for some major dialects such as BEV and Hispanic forms, but will still miss variants even within these major dialect types. We cannot hope to have speech samples to match the wide variety of dialects and foreign languages spoken in our hospitals and schools. Furthermore, a complete matched-guise design is essentially impossible to achieve in such contexts. Thus, this approach, like the matched pairs test, is most difficult to apply in the very multiethnic settings where the need for measurement of linguistic insecurity is most acute.

THE "SELF-CORRECTION" MEASURE: A PILOT STUDY

A new approach for assessment of linguistic insecurity has been designed in an attempt to avoid the problems outlined above. The method involves evaluation by subjects of recorded speech samples that they themselves have produced. An objective and quantifiable measure of the speaker's attitude to his own speech product is derived that is determined by whether he wishes to make changes in it when it is played back to him.

In the pilot study to be reported here, the self-correction measure was given to a group of dialect speakers. The goal of the study was to assess the validity of the self-correction method as a measure of linguistic attitudes, by showing its correspondence to other related data. The results of the self-correction measure were compared with socioeconomic data as to risk factors for linguistic insecurity and also with data on linguistic attitudes derived from rating sets of prepared tapes. If the self-correction measure is validated in this way, the procedure may then be used in a wide range of situations in which other approaches cannot be applied.

Subjects for the study were 18 students attending a remedial English class in a New York City community college, including six Hispanics of varied origins, two West Indians, eight native American blacks, one person from the Philippines, and one from Bangladesh. The wide variation of ethnic backgrounds in the sample was characteristic of that in community colleges in New York City, and was also similar to the psychiatric patient population discussed above.

Subjects were seen individually in a single session lasting less than an hour. The session included three parts: a background interview, the self-correction measure, and evaluation of the recorded dialect speech samples.

Background Interview

The session began with an interview to establish rapport and to collect background data as to education, occupation, and migration history of the subjects and their immediate families.

The Self-Correction Procedure

The self-correction measure was then administered. In this procedure, the subject is shown four pictures depicting situations that are intended to be interesting and evocative, and in which there is a considerable amount of perceptual detail. The pictures were selected to elicit rich and detailed verbal descriptions, in contrast to the type of stimuli used in projective measures such as the Thematic Apperception Test of Murray,[6] which are designed to evoke deep emotional response. The examiner instructs the subject to describe what is in the picture as fully and completely as possible, and tape records the descriptions.

After all the pictures have been described, the recorded verbal samples are played back to the subject. He is asked to rate the description and is given the opportunity to change it if he wishes. In the middle of this sequence, after half of the descriptions have been played back, several probe questions are used, with the goal of arousing any latent negative linguistic attitudes that might be present. The subjects are asked to imagine how certain other people, in particular persons likely to have high cultural status for them, such as an English teacher, might have described the picture, and to compare this to their own. After this intervention, which is carried out in a casual and conversational way as a rest from the experimental procedure, the subjects then return to the task of evaluating their own recorded speech samples.

Evaluation of Recorded Speech Samples

In the third part of the interview, subjects listen to prerecorded descriptions of the same pictures that they had previously described. Four taped descriptions were prepared for each picture, including SAE, BEV, Hispanic, and West Indian forms. The descriptions were produced by first generating texts for all pictures in SAE and then translating these to the other three dialect forms as spoken in New York. This yielded four texts for each picture which were the same in content and different in dialect form. The BEV and SAE versions were read by the same bidialectal speakers, providing a matched-guise design for these forms. The Hispanic and West Indian texts were read by native speakers of Spanish and Creole, respectively. This group of dialects provided at least approximate matches for all subjects in the study, except for the two from the Philippines and the one from Bangladesh. Half of the descriptions in each category were read by male and half by female speakers.

Each subject listens to one tape set consisting of one description for each of the four pictures in each of the dialect forms. The design controls for voice quality and sex of the speaker, as well as for possible variation in quality of description between pictures or between dialect translations, when data for all subjects are combined. The subjects are asked to rate the prepared tapes and rate their own in comparison to them.

Results of the Self-Correction Procedure

The subjects were divided into two groups on the basis of the number of the descriptions that they wished to change. Any type of critique was counted, including changes in content, style, and form. Subjects who wished to change less than half of their descriptions were characterized as low on the self-correction measure. Seven of the eighteen subjects were in this group.

Eleven of the eighteen subjects wished to change half or more of their descriptions; they were classified as high on this measure. Their criticisms dealt with aspects of style, vocal quality, and phonological features, as well as content and syntax.

Socioeconomic Characteristics of the Two Groups

The two groups of subjects, distinguished by the self-correction measure, were then compared as to social and demographic characteristics. As discussed above, negative linguistic attitudes are expected to be associated with upward social mobility, rather than with social class per se. In the high self-correction group, parents of nine of the eleven subjects were working class (e.g., truck drivers, maintenance workers, and farmers). Only one father had some college education and one owned a business. In contrast, in the low self-correction group, only two subjects were clearly of working class or rural farm backgrounds. Parents of four of the seven subjects had at least some college education, owned a business, or had professional career status; parents of a fifth subject were described as city employees, but the level of the position was not specified. Thus, nine of eleven (82%) of the subjects in the high-correction group were from rural or working class backgrounds and were the first members of their families to attend college; attendance at the community college was a sign of upward mobility for this group. This compares to two of seven (29%) in the low-correction group. Thus, the self-correction measure appears to differentiate subjects who would be assessed as at risk for linguistic insecurity on the basis of socioeconomic indicators from those who do not fit the "at risk" profile.

The high self-correction group included four black native Americans, four Hispanic persons of varying origins, two persons from the West Indies, and one from Bangladesh. The low self-correction group included four black native Americans, two individuals of Hispanic origins and one from the Philippines. Overall age levels were equivalent in the two groups, with the high-correction "insecure" subjects ranging from 18 to 44 years, and the low-correction "secure" subjects ranging from 20 to 50 years of age. However, the data suggested that age might be a relevant factor in the group of native black Americans, considered separately. Three of four of the black native Americans in the low-correction group were in their early 20s; all of those in the high-correction group were over 30 years old. We suggest that the younger blacks are likely to have developed a more positive attitude about their origins, and that this is reflected in greater satisfaction with their speech forms.

Ratings of Prepared Tapes

The two groups of subjects also showed corresponding differences in ratings of the prepared tapes. In the high-correction (insecure) group, 90% of the subjects placed the dialect sample like their own in last or next to last place; one subject placed this version second; no subject rated this version best. In contrast, in the low-correction (secure) group, 84% of the subjects ranked the "like" form either first or second; no subject placed this version last. The difference in assigned ranks was statistically significant, even in this small pilot sample ($t = 3.1$; $p < 0.01$).

The reasons given for preferring other speech forms over one's own varied widely, often focusing on voice quality and content, as in the following two excerpts:

(i) ". . . the way, how he speak English—very good—clearly—the expression, how he describe . . . I'd say—the tone of the—his voice, the down and up, gives some interest."

(ii) "Better command of English language—clearer—might be more insight involved."

The same bidialectal speaker whose vocal modulation was admired in SAE was not judged positively in the BEV dialect. Similarly, the same type of content that was cited as a basis for a high ranking in one form was given as a reason for a low evaluation in another. Here is a dialect speaker commenting on an SAE description:

(iii) "She was more descriptive here. She described not only the people but the day, the snow, the event, how peaceful it was, everything—beautiful, detailed description."

Compare this with comments by a Hispanic and a black subject on the same material delivered in their own dialect forms:

(iv) "I think that description is seein' too many things . . . It wasn't exactly what she saw. Used a lot of imagination and things that were subjective which may not exactly be reality. I think my description was more realistic of what I saw."

(v) "I think in a way she was a little bit repetitious about the snow and saying the cat in the window inside the house lookin' up and then the snow—snow storm—and not snow flurry. I think in a way it was a little too repetitious. I got a little bored with it."

Thus the impression created by the speech forms spilled over to affect perception of voice quality and content although these factors had been controlled in the experimental design. Material seen as showing effective use of detail in a more prestigious form appeared "repetitious" and boring in the insecure subject's own dialect; material seen as beautiful and descriptive in another speech form became overly subjective in the insecure individual's own. This corresponds to findings in studies by others in which negative attitudes toward certain forms of spoken language have been found to affect ratings of character or personality traits, even where the ratings are based on speech samples delivered by the same individual.

The subjects were also asked to rank their own recorded descriptions in relation to the four prepared tapes; the difference between the secure and insecure groups also emerges clearly in this measure. The secure group put their own descriptions in either first or second place; the insecure group tended to put their own descriptions in second, third, or fourth place. The difference in average rank was significant ($t = 2.13$, $p < .05$).

Most subjects in both groups ranked the SAE form in first place. This corresponds to findings reported elsewhere as to ratings of personality traits based on dialect speech samples versus the culturally dominant standard form.[7,8]

Implications of the Pilot Study

The approach used here has permitted us to distinguish subjects who showed general satisfaction with their own spoken language from those who showed a persistent inclination to change or correct what they had said. As demonstrated by the validation procedures, the self-correction measure does tap the phenomenon of linguistic insecurity as defined above. Subjects who tended to express dissatisfaction with a relatively large proportion of their own utterances, as manifest in a wish to change them, also showed the socioeconomic profile associated with vulnerability to linguistic insecurity, and showed dissatisfaction with their own dialect forms in rating the prepared tapes.

The measure is simple to administer, requiring only speech samples produced by the subjects themselves. It does not involve matching of language samples, and does not rest on sophisticated awareness of one's language style or readiness for self-report. Thus it appears to provide a promising approach to assessment of linguistic insecurity, which can be applied in any psychiatric or medical setting, in schools, and in any other situation in which context-induced communication problems are likely to arise.

DIRECTIONS FOR FUTURE RESEARCH

A wide range of methodological and conceptual issues remain to be explored in understanding the various types of cross-cultural communication problems, and in developing methods for their assessment. The self-correction method needs to be tested using a larger sample of subjects and a larger number of stimulus items. We will also look specifically at the impact of the probe questions used halfway through the test, and their different effects in secure and insecure groups. In addition, we will distinguish the various different types of criticisms that the subjects make of their recorded speech samples (such as critiques of content, vocal tone, accent, vocabulary, style, and grammatical form) and relate these individual categories separately to the validating criteria. On this basis, it may be possible to improve the reliability and validity of the assessment, as well as to understand the phenomenon of linguistic insecurity more clearly.

The problem of linguistic insecurity should also be considered in a more general sense as a problem that may arise in a wide range of contexts, within speech communities as well as in cross-cultural settings. Furthermore, negative attitudes towards one's own speech are not necessarily restricted to dialect speakers, but may also be experienced by SAE speakers under certain circumstances. This is particularly likely for persons who are upwardly mobile, as discussed above. Many variants of SAE, related to region, class, or other social factors, which are not sufficiently distinct to be termed separate dialects, may nevertheless carry different prestige values. A young man from the Flatbush section of Brooklyn, attending a New England college, or a white woman from the South working in a Wall Street law firm, may have negative attitudes toward his or her linguistic style which affect verbal behavior in significant ways.

The problem may also arise in any stressful situation, such as a school or employment interview, independent of the cross-cultural context. As in the cases of the dialect speakers discussed above, the occurrence of a negative speech image in SAE speakers in stressful situations may be unrecognized, and may lead to behaviors that are interpreted in terms of verbal or intellectual inadequacy or emotional impairment, rather than as specifically context-induced. This might be investigated in future studies by administering linguistic insecurity measures to SAE speakers, in different settings, varying in degree of formality.

QUESTIONS AND CONCLUSIONS

This paper has introduced the issue of specific negative attitudes towards one's own speech forms or the speech of one's dialect group, as a separate phenomenon whose etiology and impact are distinguishable from general negative attitudes towards oneself or one's ethnic background. In making this distinction, we do not intend to deny interaction between linguistic insecurity and psychological insecurity of a more general sort, but to focus attention on specific attitudes toward speech in a new way. Once the nature of the specific linguistic attitudes are better understood, the nature of their relation to general self-esteem may be more meaningfully explored. It is most likely that the specific linguistic and the general psychological attitudes will be found to interact to some degree. A negative speech image, like a negative body image, may in some cases be but one additional manifestation of an overall negative self-image. Alternatively, linguistic insecurity may be a specific negative attitude in a context of overall confidence, or a primary factor operating to reduce general self-esteem.

The problem of linguistic insecurity is further complicated by the fact that language plays a crucial role in organizing experience for oneself as well as in communicating with others. A negative feeling toward one's language thus may have serious implications of a basic nature, affecting thought as well as speech. In all the many types of examples that we have referred to above, and in many others that could be addressed, a negative attitude towards one's speech forms was shown to mean a focus on form at the expense of content, and thus a kind of dissociation of language and thought. For the linguistically insecure person, linguistic structures are split off from underlying nonverbal representational systems, including imagery, feelings, and abstract ideas. The individual rejects the language that is linked to emotion and imagery in his life experience. This interferes directly with basic linguistic functions, such as the translation of the speaker's private experience into the shared verbal code, and the role of language in directing and organizing thought. A core question that needs to be explored concerns the nature of this dissociation and its general operation and impact in a wide range of settings, not only those in which cross-cultural barriers are present.

At best, linguistic confidence is only relative for any one of us. Even in the linguistically secure group, the majority of subjects preferred the SAE form to their own. Among SAE speakers, as among dialect speakers, there is no one who has not had the experience of feeling "tongue-tied" in some situations at some time. If a poor speech image can be diagnosed and appropriate supports introduced, this may free individuals to try to say what they mean, rather than to reduce their meaning to whatever seems easiest or least embarrassing to say.

REFERENCES

1. BAXTER, M. & W. BUCCI. 1981. Studies in linguistic ambiguity and insecurity. Urban Health: 36–40.
2. BUCCI, W. & N. FREEDMAN. 1981. The language of depression. Bull. Menninger Clin. **45**: 334–358.
3. BUCCI, W. 1982. The vocalization of painful affect. Commun. Dis. **15**: 415–440.
4. MARCOS L. M., M. ALPERT, L. URCOYO & M. KESSELMAN. 1973. The effect of interview language on the evaluation of psycho-pathology in Spanish-American schizophrenic patients. Am. J. Psychiatry **130**: 549–553.
5. LABOV, W. 1966. Hypercorrection by the lower middle class as a factor in linguistic change. *In* Sociolinguistics. W. Bright, Ed. Mouton. The Hague.
6. MURRAY, H. A. 1943. Thematic Apperception Test. Harvard University Press. Cambridge, MA.
7. LAMBERT, W. E., R. C. HODGSON, R. C. GARDNER & S. FILLENBAUM. 1960. Evaluational reactions to spoken languages. J. Abnorm. Soc. Psychol. **60**: 44–51.
8. ANISFELD, M., N. BOZO & W. E. LAMBERT. 1962. Evaluational reactions to accented English speech. J. Abnorm. Soc. Psychol. **65**: 223–231.

Language Learnability, Language Variation, and Some Recent Proposals in Grammatical Theory

MARK BALTIN

Department of Linguistics
New York University
New York, New York 10003

One of the central goals of linguistics is commonly taken to be a specification of the possible grammars of natural languages. Linguistic research indicates that the set of grammars that are actually attested is a quite narrow subset of the grammars that one could imagine.[1,2] Therefore, the construction of a theory of possible grammars will have to be able to cope with the known diversity of the grammars of the world's languages while excluding logically possible, but humanly impossible grammars.[a]

One may view the construction of a theory of grammar as the statement of a child's initial hypotheses about the nature of the grammar that she or he must construct. It is accepted that knowing a language involves knowing how to use a system of rules that generates an infinite class of sentences. Therefore, learning a language involves learning the grammar, or system of rules, that generates that language. The theory of grammar, then, can be seen as a psychological construct. One may consequently impose a requirement on a proposed theory of grammar to the effect that the grammars made available by it must have an associated account of acquisition. This view, propounded within the field of linguistics most forcefully by Chomsky[5] and re-emphasized by Peters[6] and Baker[7,8] is commonly referred to as a *mentalist* view of linguistics.[9]

In this paper, I will show that the mentalist view is an extremely productive research strategy, and will show that it can play a decisive role in choosing among some competing theories of grammar.

In order to find out whether some rule of grammar is learnable, we must determine whether the evidence for that rule of grammar is evidence that is available to the child. For example, in English (but not in Japanese), the object of the verb appears after the verb, so that (1) is acceptable, while (2) is not:

(1)   The man ate the steak.
(2) * The man the steak ate.

The child can learn this fact about English word order quite simply, by hearing only sentences that conform to the rule, but never hearing sentences that violate it. One might propose, then, that children will only form rules

---

[a] I am aware that some of the technical details of syntax may be unfamiliar to some readers. The work of Baker[3] and Radford[4] offers two excellent introductory treatments of modern syntax.

on the basis of evidence available to them, and will not form rules that generate structures that are outside the set of structures to which they are exposed. In this view, the theory of grammar need not be a psychological construct, since the grammars that the theory allows will solely be accidents of the vagaries of experience. Put another way, this view of language acquisition would predict that the child could arrive at any grammar, given any presentation of any input data.

It is clear that this view of language acquisition is incorrect, and the evidence for this comes from a number of sources. One piece of evidence comes from experiments of artificial language learning. Schane *et al.*[10] showed that, of two groups of subjects who had to learn two different artificial languages differing by one grammatical rule, one group was significantly more successful than the other. The rule employed by the more successful group, while attested in various grammars of natural languages, was not attested in English. The rule employed by the less successful group was not attested in any natural language. Crucially, subjects in both conditions received the same amount of input. The implication seems to be that people have predispositions toward learning certain grammatical rules over others, and experience is not the whole story.

Secondly, children overgeneralize certain rules, in the sense that at certain stages, they apply the rules too widely, as noted for instance, by Braine.[11] For example, the normal rule for forming past tenses in English involves adding -*ed* as a suffix to verbs, as in the pairs in (3):

(3) talk, talked; bait, baited; harp, harped

Exceptions to the general rule exist, so that some verbs do not form their past tenses by a general rule. Examples are *go*, which has *went* rather than *goed* as its past tense, and *buy*, which has *bought* rather than *buyed* as its past tense. However, at a certain stage of language acquisition, children do use *buyed* and *goed* (as well as *bought* and *went*) as the past tense forms for *go* and *buy*. Therefore, children do extrapolate from their experience to a certain extent. Indeed, given the continually creative nature of language use, it would be difficult to imagine this not to be the case.

If children form rules that are not rules for the adult language, one must ask how the child revises his grammar to conform to the adult model. For instance, how does the child learn that *goed* and *buyed* are exception to the general rule for forming past tenses?

The first conceivable answer is that the child utters the incorrect past tense forms and is corrected by his parents, being told that these forms are ungrammatical. Brown and Hanlon[12] and Braine[11] show that children do not systematically receive correction for ungrammatical usage. In other words, children are not typically told by adults that words such as *buyed* and *goed* are not forms in the adult language.

In short, children must learn an adult grammar, and revise grammars that are overinclusive from the adult point of view, without being explicitly taught by adults that their grammars are overinclusive. Braine[11] suggests a model of language acquisition that does not rely on explicit correction for ungrammatical usage. He suggests that children register strings that possess certain structural properties, and store these strings with the relevant properties in memory stores. The more a string with a given property is encountered, the farther it will be pushed back in the memory store. If a string is not encountered frequently enough in a certain critical period, the memory store will decay.

Applied to the cases discussed above, a child learning English will hear numerous sentences in which the verb precedes the object, but no sentences in which the verb follows the object, and no sentences in which *buyed* and *goed* are the past tense forms.

In a sense, Braine's model can be viewed as an alternative to the mentalist conception of linguistic theory as a specification of the child's initial assumptions about the nature of a possible grammar. No assumption is made of any innate linguistic mechanism; the character of the adult grammars is nearly totally a function of experience.

In my view, the memory store model may be quite plausible for the cases that Braine considers, but cannot be the whole picture of grammar acquisition. The results of studies such as those in Schane *et al.*[10] are equally problematic for Braine's model, since the two groups in their study received equal opportunities to learn the two rules examined. Second, and this point is related to the first, Braine's model does allow for overgeneralization of rules at intermediate stages. Therefore, Braine would predict massive amounts of overgeneralization at intermediate stages.

Research in the properties of linguistic structure over the past 25 years or so has indicated that the adult grammars of the world's languages are not as diverse in structure as Braine's model might lead one to expect. Chomsky has repeatedly emphasized[1,2] that rules of grammar seem to be subject to all sorts of constraints that receive no natural extralinguistic explanation (i.e., in terms of reasoning, memory, perception, and so forth). In other words, various grammars that are logically possible are apparently not internalized. I shall now discuss two examples of such constraints on grammar, although the literature of generative grammar contains a great many more. The question to ask with respect to Braine's model is whether these constraints are violated by children in prefinal states of language acquisition.

Various languages allow elements to appear in more than one position within a sentence. An example is the alternation between (4a) and (4b):

(4a) How certain ⌐that the Mets will win¬ are you?
(4b) How certain are you ⌐that the Mets will win¬?

We see that subordinate clauses may appear either in a nonfinal position in the sentence or in final position. Linguists commonly account for situations in which an element may appear in more than one position in a sentence by positing grammatical rules that move those elements from a basic position to the other position(s). The movement rule responsible for the alternation in (4) is stated in Baltin[13] as (5):

(5) $\bar{S} - X \longrightarrow X - \bar{S}$[b]

For expository convenience, let us dub the rule in (5) *detachment*. It moves a subordinate clause rightward. However, detachment has a restriction on its functioning. If a potentially detachable subordinate clause is *itself* contained within a subordinate clause, the potentially detachable subordinate clause cannot move out of the clause in which it originates. For example, consider a sentence such as (6):

(6) John was believed to be certain that the Mets would win by everyone present.

Linguists commonly display the structural relationships in sentences by what are known as *phrase markers*. The phrase marker corresponding to (6) is (7):

(7) [John was believed [to be certain [that the Mets would win]] by every-
    $\bar{S}^0$ $\bar{S}^1$ $\bar{S}^2$ $\bar{S}^2$ $\bar{S}^1$
one present.][c]
    $\bar{S}^0$

The $\bar{S}^2$ is potentially detachable out of $\bar{S}^1$ to the end of $\bar{S}^0$. The resulting sentence, however, is unacceptable:

(8) * John was believed to be certain by everyone there that the Mets would win.

The unacceptability of (8), according to Ross,[15] is part of a more general restriction about rightward movement rules. This restriction is called the *right roof constraint*, and it is stated as in (9):

(9) *Right roof constraint*: An element cannot move rightward out of any clause in which it originates.

Any model of language acquisition must be able to provide an account of how a constraint such as (9) could be acquired.[d] The linguist's evidence for (9) is that a rule such as detachment has a restriction of some sort on it, and so a sentence that one might expect *a priori* to be grammatical, such as (8), is ungrammatical. Children, however, do not seem to receive evidence of ungrammatical usage in the primary data that they use to construct a grammar.

Braine's model might state that the child learns a constraint such as the right roof constraint by never hearing a sentence that violates it, such as (8).

---

[b] For those unfamiliar with current transformational grammar, a word of explanation is in order about the terms $\bar{S}$ and, later in this paper, COMP. The term COMP is short for *complementizer*, which is a type of clause-introducer. (In English, the word *that* in *I think that it rained* is a complementizer). Bresnan[14] proposed that all sentences in English and many other languages contain COMP at the basic level, and proposed that $\bar{S}$, which consists of COMP and an S (for sentence), is the basic unit of sentence structure.

[c] I am omitting irrelevant details in these phrase markers, such as representation of traces, and so on.

[d] I should note that I am distinguishing between *acquisition*, by which I simply mean ontogenesis, or how something comes to be known, and *learning*, which is one type of acquisition, that is, by experience.

One might therefore ask whether sentences such as (8) are uttered by children at some intermediate stage of language acquisition. Given that children overgeneralize, as in the case of past tenses, one would expect overgeneralizations of detachment that would violate Ross's right roof constraint. If such overgeneralizations never occur, one would have to assume that the child knows in advance that the constraint holds, and that the constraint, a part of the theory of grammar, is also innately specified.

In this way, evidence from language acquisition and from linguistic theory may affect the models constructed in both fields. By analyzing some feature of grammar and exploring various alternative accounts of its acquisition, one may see the aspects of language that are deeply ingrained as well as the nature of the mental apparatus that can acquire language.

The story does not end here, however. If a constraint such as the right roof constraint is a part of language and is innate, we would expect it to be universal, or at least part of the initial assumptions of a language-learner acquiring any natural language. We can assume that all human beings share the same innate capacity to learn language. Therefore, in the best of all possible worlds, with respect to the innateness hypothesis, a constraint such as the right roof constraint should be universal. If grammars differ as to whether or not the right roof constraint holds, then those who view a theory of grammar as a mental construct must be able to provide an account of the acquisition of this difference.

In other words, if Language A is subject to the right roof constraint and Language B is not, one must ask how children learning each of the two languages learn that the constraint holds in the former language but not in the latter. One might propose the right roof constraint as an unmarked case, and suggest that the child assumes the right roof constraint to be operative unless evidence is heard to the contrary, in the form of sentences that violate the right roof constraint.

In fact, various linguists have proposed that certain languages do violate the right roof constraint: German,[16] Navajo,[17] and Hindi.[18] For example, Kohrt cites the following sentence:

(10) Paul horte $_S$[wie peter   den Mann $_S$[___ zu gestehen]$_S$ zwang $_S$[dass
     Paul heard ^{S} how Peter   the man ^{S} to confess ^{S} forced ^{S} that

     er den Wagen gestohlen hatte.]$_S$]
     he the car   stolen   had.

Paul heard how Peter forced the man to confess that he had stolen the car.

The rule of detachment, which we have seen to be operative in English, is operative in German as well, and has moved the *dass* clause rightward out of the clause in which it originated.

The crucial evidence that German is not subject to the right roof constraint is (11) below, but the assumption that (11) is part of the crucial evidence that a learner of German uses in arriving at a grammar of German is most implausible. The sentence contains three subordinate clauses, and it is quite unlikely that such complex sentences are part of a child's primary data base.[19] If such sentences are the only way that the child can learn that her or his language is not subject to the right roof constraint, a theory of grammar that allows obedience to the right roof constraint to be a parameter fixed differently by different languages does not seem to provide a plausible account of acquisition.

Consideration of further data from both German and English, however, in Baltin,[13] shows that the difference between German and English is not that German lacks the right roof constraint while English has it. There are other sentences in German that indicate that the right roof constraint is obeyed, and other sentences in English that indicate that the right roof constraint can sometimes be violated in English:

(11) * Paul horte $_{\bar{S}}$[wie ich Brigitte $_{\bar{S}}$[___ anzukundigen $_{\bar{S}}$[zu versprechen
Paul heard ^{S} how I Brigitte ^{S} to announce ^{S} to promise

$_{\bar{S}}$[versuchte]]] $_{\bar{S}}$[dass Peter die schule verlassen hatte.]
tried that Peter the school left had.

Paul heard how I tried to promise Brigitte to announce that Peter had left school.

(12) Fred was forced to admit___by each of them that he had stolen the cookies.

We see from such examples, then, that German appears to both violate and obey the right roof constraint, as does English. The account proposed in Baltin[13] differs from that of Kohrt. In my view, the right roof constraint basically holds in both languages. The German example (10) does not in fact have a clause boundary between *zwang* and *gestehen*. Rather, a rule of restructuring, proposed originally by Aissen and Perlmutter[20] exists, which restructures a sequence of contiguous verbs into a single verb, erasing intervening clause boundaries. The rule is lexically governed, triggered by some complement-taking verbs, but not others. The set of verbs that trigger this restructuring process seems to be identical across several languages. The set may be universal, therefore, and does not have to be learned by the child. Thus, *force* in English governs restructuring, while *believe* does not [hence the difference between (12) and (8)], while *zwang* (*force*) governs restructuring in German, but *zu versprechen* (*promise*) does not [differentiating (10) and (11)]. As mentioned, a necessary condition for restructuring is contiguity of higher verb and complement verb, and the subject-object-verb order of German subordinate clauses, an easily learnable property of German, will often create the necessary conditions for contiguity, under the assumption that infinitival complements may appear as objects.

This analysis is justified on the basis of other facts in Baltin,[13] and a repetition of those points would go beyond the scope of this paper, but the point is that an unlearnable difference between the grammars of German and English no longer exists. If the analysis proposed in Baltin[13] is correct, I believe that it shows the viability of the mentalist conception of grammars, and of the theory of grammar, as a research program. Obviously, any theory of grammar must provide for enough grammars to be consistent with the diversity of the world's languages. Only a view of linguistics that regards the grammarian's task as being of a somewhat psychological nature would force one to examine seriously the spacing between the grammars permitted by one's theory, (i.e., the degree of distinctness between the languages generated by the various grammars) or to require that grammar differences be learnable. Viewing a theory of grammar as a psychological construct therefore places stronger constraints on the extent of grammar variation than does a view of grammars as simply abstract mathematical objects.[e]

I would now like to turn to another area in which the study of language acquisition and the study of grammar may have something to say to one another. Specifically, I shall now examine the two proposals for the proper formulation of movement rules: that of Chomsky[5] and that of Baltin.[22] The work of Wexler and Colicover[19] is an attempt to construct a learnability procedure in which the language-learner is assuming roughly the class of grammars along the lines of Chomsky,[5] and so my criticisms of Chomsky[5] will extend to Wexler and Culicover's enterprise.

Chomsky[5] views transformational movement rules as linear operations on strings. Two types of movement processes are possible: substitution and adjunction. A substitution movement rule substitutes one category for another elsewhere in the phrase marker. An adjunction rule creates a new structure, attaching a moved element to a category (A) and creating a new instance of category A over the attached element plus the category to which it is attached. For example, the rule of Q-float, responsible for the alternation between (13a) and (13b), would be formulated as (14)

(13a) Each of the men would enjoy that
(13b) The men would each enjoy that
(14) QP-X-VP
    1 2 3 - - - → 0 2 1+3

Disregarding the *of* in (13a), this rule will change phrase-marker (15) to phrase-marker (16).

(15)

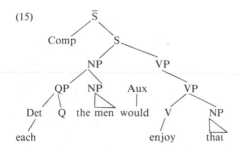

[e] Katz,[21] in his Platonist conception of language, views grammars as essentially abstract objects, akin to mathematical entities. However, in public comments at a lecture at Columbia University on November 4, 1982, he acknowledged that "indirect" evidence such as learnability considerations might prove relevant in the construction of grammars and of theories of grammar.

(16)

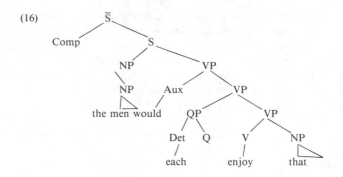

In Baltin,[21] the following theory of movement rules is proposed and justified on formal grounds. Three kinds of movement rules exist: (1) local interchange rules, which simply interchange two adjacent categories, but which do not induce adjunction; (2) stylistic movement rules, which do not move elements to defined structural positions in sentences, but simply move them as far as they can go subject to an appropriate theory of bounding of movement rules; (3) syntactic movement rules, which do not mention the structural position directly to which the moved element moves, but must pick from a fixed inventory of what I call "landing sites," the positions to which moved elements may move. The inventory of landing sites is roughly (17):

(17) (I)   VP   (a) Left periphery
      (II)   S   (b) Right periphery
      (III) S̄

In terms of the landing-site theory, Q-float would be formulated as (18):

(18) Move QP to Ia

This theory predicts a different class of movement rules from the one in Chomsky.[5] First, the landing-site theory does not view nonlocal syntactic movements as linear operations on strings, but rather as nonlinear operations on structures. (Notice that no linearity is specified in (18); see Chapter 2 in Baltin[23] for details). Therefore, it is possible to adjoin an element to a category that contains it in the phrase marker that is input to the movement rule. Such an operation is formally impossible to state in the framework of Chomsky,[5] but is shown to be empirically necessary in Baltin.[22]

Second, some adjunctions that the landing-site theory does not allow are permitted in the Chomsky theory[5] of adjunctions. The landing-site theory only allows adjunctions at the peripheries of VP, S, and S̄, while the *aspects* view of transformations allows adjunctions to any element that does not dominate the moving element. We can represent the relationship between the two classes of movement rules permitted by the two theories in the form of Venn diagram:

(19)

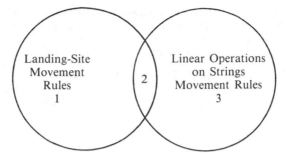

area in 1 = adjunctions to categories containing the adjoined elements;
area in 2 = linear adjunctions to landing site positions;
area in 3 = linear adjunctions to non-landing-site positions.

In Baltin,[21] I showed that the class of movements schematized in (1) and (2) was non-null, and the class of movements allowed in (3) was empty.

Because the two theories predict different classes of possible movement rules, data from language acquisition might choose between the two theories. The rules in question involve the positioning of sentential adverbs.

Sentential adverbs occur in a variety of positions in sentences, as is well known.[24] An example is the following set of variants of (20).

(20) John can eat the steak after the party.
(21) John can, after the party, eat the steak.
(22) It's obvious that, after the party, John can eat the steak.
(23) After the party, what can John eat?

In (21), the adverb occurs at the beginning of the VP, in (22) it occurs at the beginning of the S, and, in (23), it is at the front of the $\bar{\text{S}}$.

Under an *aspects* view of transformations, the language-learner will construct the following base rule plus movement rule of adverb placement:

(24) $\bar{\text{S}}$ - - - - -➤ $\bar{\text{S}}$ PP

(25)   X-PP - - - -➤   PP + X
    1   2   2+1

In other words, considering the plethora of positions before which adverbs appear, the language-learner could hypothesize a rule adjoining adverbs to any major constituent. Under the landing-site view, the language-learner would hypothesize the rule (26):

(26) Move PP

A rule as general as (26) is interpreted as an instruction to place PP at the periphery of any of the landing sites in the inventory VP, S, or $\bar{\text{S}}$. Rule (26) and rule (25) both account for the data so far, but further data are consistent with rule (26), but not rule (25):

(27) * John cannot eat after the party the steak. (Adjunction to NP)
(28) * John can after the party not eat the steak. (Adjunction to NEG)
(29) * I considered John, after the party, crazy. (Adjunction to AP)
(30) * Can, after the party, John eat the steak? (Adjunction to NP)

The problem lies in the *Aspects* view of movement. Adjunction to any category is permitted if the movement is formulable as a linear operation on strings. Consequently, (25) is the simplest rule, in the *Aspects* theory. The data that show the simplest rule to be wrong (27–30) consist of nonsentences to which the child is never exposed. The *Aspects* view might appeal to Braine's model, discussed above, which relies heavily on what Chomsky[24] calls "indirect negative evidence," that is, not hearing the sentences. However, Braine's model, in and of itself, might predict overgeneralizations of adverb placement at intermediate stages, so that (27–30) would appear at prefinal stages of language acquisition. To the extent that (27–30), or like structures, do not appear at those stages, the *Aspects* view, even supplemented with Braine's model, is insufficient to solve the projection problem, that is, how the child projects a full-fledged grammar from the set of sentences encountered.*f*

The landing-site rule (26), however, which is the simplest rule in the landing-site theory, will not permit the child to hypothesize the adjunctions exemplified by (27–30). Therefore, the landing-site rule restricts the class of hypothesized derived constituent structures to the ones exemplified by the data, and does not permit the overinclusive grammars permitted by the *Aspects* theory.

In this paper, we have seen some possible views of the interaction of the process of language acquisition and the structure of adult grammar. The discussion has been rather short on concrete conclusions, since researchers in the relevant disciplines have not, until quite recently, addressed themselves to these questions. It seems to me that many psychologists working on child language have not paid attention to the full set of facts about adult grammars that fill pages of several respectable linguistics journals, and that linguists, for their part, have not considered learnability criteria in positing theories of grammar. To the extent that the mentalist conception proves to be a fruitful research program, a much more heuristic methodology may enable us to solve the problem of induction in the area of human language, and simultaneously to define the notion of a possible human language.

ACKNOWLEDGMENTS

This paper is a revised version of a lecture presented on November 2, 1981, to the New York Academy of Sciences. In revising it, I have benefitted greatly

---

f Baker[8] independently notices the different implications of the landing-site view and the *aspects* view of movement rules with respect to learnability.

I should note here that Chomsky[25] takes a rather different view of movement rules than he did earlier.[5] According to his more recent view, movement rules are reduced to the single rule "move," and the resulting overgeneration is to be corrected by principles independent of movement. I fail to see how this can work, however, since none of these principles account for (27–30), as well as other examples in Baltin.[22]

from discussions with Guy Carden, Janet Randall, Elan Dresher, and Larry Solan, all of whom I would like to thank. In addition, Virginia Teller provided considerable assistance with the manuscript in its final versions, for which I am grateful.

REFERENCES

1. CHOMSKY, N. 1975. Reflections on Language. Pantheon. New York, NY.
2. CHOMSKY, N. 1980. Rules and Representations. Columbia University Press. New York, NY.
3. BAKER, C. L. 1978. Introduction to Generative-Transformational Syntax. Prentice Hall. Englewood Cliffs, NJ.
4. RADFORD, A. 1982. Transformational Syntax. Cambridge University Press. Cambridge, England.
5. CHOMSKY, N. 1965. Aspects of the Theory of Syntax. MIT Press. Cambridge, MA.
6. PETERS, S. 1972. The projection problem: How is a grammar to be selected? *In* The Goals of Linguistic Theory. P.S. Peters, Ed. Prentice Hall. Englewood Cliffs, NJ.
7. BAKER, C. L. 1979. Syntactic theory and the projection problem. Linguistic Inquiry **10**: 533–581.
8. BAKER, C. L. 1982. Review of K. Wexler and P. Culicover, *Formal Principles of Language Acquisition* (MIT Press). Language **58**: 182–201.
9. KATZ, J. J. 1964. Mentalism in linguistics. Language **40**: 105–140.
10. SCHANE, S., B. TRANEL & H. LANE. 1975. The psychological reality of a rule of syllable structure. Cognition **3**: 296–301.
11. BRAINE, M. 1971. On two types of models for the internalization of grammars. *In* The Ontogenesis of Grammar. D. Slobin, Ed. Academic Press. New York, NY.
12. BROWN, R. & C. HANLON. 1970. Derivational complexity and the order of acquisition in children's speech. *In* Cognition and the Development of Language. J.R. Hayes, Ed. John Wiley. New York, NY.
13. BALTIN, M. 1981. Strict bounding. *In* The Logical Problem of Language Acquisition. C.L. Baker & J. McCarthy, Eds. MIT Press. Cambridge, MA.
14. Bresnan, J. 1970. On complementizers: Toward a syntactic theory of complement types. Foundations of Language **5**: 297–321.
15. Ross, J. R. 1967. Constraints on Variables in Syntax. Unpublished doctoral dissertation, MIT, Cambridge, MA.
16. KOHRT, M. 1975. A note on bouding. Linguistic Inquiry **6**: 167–171.
17. KAUFMAN, E. 1974. Navajo spatial enclitics: A case for unbounded rightward movement. Linguistic Inquiry **5**: 507–533.
18. SATYARAYANA, P. & K. V. SUBBARAO. 1973. Are rightward movement rules upward bounded? Studies in the Linguistic Sciences **3**. University of Illinois. Urbana, IL.
19. WEXLER, K. & P. CULICOVER. 1980. Formal Principles of Language Acquisition. MIT Press. Cambridge, MA.
20. AISSEN, J. & D. PERLUMUTTER. 1977. Clause reduction in Spanish. Proceedings of the Berkeley Linguistic Society.
21. KATZ, J. J. 1964. Language and Other Abstract Objects. Ablex.
22. BALTIN, M. 1982. A landing site theory of movement rules. Linguistic Inquiry **13**: 1–38.
23. BALTIN, M. 1978. Toward a Theory of Movement Rules. Unpublished doctoral

dissertation, MIT, Cambridge, MA.
24. KEYSER, S. J. 1968. Review of Sven Jacobson's *Adverbial Positions in English.* Language **44**: 357–374.
25. CHOMSKY, N. 1981. Lectures on Government and Binding. Foris.

Topicalization and Left-Dislocation: A Functional Analysis[a]

ELLEN F. PRINCE

Department of Linguistics
University of Pennsylvania
Philadelphia, Pennsylvania 19104

INTRODUCTION

From the point of view of sentence grammar, the Topicalization (TOP) in 2a and the Left-Dislocation (LD) in 2b are paraphrases in that they differ in a systematic way in syntactic form and, at the same time, are "cognitively synonymous,"[2] the propositions they represent being truth-conditionally equivalent, identical to those of the proposition represented by the canonical word-order variant in 1:

(1) John saw Mary yesterday.
(2) a. Mary John saw yesterday.
    b. Mary, John saw her yesterday.

The question then arises as to what, if anything, guides a speaker in choosing one of these over the other in discourse. It is the thesis of this paper that such choices are not random, but rather are made on the basis of the discourse functions of each construction. These functions, which turn out to be surprisingly specialized, consist mainly of the marking of the information status of what is being talked about.

In what follows, I shall first present some evidence for the claim that the choice of one over the other is not random, and then I shall outline briefly what it is that guides the choice, that is, what discourse functions each serves.

DEFINITIONS

For the purposes of this study, TOP and LD are those sentences that have the structural analysis shown in 3:

(3) [[X1] [. . . [X2] . . .]],
    S NP S   NP
    where X1 and X2 are coreferential,
        X1 is nonvocative, and,
    for TOP, X2 is a gap, while,
    for LD, X2 is a personal pronoun/possessive adjective.[b]

---

[a] Earlier versions of this paper were presented at Harvard University and the University of Chicago. A more detailed approach is presented in Prince.[1]

[b] Although the constructions are defined here on formal grounds, this paper will not deal with their syntax, although it is hoped that some of the issues that it raises may be found relevant to syntactic analysis.

Furthermore, TOP has a characteristic intonation contour, having a secondary stress on/within the leftmost NP and a primary stress within the following clause.[c]

For ease of exposition, I shall call the leftmost NP in both TOP and LD (X1, or *Mary* in 2a,b) the *NP*, I shall call what follows the NP the *Clause* (*John saw O yesterday* in 2a, *John saw her yesterday* in 2b), and I shall call the proposition that the whole sentence (NP plus Clause, equivalent to the proposition represented by the canonical word-order variant) represents the *Proposition*.

NONRANDOMNESS OF DISTRIBUTION

If the distribution of canonical word-order, TOP, and LD were random, it would follow that, wherever canonical word-order were possible, so would be TOP and LD. Likewise, TOP and LD would themselves be interchangeable in discourse, preserving felicity/coherence. Neither of these situations obtains, however, as shown below:

(4) Q: What did you do over vacation?
    a. A: I read two books.
    b. A: #Two books I read.
    c. A: #Two books, I read them.[d]

In 4, we see that canonical word-order may occur felicitously (4a) where neither TOP (4b) nor LD (4c) can. Now compare TOP and LD:

(5) Q: Why do you like horses so much?
    a. A: Well, *this one book, I read it when I was a kid* and it really made a lasting impression on me. It was about a really smart horse and I guess I've loved horses ever since.
    b. A: #Well, *this one book I read when I was a kid* and . . .

In 5, we see that LD may occur felicitously (5a) where TOP cannot (5b).[e] However, what I have not found are: *first*, environments that permit TOP and/or LD but not canonical word-order, and, *second*, environments that permit TOP but not LD.[f] Thus it seems that the sets of environments of

---

[c] Note, therefore, that this paper is not considering certain other TOP-like constructions, such as Focus-Movement (i) and Yiddish-Movement (ii). For a discussion of their functions, see Prince.[3]
    (i) FIDO they named it.
    (ii) A BITE he wouldn't eat!

[d] # indicates discourse infelicity/incoherence.

[e] Of course, there are many other instances where LD but not TOP can occur, but in which there are obvious syntactic reasons for the difference, e.g., when the pronoun/gap would be in subject position (i) or in an island (ii):
    (i) "The younger women, *O/they don't pay you too much attention." (Ref. 4, p. 167)
    (ii) "My first book, I paid half of each trick to the person who gave *O/it to me." (Ref. 4, p. 95)
See Ross[5], among others.

[f] First, however, see Rodman,[6] called to my attention by an anonymous reader, where it is claimed that TOP and LD are in fact in complementary distribution. Unfortunately, my intui-

the three constructions are not disjoint, but rather fall into an inclusion relation, as shown in 6, where *ENV* = set of environments:

(6) ENV(TOP) ⊂ ENV(LD) ⊂ ENV(SVO)

From this, we draw certain inferences. First, the set of discourse functions of LD properly includes the set of discourse functions of canonical word order (which is null). From this it follows that the set of discourse functions of LD is nonnull, i.e., LD has come discourse function. Second, if LD, in each of its occurrences, always has the same discourse function or set thereof (i.e., LD exhibits no constructional homonymy), then the set of discourse functions of TOP properly includes the set of discourse functions of LD, from which it follows that TOP has at least two discourse functions. Third, if LD occurs sometimes with one discourse function or set thereof and sometimes with another (i.e., LD exhibits constructional homonymy), then we can infer only that the set of discourse functions of TOP properly includes a subset of the set of discourse functions of LD, the complement of which is not in the set of discourse functions of TOP. These two possibilities are illustrated in the Venn diagrams in 7, where *DF* = set of discourse functions:

(7) a. If LD is nonhomonymous:
     b. If LD is homonymous:

Minimally, then, we must look for some discourse function that LD and TOP share and some discourse function that TOP has and that LD lacks.[g]

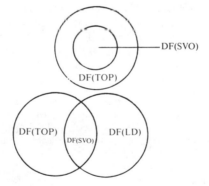

tions and my data are not consistent with Rodman's, and I find nothing unusual with his starred LDs' involving quantified NPs. On the other hand, the same reader supplied cases permitting TOP but not LD involving *there* sentences, e.g.
  (i) "Something there is O/*it that doesn't love a wall."
I have no explanation either for the acceptability of the TOP version or for the unacceptability of the LD version.

  Second, see Ward[7] for an insightful analysis of a TOP-like construction that appears to have no canonical word-order or LD variant which may be substituted for it in discourse, preserving felicity/coherence.

  [g] This seems to be an uncontroversial inference in linguistics. For example, a distributional analysis would note that the set of (sentence) environments of *puppy* was a proper subset of the set of (sentence) environments of *dog* (excluding metalinguistic statements, i.e., analytic truths) and infer that, if the latter were univocal, its (single) set of meaning components was a proper subset of the set of meaning components of *puppy*. Of course, in the event that *dog* represents two (or more) homonymous morphemes, only a subset of its meaning components would constitute a subset of the meaning components of *puppy*. See Lounsbury.[8]

BRIEF SURVEY OF THE LITERATURE

Although the syntax of TOP and LD has received a great deal of attention, far less work has been done on the pragmatics of these constructions. Furthermore, what does exist is often difficult to compare, since functional syntax still lacks a uniform terminology and framework. TABLE 1 is an attempt to sidestep this problem by extracting the functions attributed to these constructions in six previous studies. For ease of comparison, but at the risk of distortion, the original terminology has in some cases been changed.

(8) **TABLE 1.** Comparison of Six Relevant Studies

Author	Year	TOP	LD
Chafe[9]	1976	Contrast	Contrast
Creider[10]	1979	Marked topic	Marked topic; "topic-bridging"
Gundel[11]	1974	New topic	New topic
Halliday[12]	1967	Marked topic	Marked topic; separate information unit
Reinhad[13]	1981	Marked topic	Marked topic
Rodman[6]	1974	Old topic	New topic

Note that five of the six studies cite marking a topic as the main or only function of both TOP and LD. It is not clear how to test this claim, since there is no generally accepted method of determining, for English, what the topic of a sentence is. Gundel[11,14] addresses this difficult problem and proposes two tests, which have by now become classic: first, can *as for* precede the leftmost NP?, and, second, is the full sentence understood as an answer to *What about X?*, where X is coreferential with the leftmost NP? However, the TOP examples in 9 and the LD examples in 10 fail both tests, which I leave to the reader to administer:

(9) a. "The only time a guy isn't considered a failure is when he resigns and announces his new job. That's a tipoff. 'John Smith resigned, future plans unknown' means he was fired. 'John Smith resigned to accept the position of X Company'—then you know he resigned. *This little nuance you recognize immediately when you're in corporate life.*" (Ref. 4, p. 537)

   b. "I became a waitress because I needed money fast and you don't get it in an office. My husband and I broke up and he left me with debts and three children. My baby was six months. The fast buck, your tips. *The first ten-dollar bill that I got as a tip, a Viking guy gave to me.* He was a very robust, terrific atheist . . ." (Ref. 4, p. 390)

(10) a. "They said, men from the company, we'd get a road up to the cemetery that's on top of the hill. I said, 'Well, it won't be any use going up there, because there won't be any dead up there. Because the coal is under the graves.' *An old preacher down there, they augured under the grave where his wife was buried.* And he's nearly blind and he prayed and everything." (Ref. 4, p. 44)

   b. "I know what this piece of equipment's raised to do. I always try to get that and to better it. *Any company, if they're worth 150 million dollars, you don't need to think for a minute that they're not going to know what you're doing.* They didn't get there that way." (Ref. 4, p. 46)

Reinhart[13] accepts Gundel's *as for*-test (recognizing its defect in that it cannot occur with an NP representing a brand-new entity in the discourse), but, in place of the *what about*-test, she substitutes acceptability in the frame *He said about X that S*, Akmajian's bound-sentence type.[15] However, this test does no better on data like 9 and 10 than the preceding ones, which I likewise leave to the reader to check.

Therefore, before a sharper test for "topichood" is proposed, it is not clear that the explanation of marking, introducing, or "bridging" topics is a useful one, although it may well turn out ultimately to be correct.[h] Chafe's "contrast" and Halliday's "new information unit" will be discussed below.

TOPICALIZATION

I shall try to show that TOP has two simultaneous functions. First, TOP marks the entity represented by the NP as being either *already evoked* in the discourse or else in a salient *set relation* to something already evoked in or inferable from the discourse. Second, TOP marks an open proposition, arrived at by replacing the (translation of) the tonically stressed constituent with a variable, as *given*, in Chafe's sense,[9,16] i.e., assumed to be appropriately in the hearer's consciousness at the time of hearing the utterance.

TOP: NP

To see the marking effect on the referent of the NP, note first that, if the NP is nonreferential, TOP is ungrammatical:

(11) a. I didn't think you would leave.
     b. I told Mary that I wasn't chosen.
     c. I brought some books with me.
(12) a. You I didn't think would leave.
     b. Mary I told that I wasn't chosen.
     c. Some books I brought with me.

[h] That it may not be correct, however, is suggested by the following: 67% of the LDs in the Terkel corpus involve the full main subject of the S. Since everyone who has ever discussed the notion of topic seems to agree that subjects are unmarked topics, one must wonder why speakers go to so much trouble to mark something for a feature that it would have anyway. Conversely, a sentence-final constituent would seem to be a likely candidate for topic-marking, since, in its natural (canonical) state, it would never (or hardly ever) be construed as topic, and yet only 7% of the LDs in the Terkel corpus involve a full sentence-final NP.

(13) a. I didn't think there would be a fight.
        b. I resented it that I wasn't chosen.
        c. I brought few books with me.
(14) a. *There I didn't think would be a fight.
        b. *It I resented that I wasn't chosen.
        c. *Few books I brought with me.[i]

Second, while referentiality of the NP may be sufficient to ensure gram-maticality, it is not sufficient to ensure discourse felicity, as shown in 15 and 16:

(15) a. A: You want to see *Annie Hall?*
           B: *Annie Hall* I saw yesterday.
        b. A: You see every Woody Allen movie as soon as it comes out.
           B: No — *Annie Hall* I saw (only) yesterday.
(16) a. A: Why are you laughing?
           B: #*Annie Hall* I saw yesterday. I was just thinking about it.
        b. A: Sue told me that you were away.
           B: #Yes, I was. Oh, by the way, *Annie Hall* I saw yesterday.

Although *Annie Hall* is referential in all the sentences of 15 and 16, only in the contexts of 15 is TOP felicitous. One difference between 15 and 16 is that, in the former, the NP represents old information in the discourse, an evoked entity in 15a and an inferable entity in 15b, whereas, in 16, the NP represents new information in the discourse (an "unused" entity[17]). How-ever, not all inferable entities are possible in TOP, as shown in 17 and 18, where "functionally dependent" entities, i.e., entities related by cultural in-ferences, are disallowed:

(17) a. I went to his house and I rang the bell.
        b. #I went to his house and the bell I rang.
(18) a. That newspaper infuriates me. I think I'll call the editor.
        b. #That newspaper infuriates me. The editor I think I'll call.

In 17, *the bell* is inferentially related, via functional dependency, to *his house*,[17-19] but TOP in 17b is infelicitous; likewise for *the editor* in 18. Now compare the following naturally occurring tokens:

(19) a. "I have *a recurring dream* in which . . . I can't remember what I say.
           I usually wake up crying. *This dream* I've had maybe three, four times."
           (Ref. 4, p. 118)
        b. "*They* [the patients] were in long wards and *they* had curtains around
           the bed. I'd start out with just the shirt, work on getting the affected
           arm into the sleeve. *Some people*, it would take ten days to learn. Some
           could do it in one day — getting their shirt on, their pants on, how to
           wash themselves with one hand." (Ref. 4, p. 644)

---

[i] There seems to be a relevant ongoing change in the language. Both an anonymous reader and a number of younger speakers I have polled find 14c acceptable, whereas its only accept-able variant for me is:
    (i) Few books did I bring with me.
However, there is independent evidence that, for these speakers, NPs like *few books* have be-come referential and hence this does not constitute a counterexample to the referentiality claim.

On the basis of data like 19, the following hypothesis is proposed:

(20) Discourse function of TOP with respect to NP: TOP marks an entity as being already *evoked* in the discourse or else in a salient *set relation* to something already evoked. The entity thus marked is represented by the NP.

Thus, in 19a, we find an entity, *this dream*, that has been explicitly introduced into the discourse. In 19b, on the other hand, *some people* represents an element (here subset) of an already evoked set, *the patients*.[j]

Now consider the following:

(21) a. "[I graduated from high school as] an average student. My initiative didn't carry me any further than average. *History* I found to be dry. Math courses I was never good at. I enjoyed sciences . . . Football was my bag." (Ref. 4, p. 590)

b. "Sunday I was taking paper and pasting it together and finding a method of how to drop spoons, a fork, a napkin, and a straw into one package. *The napkin feeder* I got. The straw feeder we made already. That leaves us the spoon and the fork." (Ref. 4, p. 516)

Note that the underlined NP in 21a, *history*, is not evoked and is not in a set-to-element or element-to-set relation to any already evoked entity. However, it *is* inferable, via a set-to-element inference, from a set that is not mentioned but that is itself saliently inferable from the high school "frame." Put differently, if a hearer did not know that associated with high school is a set of courses or subjects and that *history* (and then *math courses*, and so forth) represents an element of that set, then, I claim, s/he could not process this text effectively. Likewise, in 21b, upon hearing *the napkin feeder*, a hearer must infer a set of parts of the device that the speaker is designing and must infer that *the napkin feeder* (and then *the straw feeder*) is an element of that set. Thus, examples like 21 are accounted for by the hypothesis in 20, their peculiarity being that the relevant set is not explicitly evoked, but must be saliently inferable from the prior context.

In addition to invoking co-elements of a set, the TOPs in 21 share a second feature: they have the flavor of belonging to a *list*. The first feature, I claim, is prerequisite to the second: to understand items as belonging to a list, one must infer that they are co-elements of some single, independently nameable, set. Consider, for example, 22:

(22) a. I used to live in Philadelphia and I often went to Atlantic City.
b. Philadelphia I used to live in and Atlantic City I often went to.

In 22a, it is easy (for someone who is familiar with the area) to take the sentence as an asymmetric coordination,[20] i.e., to understand the first clause, *I used to live in Philadelphia*, as the setting for the whole sentence: while living in Philadelphia, the speaker often went to Atlantic City. However, this understanding does not seem to be available for 22b; rather, we find a symmetric coordination, a *listing* of the speaker's relation to two (Eastern U.S.)

---

[j] Set-to-element inferences like that in 19a are far more common in the data than element-to-set inferences, but both occur. See Prince.[3]

cities. This, I claim, is forced by the TOP construction which requires us to construe *Philadelphia* and *Atlantic City* as co-elements of a single set (since more than one element is evoked) induces a list understanding.

Now, if we reconsider the examples in 21, we see that, in addition to being lists, they also exemplify the phenomenon of *contrast*, claimed by Chafe[9] to be the function of TOP (and of LD). Contrast, in turns out, is *not* a necessary effect of TOP, as seen, for example, in 19a, but rather obtains just in case, first, a *list* understanding is induced, and, second, a salient *opposition* is inferred in the new information represented in the Clause associated with each element. Contrast is clearly not inferred, therefore, in cases like 19a, where the NP represents simply an evoked entity and not one of at least two elements of a set.

TOP: Proposition

Let us now turn to the second discourse function of TOP, the marking of a certain relation between the Proposition and the context. Consider first the case where the NP represents an already evoked entity, e.g., 19a. The Proposition associated with 19a is presented in 23:

(23) I've had this dream maybe three, four times.

It turns out that, if one constituent is replaced by a variable, the resulting open sentence is already known and salient, i.e., Chafe-given, in the discourse:

(24) I've had this dream X/some number of times.

That is, since we have just been told that the speaker has had a recurring dream, we know and are attending to the fact that she has had this dream some number of times. The *new* information in the TOP in 19a, then, is not a proposition, but the value of some variable in an already known proposition. Note further that the constituent representing this new information is just the one that receives primary/tonic stress. This suggests that the open proposition resulting from the replacement of the tonically stressed constituent (in the Clause) by a variable represents Chafe-given information.

But now consider the case where the NP represents an entity that is in a salient set-relation to something already known or saliently inferable, e.g., 21b. It cannot be the case that it is already Chafe-given that the speaker is in some state with respect to the napkin feeder, since the average hearer has presumably never even heard of a napkin feeder. What is presumed to be Chafe-given here is that the speaker is in some state with respect to whatever goes into making the desired device. Therefore, the following hypothesis is proposed:

(25) Discourse function with respect to Proposition in TOP: TOP marks an open proposition as Chafe-given in the discourse. The open proposition is determined as follows: First, if the NP represents an element of a set, replace it by that set, yielding a new Proposition. Then, in all cases, replace the tonically stressed constituent in the (new) Proposition by a variable.

LEFT-DISLOCATION (LD)

Turning now to LD, we expect, on distributional grounds, that one of the following holds: First, barring constructional homonymy (i.e., all occurrences of LD have the same discourse function[s]), LD should have one, but not both, of the discourse functions of TOP, and no discourse function that TOP does not have. Second, in the event of constructional homonymy, a proper subset of the occurrences of LD will exhibit a pattern as just described, while the complement of that set will have different discourse functions.

LD-1

Analysis of naturally occurring tokens of LD suggests that the second situation obtains. That is, a good number of LD sentences, though not all, seem to share the first discourse function of TOP: the entity represented by the NP either is already evoked in the discourse (26a) or else is in a salient set-relation to something already evoked (set-to-element, 26b; element-to-element, 26c):

(26) a. *"The machine dictates. This crummy little machine with buttons on it*—you've got to be there to answer it." (Ref. 4, p. 59)
  b. "As for making out with *tenants*, it's not like they say. *Good-looking broads*, if they're playing, they ain't going to monkey around with a janitor." (Ref. 4, p. 173)
  c. "Everybody has their little bundle, believe me. I'll bet she had a *nervous breakdown*. That's not a good thing. *Gallstones,* you have them out and they're out. But a nervous breakdown, it's very bad . . ." (Ref. 21, p. 162)

Note, by the way, that the set-relation inference is crucial to discourse understanding in 26b,c: in 26b, the speaker is not necessarily making a statement about "good-looking broads" in general, but only about those who are his tenants. Likewise, in 26c, the speaker is not simply asserting a tautology about gallstones, but is rather considering them only insofar as they constitute an element of the set "bad things," another element of which is the discourse-relevant "nervous breakdown."

On the other hand, the second function of TOP, the marking of an open proposition as Chafe-given, does not appear to be a function of LD.[k] Thus, for a subset of the LD data, which I shall characterize as tokens of LD-1, the following hypothesis is proposed:

(27) Discourse function of LD-1: LD-1 marks an entity as being already evoked in the discourse or else in a salient set-relation to something already evoked. The entity thus marked is represented by the NP.

---

[k] Of course, some LD sentences can also be viewed as presenting a Chafe-given open proposition, but no more so than can some canonical word-order sentences. Thus they are not considered to be *marking* these open propositions. It should further be pointed out that intonation, which is not transcribed in much of the corpus used here (e.g., Terkel[4] and Carterette and Jones[22]), can mark information status as effectively as syntax can.

If TOP and LD-1 have the same function with respect to NP but differ with respect to the open proposition, one might expect the two constructions to co-occur in discourse in the following way: Given that some set of entities is evoked, one might expect an occurrence of LD-1, where NP represents an element of that set. But LD-1 also introduces a proposition; if that proposition forms the basis of some open proposition which will then be predicated of other elements of that set, we might expect one or more occurrences of LD-1 to be followed by one or more occurrences of TOP. In fact, such situations do occur:

(28) a. "She had an idea for a project. She's going to use three groups of mice. *One, she'll feed them on mouse chow,* just the regular stuff they make for mice. *Another, she'll feed them veggies.* And *the third she'll feed junk food.*" (S.J., 11/7/81)
      b. (There were two things I promised to talk about. *The first thing, I looked at it with care. The second thing I didn't look at.*) (S.V., 12/14/81)

As might be expected, sequences of TOP followed by LD-1 do not occur in the corpus.

LD-2

Of course, the hypothesis in 27 is compelling only insofar as some co-herent pattern can be seen in those LD tokens that are not claimed to be instances of LD-1. In fact, the other LD tokens do seem to form coherent patterns: they appear to serve to introduce an entity, represented by the NP, which is not currently salient, or "in focus."[23] Whether this entity was formerly evoked and has moved out of focus or has not yet been evoked and is new in the discourse does not seem to be relevant. What is relevant, however, is the syntactic position the NP would occupy were the sentence in canonical word-order: it is very frequently the subject position, occasionally direct or indirect object before another constituent, but apparently never in sentence-final position.[l] Examples are presented in 29:

(29) a. "I watch strange film science fiction it was about I forgot it its like a grasshopper. But they made the grasshopper bigger because they put a magnifying glass. And these *a girl it was a lady who collects books she said to the policeman what are they doing.* He said sorry lady but I cant tell you." (Ref. 22, p. 74)
      b. "Once when we went to Big Bear and we caught a lot of fish and and Suzie Kathy and Betty went to a park and me my mom and dad went fishing. *And this guy his fishing pole fell down in the water* and he had to go down and get it." (Ref. 22, p. 134)

---

[l] For a discussion of the correlation between syntactic position and the information status of entities, see Joshi and Weinstein.[24] In their terms, this class of LD involves entities whose NPs would have, in canonical word-order, the position of a "backward-looking center." For LD-2, then, the NP would be a "forward-looking center." This would, of course, not be the case for LD-1.

Note that, if we replace, in context, the LD sentences of 29 with those of 30, the texts are far less coherent:

(30) a. A lady who collects books the policeman talked to her.
　　 b. And this guy we saw him.

Thus it appears that there are two homonymous LD constructions, LD-1, discussed above, and LD-2, for which the following hypothesis is proposed:

(31) Discourse function of LD-2: LD-2 creates a separate information-unit for an entity not currently in focus and not represented by an NP in a favored position, e.g., sentence-final, for introducing out-of-focus entities.

Perhaps, then, it is LD-2 that Halliday[12] is considering in ascribing the function of creating a "new information unit" to LD.

Comparison of LD-1 and LD-2

Note that the claims made for LD-1 and LD-2 lead to an empirically testable prediction. Given an LD sentence in which the NP would, in canonical word-order, occupy sentence-final position, that sentence should be felicitous just in case it can be construed as an instance of LD-1, i.e., where the NP is understood as representing an entity already evoked in the discourse or else in a salient set-relation to something evoked. If it is not construable as such, the sentence should be infelicitous. The data in 32 seem to bear out this prediction:

(32) a. A: I heard John baked a lot for the party. How'd he do?
　　　 B: *Some cookies, I ate them* and they weren't bad, but I heard the cake was really fantastic. [LD-1]
　　 b. A: How come you're not hungry?
　　　 B: #*Some cookies, I ate them.* [LD-2][m]

Furthermore, the data suggest that LD-1 and LD-2 differ dialectally: while both are colloquial rather than formal, LD-1 appears to occur in a very wide range of social dialects, while LD-2 seems characteristic of the speech of children and of lower-prestige dialect speakers.[n] Obviously, this is merely an impressionistic observation and requires sociolinguistic investigation.

CONCLUSION

In this paper, which is a brief presentation of a larger study of OSV word order in English, I have studied the discourse functions of TOP and LD and I have tried to show that TOP has two simultaneous functions, one marking

---

[m] Note, of course, that the canonical word-order variant, *I ate some cookies*, is felicitous in both contexts of 32. Note also that the intonation would be different in the two contexts.

[n] It is perhaps worth noting that the tokens of LD-1 cited in 28 were both uttered by highly educated adults, both, in fact, university professors (28a by an Englishwoman and 28b by a Brazilian who learned English as an adult in an academic environment).

a certain information status of the entity represented by the NP, the other marking a certain information status of an open proposition. The first of these relates to the NP appearing noncanonically in initial position and the second to the gap in the clause. The two functions and their syntactic reflexes appear to be separable in that a sentence having a noncanonical sentence-initial NP but no gap, i.e., an occurrence of LD-1, exhibits the first function but not the second. At the same time, there appears to be another, homonymous, LD construction, LD-2, which functions to create a new information unit for a new entity whose NP would not otherwise be in a position favored for introducing new entities. Obviously, much more research is required before the correctness of this analysis can be claimed.

ACKNOWLEDGMENTS

Among those to whom I am deeply indebted for their helpful comments and criticisms are John Fought, Georgia Green, Barbara Grosz, Tony Kroch, Susumu Kuno, David McNeill, Sebastiao Votre, Greg Ward, Bonnie Webber, and Annie Zaenen.

REFERENCES

1. PRINCE, E. F. 1982. A comparison of Topicalization and Left-Dislocation in discourse. Unpublished manuscript.
2. CHOMSKY, N. 1965. Aspects of the Theory of Syntax. MIT Press. Cambridge, MA.
3. PRINCE, E. F. 1981. Topicalization, Focus-Movement, and Yiddish-Movement: A pragmatic differentiation. In D. Alford, et al., Eds. Berkeley Linguistic Society VIII.: 249–264.
4. TERKEL, S. 1974. Working. Avon Books. New York, NY.
5. ROSS, J. R. 1967. Constraints on Variables in Syntax. Ph.D. dissertation, Massachusetts Institute of Technology.
6. RODMAN, R. 1974. On left-dislocation. Papers in Linguistics 7: 437–466.
7. WARD, G. 1982. A pragmatic analysis of Epitomization: Topicalization it's not. LSA Summer Meeting, College Park, MD.
8. LOUNSBURY, F. 1964. Structural analysis of kinship semantics. In Proceedings of the 9th International Congress of Linguists. : 1073–1089. Cambridge, MA.
9. CHAFE, W. 1976. Givenness, contrastiveness, definiteness, subjects, topics, and point of view. In Subject and Topic. C. Li, Ed. : 25–55. Academic Press. New York, NY.
10. CREIDER, C. 1979. On the explanation of transformations. In Syntax and Semantics. XII. Discourse and Syntax. T. Givon, Ed. : 3–22. Academic Press. New York, NY.
11. GUNDEL, J. 1974. The Role of Topic and Comment in Linguistic Theory. Ph.D. dissertation, University of Texas.
12. HALLIDAY, M. A. K. 1967. Notes on transitivity and theme in English. Part 2. J. of Linguistics 3: 199–244.
13. REINHART, T. 1981. Pragmatics and linguistics: An analysis of sentence topics. Unpublished manuscript.
14. GUNDEL, J. 1975. Left dislocation and the role of topic-comment structure in linguistic theory. In Ohio State Working Papers in Linguistics. 18: 72–131.

15. AKMAJIAN, A. 1979. The Bound-Sentence Constraint. Unpublished manuscript.
16. CHAFE, W. 1974. Language and consciousness. Language **50**: 111–133.
17. PRINCE, E. F. 1981. Toward a taxonomy of given/new information. *In* Radical Pragmatics. P. Cole, Ed. : 223–255. Academic Press. New York, NY.
18. CLARK, H. & S. HAVILAND. 1977. Comprehension and the given-new contract. *In* Discourse Production and Comprehension. R. Freedle, Ed. : 1–40. Erlbaum. Hillsdale, NJ.
19. HAWKINS, J. A. 1978. Definiteness and Indefiniteness. Humanities Press. Atlantic Highlands, NJ.
20. SCHMERLING, S. 1975. Asymmetric conjunction and rules of conversation. *In* Syntax and Semantics. Vol. 3. Speech Acts. P. Cole & J. L. Morgan, Eds. : 211–231. Academic Press. New York, NY.
21. ROTH, P. 1963. Goodbye Columbus. Bantam Books, New York, NY.
22. CARTERETTE, E. & M. JONES. 1974. Informal Speech. Alphabetic and Phonemic Texts with Statistical Analyses and Tables. University of California Press. Berkeley and Los Angeles.
23. GROSZ, B. 1981. Focusing and description in natural language dialogues. *In* Elements of Discourse Understanding. A. K. Joshi, B. L. Webber & I. A. Sag, Eds. : 84–105. Cambridge University Press, Cambridge, England.
24. JOSHI, A. K. & S. WEINSTEIN. 1981. Control of inference: Role of some aspects of discourse structure-centering. Proceedings of the IJCAI.